SUCCESS, FAILURE, AND WASTAGE
IN HIGHER EDUCATION

UNIVERSITY OF LONDON INSTITUTE OF
EDUCATION

SUCCESS, FAILURE, AND WASTAGE
IN HIGHER EDUCATION

*An Overview of the Problem derived
from Research and Theory*

by

GORDON W. MILLER, B.A., Ph.D.

Published for

THE UNIVERSITY OF LONDON INSTITUTE OF
EDUCATION

by GEORGE G. HARRAP & CO. LTD
London   Toronto   Wellington   Sydney

First published in Great Britain 1970
by GEORGE G. HARRAP & CO. LTD
182 High Holborn, London, W.C.1

SBN 245 59792 1

*Composed in Baskerville type and printed at the
St Ann's Press, Park Road, Altrincham. Made in Great Britain*

PREFACE

Universities' and colleges' study of themselves has been increasing in volume in the United Kingdom in recent years. Considering all the fields of knowledge with which institutions of higher education are concerned, it is strange that they have studied themselves so little except for some isolated but significant efforts by a few pioneers. There is growing awareness that educated people are among the nation's best resources, whether economic or other criteria are applied. Equally, education is one of the chief assets of an individual. Gains from research in scientific fields could to some extent be paralleled if research findings were applied to educational practice. There is undoubtedly need for research on which to base policy decisions involving rapidly increasing education budgets.

In education and the comparatively young social sciences it would be rash to think that the spectacular outcomes of research in physical sciences will quickly be paralleled. However, the literature already contains some research findings of considerable significance, and in Great Britain research into higher education is gathering momentum. The Department of Education and Science has been spending larger sums on selected projects, the Social Science Research Council was established in 1966 and is taking a special interest in education, and some appointments have been made to chairs of higher education and educational research. The Society for Research into Higher Education exercises a co-ordinating influence which helps to rationalize research throughout the country and disseminate the findings from British studies and those from other countries. A national data bank for higher education should now be established.

When the Department of Higher Education was established at the University of London Institute of Education, H. L. Elvin, the Director of the Institute, said that one of the hopes in establishing it was that it would form a bridge between research and policy. The fact that much of the research in this field has been done in America raises the question to what extent the findings can be applicable to universities and colleges in Britain and other countries.

The limitations of using research in other countries to formulate policy in institutions other than where the research was conducted are fully recognized. There are enormous differences between universities and colleges of Britain and those of the United States. They are probably almost as great between institutions within any one country. There are even differences between the characteristics of departments within quite small universities of any given country. For example, the problems of a history department are different in many ways from those of an engineering, medical, or law department.

These are valid objections, but it would be wrong to assume that no study is relevant to more than one college or department. To argue this is tantamount to arguing in favour of an education research unit in every university and college. It is left to readers to decide which of the studies discussed in this volume have any significance for their own institutions and departments. Some will be capable of direct application, while others will require local replication. The main aim is to show wastage in perspective and to stimulate further research in related fields. It may well be that each university should have its own education research office, and it should also be possible for homogeneous groups of colleges of education and technology to support research jointly to test ideas and methods which sometimes originate by hunch and become established practice.

This volume covers several major topics that at first might seem peripheral to the central topic of student wastage. Among the associated topics are schools, guidance, residence, teaching, selection, institutional characteristics, curricular inflexibility, student-teacher relations, and student problems. Wastage is a highly ramified problem, and it will soon be seen that each topic discussed is integral to the main problem.

G.W.M.

Acknowledgments

I am grateful to my colleagues at the University of London Institute of Education, particularly the Director, H. L. Elvin, and the former Dean, Professor W. R. Niblett, who is now the Head of the Department of Higher Education in the Institute, for the opportunity to examine such a large proportion of the literature. Though a heavy task, it has been most illuminating.

Thanks are due to Her Majesty's Stationery Office, the University Grants Committee, the Clarendon Press, Oxford, the Pergamon Press, Mr A. J. Jenkinson, O.B.E., Professor W. D. Furneaux, Professor John Nisbet, the late Sir Fred J. Schonell, and Professor C. Sanders for permission to use material.

Dr Ruth Beard, Dr Joan Brothers, Mr T. W. Eason, Mr J. W. Thompson, a former colleague, Professor Niblett, and Dr W. D. Wall, our Dean, were very generous with their time in reading drafts and offering helpful suggestions, as also were Miss Elisabeth Clark, Mrs Jennifer Dunn, and Mrs J. Storey in typing and checking the drafts.

G.W.M.

CONTENTS

Chapter 1 THE NATURE AND EXTENT OF WASTAGE 10

2 STUDENT FACTORS 28

The Reasons Students give—Least Influential Variables—Ability—Social Class and Other Social Factors—Birth Rank and Family Size—Home Location and Cultural and Ethnic Differences —Family Characteristics—Financial—Age and Maturity—Extra-curricular Interests, Need for Affiliation, Sociability—Study Habits of High and Low Achievers—Personality and Motivation —Extrinsic Motivation and Incentives—Intrinsic Interest and Curiosity—Students under Stress— Summary and Conclusions (Student Variables of Least Influence in Academic Performance— Student Variables producing Inconsistent Findings —Student Variables producing Consistent Findings)

3 STUDENT SELECTION 95

School Performance as Selection Criteria— Scholastic Aptitude Tests and Creativity Tests— Personality, Motivation, Interests, Ambition— Sixth Form and University First Year—Selecting Postgraduate Research Students—A Preliminary Outline for Research into Criteria for selecting Postgraduate Research Students—Summary

4 OTHER INSTITUTIONAL FACTORS 149

Teaching—Staff-student Relations and Institutional Ethos—Counselling, Health, and Psychiatric Services (When is Counselling needed?—Kinds of Services needed—Who should counsel Students? —Helping to reduce Wastage)—Student Residence —Schools and Preparation of Students for Higher Education—Examinations—Academic Flexibility —Summary

5 FUTURE RESEARCH STRATEGY 226

Student Variables—Selection of Undergraduates and Postgraduates—Postgraduate Research Students—Wastage among Research Students—Teaching—Examinations—Halls of Residence—Schools—A National Data Bank—Pass Rates and Measures of Productivity—Responsibilities of Institutions and assessing the Effectiveness of Student Services—Studies of Special Groups of Students—Philistines and the All-round Scholar —Summary

INDEX 255

THE NATURE AND EXTENT OF WASTAGE

THE simplest criterion of wastage is whether or not the student has left his institution of higher education without gaining the degree or other qualification intended. This is a crude and not altogether satisfactory criterion because it assumes that the student has gained nothing from the institution in the time spent, which can rarely be true. Yet in a great number of faculties and departments failure to graduate in minimum time can mean rejection and disqualification in the field in which study was undertaken.

The aims of academic education are not limited to examination success or qualification to enter a profession. Few educationists would be prepared to accept such a restricted view, however important they feel examinations and formal qualifications to be. Sanford has said:

It seems clear that liberal education has accepted the task of familiarizing the student with his cultural heritage and of exercising his intellect, and, in addition, is concerned with the development of the individual as a whole person. The kinds of intellectual, moral, social and emotional characteristics which the liberal college usually seeks to develop and foster, and those which it seeks to eliminate, are much like those which concern the psychologist when he thinks about the maturity or health or optimum functioning of the individual. (1)*

The problem of academic failure, or, as it is variously called, dropping out, attrition, wastage, or student mortality, is one which has been widely investigated for many years in the United States, but markedly less in other countries. In Australia some valuable studies have been undertaken, and reference to them is made in later pages.

The United Kingdom in the past has been less concerned about this problem, probably because of traditionally low overall failure rates. But there are very great differences in the wastage rates of different British universities and particular departments

---

* The notes relating to each chapter will be found at the end of the chapter.

within them which have shown the need for a hard look at the problem. The Robbins Committee (2) considered that, in a system so highly selective as in Britain, the 14 per cent overall wastage hardly merited congratulation. The 1968 University Grants Committee Report on Student Progress has shown a reduction of wastage to 13.3 per cent. (3)

It is taken for granted that the wider aims of education are of fundamental importance in higher education, but at the present day, when the demand for higher education is increasing and budgets are expanding, it is proper to study in what ways wastage might be lessened and productivity improved and how places in higher education and the grants that go with them may best be allocated. In 1957, 74 per cent of students with the requisite number of A-level results for admission to university were being admitted. In 1967 the proportion fell to 54 per cent. The proportion will probably continue to diminish as more young people stay on in sixth forms.

Besides failure to attain any formal qualification, numerous other criteria of failure can be applied. Some of these are: failure to graduate in minimum time, failure to graduate with some delay, and failure in first or subsequent years. Wastage criteria include percentage of students failing to complete a course or a year, failure of students to remain in one particular institution until graduation, and failure to transfer to another institution to complete a qualification.

In the United States in 1938 McNeely (4) defined wastage in two ways: gross wastage as failure or withdrawal of students from courses without account being taken of whether they enrolled in another university or re-enrolled at a later date in the same university, and net wastage as when account was taken of later enrolment of students in another university or re-enrolment in the same. On this basis gross wastage in the twenty-five universities McNeely studied was 62.1 per cent. Net wastage was estimated at 45 per cent, with an approximate ultimate graduation rate of 55 per cent for all twenty-five universities. This was estimated on the evidence that 10.1 per cent of students had transferred and graduated or were continuing to study in other institutions, while there was a probability that 6.8 per cent would return and complete their degrees in their own or another university later.

There are vast differences between individual institutions, of course, but present rates of wastage in American universities are, on average, probably not greatly different from then. Summerskill (5) cites thirty-five studies of attrition rates for classes entering hundreds of varied colleges and universities from 1913 to 1962, which show that attrition rates have not changed appreciably during that time. In each decade attrition over four years of undergraduate time was about 50 per cent, with only 40 per cent graduating in the minimum time and a further 20 per cent graduating at some college at a later time. Australian and Canadian universities (6, 7) have somewhat similar rates, only about 35–40 per cent finishing in minimum time and about 65–70 per cent ultimately with delays, about one-third never attaining their degrees.

Colleges and universities do not often have detailed information on their wastage rates and the reasons for them, but from the literature it is clear that wastage is due to a complex of factors, some of which apply directly to students and others to institutions, in various combinations. Contrary to popular interpretation that the calibre of students has declined, there is evidence from many studies that it has been improving; yet wastage is about constant, with the exception of a few departments and institutions where it has been reduced. Instances are given in the chapter on selection.

Kelsall (8) cites studies of faculties and departments in such British universities and colleges as Keele, Liverpool, Sheffield, University College, London, the London School of Economics, and Queen's University, Belfast, which have disclosed failure rates ranging from 12 per cent to 25 per cent—this from very highly selected groups of students. Table 1 shows the percentage of undergraduates entering British universities in 1957 who failed to graduate. In one faculty wastage was as high as 56 per cent, and in seventy other instances over the three years it was 20 per cent or higher. The table also shows the marked stability of wastage rates in most faculties—an almost constant factor to which Vernon also has referred. (9)

Table 2, taken from the University Grants Committee Report of 1968*, shows there has not been a great change in overall wastage rates in ten to fifteen years, and that scientific and technological faculties still have the greatest proportion of failure.

* *Enquiry into Student Progress, 1968,* University Grants Committee (H.M.S.O.).

12

TABLE I

Wastage Rates of Undergraduate Entrants: by Faculty, University, and Year of Entry (Great Britain).
Percentage of Students failing to gain Degrees

University	Arts 1952 entrants	Arts 1955 entrants	Arts 1957 entrants	Science 1952 entrants	Science 1955 entrants	Science 1957 entrants	Technology 1952 entrants	Technology 1955 entrants	Technology 1957 entrants
A	20	13	20	22	21	21	19	16	22
B	19	17	16	23	22	23	33	19	36
C	6	5	3	4	3	3	6	5	5
D	13	12	14	11	10	12	23	16	19
E	16	16	14	17	16	17	19	18	18
F	5	9	11	13	10	9	19	7	32
G	28	14	18	23	19	19	35	31	28
H	14	11	11	32	17	19	—	—	—
I	12	11	14	18	19	14	21	21	22
J	24	21	20	40	33	22	—	—	—
K	28	16	17	21	16	12	19	25	24
L	16	8	15	20	15	22	28	26	21
M	18	13	16	10	4	12	23	22	20
N	10	6	8	11	12	12	18	19	17
O	25	19	18	29	14	19	33	26	28
P	—	—	—	44	19	23	31	30	34
Q	25	22	10	—	—	24	—	—	—
R	10	12	11	20	17	13	18	18	22
S	14	15	11	22	22	20	33	24	9
T	7	10	11	11	12	9	40	22	14
U	34	12	8	56	25	28	—	—	—
V	19	11	9	12	17	17	—	—	—
W	38	18	19	44	30	26	7	—	—
X	7	8	8	6	5	4	—	14	11
All universities	15	12	12	18	15	15	22	20	21

Source: University Grants Committee. Note: The universities are listed in random order.

13

TABLE 2

Students who left without having obtained a first degree by time of leaving

All Subject Groups

Period of Study: All periods

Reason for leaving: All reasons
Men and Women
Home and Oversea

University	Number who would normally have graduated in 1965–66 (1)	1st Term (2)		Remainder of 1st year (3)		Second Year (4)		Third Year (5)		Fourth Year (6)		Fifth Year (7)		Sixth Year (8)		Number	% of Col.1
		Number	% of Col.1	Number	% of Col.1	Number	% of Col.1	Number	% of Col.1	Number	% of Col.1	Number	% of Col.1	Number	% of Col.1		
Aston	495	4	0·8	88	17·8	38	7·7	13	2·6	1	0·2	—	—	—	—	144	29·1
Bath	125	—	—	13	10·4	7	5·6	15	12·0	—	—	—	—	—	—	35	28·0
Birmingham	1,255	4	0·3	60	4·8	41	3·3	14	1·1	1	0·1	1	0·1	—	—	121	9·6
Bradford	402	3	0·7	44	10·9	50	12·4	17	4·2	8	2·0	2	0·5	—	—	124	30·8
Bristol	1,110	7	0·6	50	4·5	31	2·8	17	1·5	1	0·1	—	—	—	—	108	9·7
Brunel	161	3	1·9	18	11·2	13	8·1	10	6·2	—	—	3	1·9	2	0·2	47	29·2
Cambridge	2,263	1	—	34	1·5	24	1·1	17	0·8	1	—	—	—	—	—	77	3·4
City	414	—	—	55	13·3	40	9·7	14	3·4	8	1·9	3	0·7	—	—	121	29·2
Durham	550	4	0·7	12	2·2	8	1·5	10	1·8	—	—	—	—	—	—	34	6·2
Exeter	569	—	—	39	7·0	18	3·2	8	1·4	—	—	—	—	—	—	65	11·4
Hull	769	2	0·3	37	4·8	16	2·1	7	0·9	—	—	—	—	—	—	62	8·1
Keele	241	—	—	15	6·2	8	3·3	3	1·2	—	—	—	—	—	—	26	10·8
Leeds	1,509	7	0·5	82	5·4	50	3·3	23	1·5	12	0·8	2	0·1	1	0·1	177	11·7
Leicester	590	2	0·3	43	7·3	11	1·9	6	1·0	—	—	—	—	—	—	62	10·5
Liverpool	1,240	9	0·7	14	1·1	34	2·7	30	2·4	19	1·5	10	0·8	—	—	117	9·4
London	5,048	29	0·6	332	6·6	190	3·8	112	2·2	35	0·7	5	0·1	4	0·1	707	14·0
Loughboro'	473	6	1·3	93	19·7	48	10·1	13	2·7	—	—	—	—	—	—	161	34·0
Manchester	1,500	7	0·5	58	3·9	32	2·1	40	2·7	9	0·6	1	0·1	1	0·1	148	9·9
U.M.I.S.T.	617	1	0·2	42	6·8	19	3·1	8	1·3	6	1·0	—	—	—	—	76	12·4
Newcastle	1,135	5	0·5	60	5·3	40	3·5	12	1·1	—	—	—	—	—	—	113	10·0
Nottingham	988	7	0·7	60	6·0	28	2·8	10	1·0	—	—	—	—	—	—	103	10·4
Oxford	2,298	3	0·1	59	2·6	22	1·0	25	1·1	2	0·1	—	—	—	—	115	5·0
Reading	571	—	—	39	6·8	8	1·4	8	1·4	—	—	—	—	—	—	58	10·2
Salford	461	1	0·2	79	17·1	43	9·3	22	4·8	—	—	1	0·2	—	—	146	31·7
Sheffield	1,077	—	—	65	6·0	43	4·0	40	3·7	2	0·2	2	0·2	—	—	153	14·2
Southampton	600	2	0·3	37	6·2	14	2·3	12	2·0	—	—	—	—	—	—	65	10·8
Surrey	380	3	0·8	48	12·6	48	12·6	16	4·2	7	1·8	—	—	—	—	122	32·1
Sussex	422	4	0·9	15	3·6	5	1·2	5	1·2	2	0·5	—	—	—	—	31	7·3

Numbers leaving without having obtained a first degree

Institution																		
Total England	27,479	119	0·4	1,599	5·8	941	3·4	531	1·9	117	0·4	30	0·1	—	9	—	3,346	12·2
Aberystwyth	539	3	0·6	51	9·4	13	2·4	6	1·1	—	—	—	—	—	—	—	73	13·5
Bangor	445	2	0·4	23	5·2	10	2·2	14	3·2	3	0·7	—	—	—	—	—	52	11·7
Cardiff	645	2	0·3	36	5·6	27	4·2	11	1·7	2	0·3	—	—	—	—	—	78	12·1
Swansea	557	1	0·2	24	4·3	16	2·9	7	1·2	4	0·7	—	—	—	—	—	52	9·3
W.N.S.M.	65	—	—	—	—	—	—	1	1·5	—	—	—	—	—	—	—	1	1·5
Total U. of Wales	2,251	8	0·4	134	6·0	66	2·9	39	1·7	9	0·4	—	—	—	—	—	256	11·4
St. David's Lampeter	84	2	2·4	21	25·0	10	11·9	1	1·2	—	—	—	—	—	—	—	34	40·5
Welsh C.A.T.	172	—	—	29	16·8	11	6·4	5	2·9	1	0·6	—	—	—	1	0·6	47	27·3
Total Wales	2,507	10	0·4	184	7·3	87	3·5	45	1·8	10	0·4	—	—	—	1	0·6	337	13·4
Aberdeen	720	—	—	61	8·5	25	3·5	15	2·1	14	1·9	—	—	—	—	—	115	16·0
Dundee	442	2	0·4	22	5·0	15	3·4	6	1·4	5	1·1	—	—	—	—	—	50	11·3
Edinburgh	1,553	5	0·3	125	8·1	65	4·2	31	2·0	24	1·5	2	0·1	—	—	—	252	16·2
Glasgow	1,423	6	0·4	104	7·3	65	4·6	66	4·6	17	1·2	3	0·2	—	—	—	261	18·3
Heriot-Watt	238	—	—	46	19·4	21	8·8	12	5·0	1	0·4	—	—	—	—	—	80	33·6
St. Andrews	368	1	0·3	29	7·9	11	3·0	7	1·9	5	1·3	—	—	—	—	—	53	14·4
Strathclyde	656	5	0·8	81	12·3	73	11·2	31	4·7	4	0·6	—	—	—	—	—	194	29·6
Total Scotland	5,400	19	0·4	468	8·6	275	5·1	168	3·1	70	1·3	5	0·1	—	—	—	1,005	18·6
Total Great Britain	35,386	148	0·4	2,251	6·4	1,303	3·7	744	2·1	197	0·6	35	0·1	—	10	—	4,688	13·3

Reproduced from "Enquiry into Student Progress, 1968" (University Grants Committee; H.M.S.O.) with the permission of the Controller of Her Majesty's Stationery Office.

The Robbins Report compared the rates of wastage in the United Kingdom with those of other countries. In the United States, of students who enrolled for degree courses in four-year colleges in the 1950's, about 40–50 per cent left without obtaining a Bachelor's degree, while a further 10 per cent took longer than the normal four years. The College Entrance Examinations Board estimated that overall wastage was 45 per cent for men and 48 per cent for women. (10) But, of course, these data conceal enormous differences between institutions' wastage rates. For example, at Stanford 80 per cent of students graduate, and after transfer most of the remaining 20 per cent graduate from other universities, and it has been estimated that only 2 per cent of Stanford students who left Stanford did so because of academic failure. (11)

Such striking differences in wastage rates between different universities and different faculties in the same university (12) are probably common in all countries.

University Grants Committee statistics also show that even when taken on a national basis these differences in wastage between different fields of study are marked. In taking a national average it is expected that the differences would smooth out to some extent, but they are still quite large, as Tables 3 and 4 show, even though individual differences between institutions and faculties are masked. (13, 14)

TABLE 3

Percentage of Progress after Four Years (1952 Entry) of First-degree Students in Arts and Social Studies, Pure Science, Applied Science

Faculty	Successful	Readmitted	Left without Success	All
(1) Arts and Social Studies	84.1	1.6	14.3	100
(2) Pure Science	80.5	1.7	17.8	100
(3) Applied Science	69.4	8.2	22.4	100

Source: University Grants Committee, *University Development* 1957–62, Cmnd. 2267 (H.M.S.O., 1963).

From Tables 2, 3, and 4 three things are clear. First, wastage in applied science or technology was nearly twice that in arts and social studies, with pure science falling roughly midway;

TABLE 4

Percentage of First-degree Students who left without Success (1954–57 Entry) for Academic and Other Reasons

Faculty	Year of Entry	Year of Study							
		1st	2nd	3rd	4th	5th	6th	7th	Total
Arts and Social Studies	1957	5.9	2.9	2.4	0.7	n.a	n.a	n.a	11.9
Pure Science	1957	6.2	4.6	2.9	1.0	n.a	n.a	n.a	14.7
Applied Science	1957	10.4	6.3	2.7	1.4	n.a	n.a	n.a	20.8
Agriculture, Forestry	1957	7.3	0.9	2.5	1.5	n.a	n.a	n.a	12.2
Veterinary Science	1954	5.3	3.9	4.8	1.3	0.9	n.a	n.a	16.2
Dentistry	1955	3.7	3.9	0.6	0.6	0.2	0.4	n.a	9.4
Medicine	1954	1.3	3.7	2.7	2.1	0.5	0.3	0.1	10.7

Source: University Grants Committee, *University Development* 1957–62, Cmnd. 2267 (H.M.S.O., 1963).

1. Compared with Table 2, there has been a slight overall lessening in wastage in the two quinquennia.
2. First year has the greatest attrition in most instances.

second, the greater amount of wastage occurs in first year; and, third, there was a very slight overall improvement in wastage rates over the years. The proportional wastage between science and arts was still about the same throughout all periods.

Mountford's study provides an example in one institution of the differences between faculties in their wastage rates. (15, 16) Of students admitted to arts, science, medicine, and engineering, which were the biggest faculties and those which to some extent took over where the sixth form of the grammar school left off, one in ten failed to complete. Failure to complete was twice as great in dentistry, law, and veterinary science. In architecture it was three times as frequent, 30 per cent failing to complete. It is notable that in the two groups of departments where the greatest wastage occurred the studies were least related to specific school subjects.

The cost of wastage is enormous. Malleson (17) has pointed out that in financial terms one 'student year' of wastage costs about £700. Considering the national average of 1½ years which is spent by non-graduating students in higher education, he calculated the annual cost of wastage in the country as a whole to be about £5 million. Because of increased student numbers and increased costs this figure must by now have risen significantly,

S.F.W.H.E.—B

assuming wastage rates to be the same. Malleson, therefore, considers that reducing the wastage rate would be the most rapid and economical way of increasing the effective number of university places and, therefore, academic productivity. He calculated that in the sciences and technologies alone a reduction of the wastage rate from 20 per cent to 10 per cent would be the effective equivalent of two entire new universities.

Though not directly comparable because of the high part-time component, wastage in other sections of higher education is much worse. Venables (18) indicates that similar phenomena to those found in universities exist in technical colleges. For example, pass rates in certain examinations have been amazingly constant for many years, at about 54 per cent. Even when colleges set their own examinations the expectation that half the students will fail appears to operate. Although heads of colleges maintain that no conscious effort is made to keep the pass rate at 50–60 per cent, this is what they managed nevertheless to do. Venables cites instances in which heads of colleges, having raised the pass rate to 80 per cent or so of students, were said to have been honoured by an inspectorial visit.

Venables and Jenkinson (19) give evidence of built-in wastage in technical institutions, where established percentages are failed in each year and thereby disqualified from proceeding to the following year. Table 5 shows how, when six different pass rates are applied to a given 100 candidates in courses of up to seven years' duration, severe reduction in student numbers occurs.

TABLE 5

The Effect of consistently applying Six Different Pass Rates to 100 Candidates in Courses of up to Seven Years' Duration

years completed	Year	50%	60%	70%	75%	80%	90%
—	1	100	100	100	100	100	100
1	2	50	60	70	75	80	90
2	3	25	36	49	56	64	81
3	4	13	22	34	42	51	73 gain O.N.C.
4	5	6	13	24	32	41	66 gain O.N.C.
5	6	3	8	17	24	33	59 gain H.N.C.
6	7	2	5	12	18	26	53 gain H.N.C.
7	8	1	3	8	14	21	48 gain graduateship

Source: A. J. Jenkinson, *The Vocational Aspect* (Pergamon Press, 1959).

Even a pass rate of 90 per cent applied year by year produces a grievous wastage. At this rate, of 100 starters only 73 would gain the Ordinary National Certificate, 59 the Higher National Certificate, and in eight years only 48 would gain graduateship of an institution. On a three-year course where 66 per cent are passed in each year, only about 30 per cent would finish in minimum time. The question whether built-in wastage is effective in maintaining academic standards or justifiable on other grounds is worth serious consideration, and must be asked in conjunction with the question of how institutions can maintain or improve productivity. Consideration might also be given as to whether the remedy is to be found in greater examination rigour. Perhaps better teaching rather than more rigorous examinations would be more instrumental in raising or maintaining academic standards and productivity.

Darley (20) studied students at Minnesota, Wisconsin, Texas, and Ohio, and the relationships between their achievements and the institutions themselves. He found a significant relationship between the types of institution entered and the academic results of high-potential students. Overall there was only a 60 per cent chance that they would ever graduate, even though they were a group which might be expected to succeed without excessive effort if, as Darley stated, they were "properly stimulated, advised and taught". The fact that, among those who do not initially succeed, a proportion do succeed by transferring to another institution raises questions about the nature of educational environments as they bear on student behaviour, especially as, according to Knoell, (21) the institutions to which students transfer are generally equal to, if not better than, the ones in which they were originally enrolled. Fuller discussion of institutional variables which impinge on student performance follows in later chapters.

Studies of Ford Scholars in eleven different medical colleges by Funkenstein, (22) who made visits to colleges where he studied Deans' records and talked with physicians, psychiatrists, teachers, and students, led him to call for a national study of reasons for failure to graduate. He found that attrition in these colleges had increased by two-thirds, to a wastage of graduates on a scale equivalent to the graduating classes of three medical schools, yet there was evidence that the quality of students at entry had not deteriorated.

Shuman, (23) Jex and Merrill, (24) and MacIntosh (25) also

refer to the costliness of up to 50 per cent of students dropping out of U.S. colleges. Jex and Merrill in their study of persistence reported a study in which only 20.2 per cent graduated on schedule, but 45 per cent graduated over a very extended period of thirteen years, and Eckland (26) reported on another large institution where 60 per cent of a year's male intake dropped out before graduation, but only one-third of the drop-outs were permanent, and half of the original 60 per cent graduated within ten years.

Although such periods are longer than most academics would care to tolerate, these studies provide evidence of a rarely considered aspect of the nature of wastage. They support the hope that a large number of students who do not graduate in the minimum time nevertheless gain an abiding interest in learning from their period in higher education, which is one of the supposed goals of education apart from the formal degree.

By contrast, the University of Wurzburg (27) in 1966 published its intention of discouraging the perennial students who occupy for too long places which are needed by more serious students. In future students will be expected to take the final examination not more than two years beyond the norm of the four years' course. In one course it was discovered that of students who stayed on for six years, 53.6 per cent failed the examination, compared with the 8.8 per cent who failed after only four years. Obviously policies will vary between universities on how long to encourage failing students to stay on until graduation, but unless diminishing returns are evident, as they were at Wurzburg, a case could be made for not creating wastage of students who have gone some way towards attaining their degrees. If they are forced to leave the investment in them is then lost. In the United States most students take longer because of the custom of working their way through college. In the report from Wurzburg it was evident that the new rule was meant to exclude not industrious students but the idle dilettantes whose families could afford to support them indefinitely. English universities generally seem to be more exacting than universities in other countries in so far as students who fail in finals are not so often given such long periods to regain lost ground. In certain universities this may be a source of wastage that is avoidable by an adjustment of departmental policy.

In Australian universities the wastage rate of 30–40 per cent has been stable for at least twenty years. The Royal Commission on the University of Western Australia in 1942, Hohne in 1952, and the Murray Report on Australian Universities in 1957, all made reference to overall wastage rates of 30–40 per cent. (28) The Murray Commission reported that in 1957 in New South Wales only 4.4 per cent of the 17–18 age group entered universities, while the evidence suggested that 16 per cent of any age group of the Australian community had intellectual ability above the minimum generally considered necessary for success at the university. In spite of this apparently highly selective nature of Australian students the Murray Committee found it necessary to say that the most disturbing aspect of university education was the high failure rate. In 1951 only 61 per cent passed the first-year examinations, only 35 per cent graduated in the minimum time possible, and only 58 per cent had graduated six years after enrolment or were expected to graduate at all. The Murray Committee considered that such a high failure rate was a national extravagance which could ill be afforded, and recommended a graduation target of 80 per cent—a cut of 50 per cent in wastage. As Frederick (29) wrote, the cost of wastage must be reckoned not only in terms of money but in terms of time and effort of students and staffs. The cost to the student is loss of professional certification and perhaps loss of morale, and to society it represents a loss of professional people, of whom there are too few. The situation would seem to be the more extravagant when evidence indicated that in the years immediately leading up to the Murray Report the quality of student intake had risen. (30) Gray and Short (31) reported that in one Australian university about 25 per cent of selected scholarship-holders were being failed in first year.

One of the most important aspects of the nature of wastage is the frequency with which promising students fail and the less promising succeed. Schonell et al. (32) studied 1478 students, 400 intensively, over seven years, in arts, science, medicine, and engineering, having a mean I.Q. of 125.8 and standard deviation of 7.0. They found that 40 per cent of students of above-average intelligence were unable to make normal progress and finish in minimum time, while 40 per cent of below-average students were able to make normal progress; and 17.8 per cent of the lowest range of I.Q. 105–114, scarcely promising as university students, were able to finish their studies in minimum time. Parkyn (33) in New Zealand reported similar wastage rates to those cited by Sanders for Australian universities. Like Schonell, he found that success and failure was not proportionately distributed over the whole range of ability, but that students of low ability sometimes did well and those of high ability did poorly.

Productivity is not a popular word in the field of education because of the dangers of oversimplification whereby factors such as academic standards, general education, and research growth and its significance can perhaps too easily be ignored and are certainly not yet accurately measurable. But there is a developing interest in productivity in higher education, and refinements in its measurement are being attempted, notably by Claus Moser's Unit for Economic and Statistical Studies in Higher Education at the London School of Economics, Mark Blaug and Maureen Woodhall at the University of London Institute of Education, and John Vaizey at Brunel. Blaug and Woodhall (34) have calculated that productivity in British universities declined in the period of their survey of productivity trends, 1938–52. While the authors recognize that their cultural, educational, and economic indices are necessarily crude, their results are certainly startling, and have implications for policies of institutions and departments regarding teaching and other services which might reduce wastage.

What are some of the possibilities? Students vary in their motivation, personality, background, intelligence, and in diverse other ways, but so long as the perpetual puzzle of how to improve selection is not close to solution it is appropriate that institutional characteristics should be closely examined. Much of the thinking about academic performance still centres around the student and his limitations. It is a commonly held view that if selection could be improved the problem of wastage and failure would be solved, but, from the literature, it is clear that this is a limited and oversimplified view that cannot possibly lead to any solution, because of the intervening variables which are overlooked.

As long ago as 1952 opinions about wastage were expressed at the Conference of the Universities of Great Britain and Northern Ireland; (35) several points were debated which went far beyond the simple view that improved selection would eliminate wastage, and recognized institutional factors. These points included (i) that student failure was in part a function of the interaction between the student and his teacher, (ii) that the social problems of students can affect their work, (iii) that variations in temperament and physique may affect performance, (iv) that lecturing can be improved, (v) that it is necessary for faculty to be able to recognize when a student is meeting difficulties, and to be able to do something to help, presumably directly or by referring him to a suitable person, (vi) that a sense of vocation and maturity were important factors in achievement, and (vii) that too often institutions unconsciously raised standards. The Robbins Committee listed similar possible explanations for poor performance, including lack of intellectual ability, lack of application, defective teaching, difficulties of psychological adjustment to university life, and extraneous personal troubles and other factors. (36)

Summerskill (37) in the United States, in an extensive review of the literature on drop-outs, concluded that in any study of motivational factors in attrition it is most important to pay attention to institutional characteristics and values. Sanders (38) in Australia made a similar point, saying, "The problem of selection, wastage and failure cannot be considered apart from the university systems in which they occur, nor apart from the underlying educational theory which motivates academic action in [particular] systems. The point needs to be borne in mind that academic failure involves questions of aims and objectives"—*i.e.*, the educational policies of institutions or their responsibility towards the students in helping them to achieve the standards set.

Summerskill (39) also concluded that attrition problems involve students' failure to meet the psychological, sociological, or economic demands, as well as the strictly academic demands of the college environment. In so far as the objectives of colleges are to educate and admit to graduation the students they accept, academic failure must be viewed as a failure on the part of institutions as well as individual students. Sanford, (40) making the same point, asks, "How can one discuss attrition without recognition of the goals of the institution, the qualities fostered in students, means of progress in these directions, and degrees of success?" Institutional variables cannot be regarded as constants. Sir James Mountford once wrote:

> As a general proposition I would suggest that when more than 10 per cent of a class fails, something is seriously wrong with the selection of students, or the teaching they have received or the examining to which they have been subjected; and that when the failure rate reaches 25 per cent, it is time

for what may be euphemistically called a staff re-organization. (41)

In the following chapters there will be discussion of student variables, but greater importance will be attached to research on institutional variables which affect students and their academic performance.

The research which has been studied has led to the consideration of the problem of success and failure in higher education on the model proposed by Astin *et al.** and elaborated as shown.

A. *STUDENT INPUTS*
Background, Aptitudes,
Personality, Attitudes,
Social Class, Age and Sex,
Family Characteristics,
Cognitive Style and Study Habits,
Motivations, Ambition,
Scholastic Aptitude, School Qualification,
Financial Status

B. *INSTITUTIONAL OPERATIONS*
Selection Methods, Administrative Policies,
Ethos, Curricula, Teaching Methods,
Staff-Student Relations,
Counselling and Guidance Facilities,
Diversity, Flexibility, and Rigidity of
   Course Arrangements,
Allowance for Student Mobility—
   between Courses
   between Institutions
Pass Rates and Policies,
Examinations and Other Assessment Methods,
Research and Application of Research Findings,
Student Residence, Appointments Boards

C. *STUDENT AND
INSTITUTIONAL OUTPUTS*
Degree-holders, Attainment,
Qualifications,
Liberal Education,
Dissemination of Knowledge,
Research,
Vocational Choice,
Professionals,
Drop-outs and 'Wastage'

Inputs and Outputs

It can easily be visualized how student inputs (Box A) may be modified, by variables in Box B, and how, in turn, outputs (Box C) may be affected.

* A. W. Astin, R. J. Panos, and J. A. Creager, *A Program of Longitudinal Research on the Higher Education System*, A.C.E. Research Reports, vol. 1, p. 1, 1966 (A.C.E. Office of Research).

REFERENCES

1. N. Sanford, "Personality Development during the College Years", *Journal of Social Issues*, 12, 1956.
2. Committee on Higher Education, *Higher Education: Report on the Committee appointed by the Prime Minister under the chairmanship of Lord Robbins*, 1961–63, Cmnd. 2154, para. 576 (London, H.M.S.O., 1963).
3. University Grants Committee, *Enquiry into Student Progress*, (H.M.S.O., 1968).
4. J. H. McNeely, *College Student Mortality* (U.S. Office of Education, Washington, 1938).
5. J. Summerskill, "Dropouts from College", in N. Sanford (ed.), *The American College* (New York and London, Wiley, 1962).
6. C. Sanders, "Report on Academic Wastage and Failure among University Students in Australia and Other Countries: A Review of Research and Opinion" (Mimeo), (Faculty of Education, University of Western Australia, 1958).
7. T. H. Matthews, "Academic Failures", In C. Bissell (ed.), *Canada's Crisis in Higher Education* (University of Toronto Press, 1957).
8. R. K. Kelsall, "University Selection in Relation to Subsequent Academic Performance: A Critical Appraisal of the British Evidence", in P. Halmos (ed.), *The Sociological Review Monograph, No. 7* (University of Keele, 1963).
9. P. E. Vernon, "The Pool of Ability", in P. Halmos (ed.), *The Sociological Review Monograph, No. 7* (University of Keele, 1963).
10. Robbins Report, para. 576.
11. Robbins Report, Appendix II (A), pp. 176–177.
12. Robbins Report, para. 579.
13. University Grants Committee, *University Development 1952–1957*, University Grants Committee Report, Cmnd. 534 (H.M.S.O. 1958).
14. University Grants Committee, *University Development 1957–62*, University Grants Committee Report, Cmnd. 2267 (H.M.S.O., 1963).
15. Sir James Mountford, "Success and Failure at the University", *Universities Quarterly*, 11, May 1957.

16. Sir James Mountford, *How they Fared: A Survey of a Three Year Student Entry* (Liverpool University Press, 1956).

17. N. B. Malleson, "Must Students be Wasted?", *New Society*, May 2nd, 1963.

18. Ethel Venables, *The Young Worker at College* (London, Faber, 1967).

19. A. J. Jenkinson, "Wastage—Natural, Built-in or Imposed", *The Vocational Aspect*, **9**, 2, 1959.

20. J. G. Darley, *Promise and Performance*, Berkeley: Center for the Study of Higher Education (University of California, 1962).

21. Dorothy Knoell, "Undergraduate Attrition: Mortality or Mobility", paper given at Princeton University Conference on the College Drop-out and Utilization of Talent, 1964.

22. D. H. Funkenstein, "Failure to Graduate from Medical School", *Journal of Medical Education*, **37**, 1962.

23. R. B. Shuman, "College Dropouts: An Overview", *Journal of Educational Sociology*, **29**, 1956.

24. F. B. Jex and R. M. Merrill, "A Study in Persistence: Withdrawal and Graduation Rates at the University of Utah", *Personnel and Guidance Journal*, **40**, 1962.

25. A. MacIntosh, *Behind the Academic Curtain* (New York, Harper).

26. R. B. Eckland and Anita Smith, *A Follow-up Study of Male Members of the Freshman Class of the University of Illinois in September* 1952, Office of Instructional Research Report No. 105. Urbana, Illinois, University of Illinois, 1963. Cited in Dorothy M. Knoell, *op. cit.*

27. Report in *The Times Educational Supplement*, June 3rd, 1966.

28. Report of Royal Commission on the Administration of the University of Western Australia, Government Printer, Perth, 1942; H. H. Hohne, "The Prediction of Academic Success (Faculty of Arts)", Australian Council for Educational Research, Melbourne, 1951; Commonwealth of Australia, *Report of the Committee on Australian Universities,* Canberra, Commonwealth Government Printer, September 1957.

29. W. H. Frederick ,"Components of Failure", in E. L. French (ed.), *Melbourne Studies in Education* (University of Melbourne Press, 1957).

30. C. Sanders, *op. cit.*
31. G. A. Gray and L. N. Short, *Student Progress in the University*, 1958–60 (Mimeo), (University of New South Wales, 1961).
32. Sir Fred J. Schonell, E. Roe, and I. G. Meddleton, *Promise and Performance: A Study of Student Progress at University Level* (University of Queensland and University of London, 1962).
33. G. W. Parkyn, *Success and Failure at the University*, 1: *Academic Success and Entrance Standards* (Wellington, N.Z.C.E.R., 1959).
34. Maureen Woodhall and Mark Blaug, "Productivity Trends in British University Education 1938–52", *Minerva*, 3, 4, 1965.
35. Report of the Proceedings of the Conference of the Universities of Great Britain and Northern Ireland, 1952.
36. Robbins Report, para. 578.
37. J. Summerskill, *op. cit.*
38. C. Sanders, *op. cit.*
39. J. Summerskill, *op. cit.*
40. N. Sanford, *op. cit.*
41. Sir James Mountford, 1957, *op. cit.*

CHAPTER 2

STUDENT FACTORS

R E S E A R C H, theory, and opinion about wastage and performance is most readily centred on the student himself. The aspects
which have attracted most thought and research have been the
following:

(i) social class, sub-culture, and family variables.
(ii) ability, age, and maturity,
(iii) peer relationships, need for affiliation,
(iv) the effects of participation in extra-curricular activities and
of taking vacation or other part-time employment,
(v) psychiatric and other stress variables,
(vi) the reasons students themselves perceive as being instrumental in their failure,
(vii) vocational orientation,
(viii) intrinsic interest in the subjects studied,
(ix) persistence, motivation, and other personality attributes,
study habits and discipline.

Studies up to 1940 reviewed by Harris (1) suggested that
scholastic ability and aptitude, effort, drive and motivation, and
social, personal, economic, and academic circumstances were of
major importance, in that order. In this chapter most of these
areas will be examined. Sir Alexander Carr-Saunders's statement
(2) is a good example of the kind of well-informed opinion which
is often expressed, sometimes based on experience over a long
career but less frequently backed by research findings. In a study
at the London School of Economics and Political Science from
1949 to 1952, of 305 B.Sc.(Econ.) candidates, he discovered
little evidence that difficult circumstances were a frequent cause
of failure. His impression was that the failures are people who are
inconspicuous in the student body, rather lost, and not coping
with things generally. These are indicators of ineffectual behaviour which may be general in all situations, not only in the
university setting. Headmasters of English grammar schools were
asked by Furneaux (3) which pupils they thought would be

handicapped in university studies, and their opinions were quite similar to those expressed by Carr-Saunders. The reasons they gave are shown in Table 6.

TABLE 6

*Percentages of Reasons given by Headmasters for Students'
Inability to succeed at the University*

Lack of ability to work in a university atmosphere.	6
Lack of perseverance	6
Lack of ambition	5
Lack of ability	17
Lack of any strong interest	5
Lack of right home background	4
Interests not in line with abilities	3
Nervousness, excitability, temperamental difficulties	6
Poor physical health	3
One or more of above	40

Source: W. D. Furneaux, *The Chosen Few* (Nuffield Foundation, Oxford University Press).

The views of headmasters should carry a great deal of weight, but few can have been in a position to make the necessary follow-up studies of sufficiently large groups to enable significant generalizations to be made concerning the large and varied populations of school-leavers entering on higher education.

It would at first appear a truism that demonstrated scholastic ability is of paramount importance in the selection of students. But those who are selected for universities and colleges of education in Great Britain are in or near the top 10 per cent as measured by school achievement, and this degree of selection implies a shrinkage in the standard deviation or the spread about the mean, making factors other than ability more important for academic performance.

The fact that the most promising students do not always live up to their promise need not be regarded as a mystery. Even when quotas operate and only the most highly promising candidates are admitted to studies it is almost certain that some will fail.

Broe (4) and Matthews (5) and many others have noted the incidence of failure amongst the most carefully selected and intelligent students. Matthews suspected that the greatest single cause of academic failure was lack of interest, and sought to discover why students with adequate ability were not interested in their university courses and did not work hard enough. A Committee of Toronto Vice-Principals in a report on able students who failed stated that in no case did the student admit that the work was beyond his ability. There are numerous studies showing that factors other than ability or lack of it enter into academic success and failure.

Other frequently expressed views are that student performance is influenced by students' adaptability, maturity, self-discipline, ambition, and perseverance, failure to budget time sensibly between study and extra-curricular activities, (6) intrinsic motivation, external incentives, student-lecturer rapport, motivation by peers, motivation by parents, personality factors, emotional problems, attitudes, and organization and study methods, (7) previous scholastic attainment, social and scholastic adjustment to the higher education institution especially in first year, intrinsic interest in subjects, drive to achieve, vocational aims, family aspirations, personal qualities of persistence and toughness, and secondary factors such as accommodation, finance, and living conditions. (8) The influence of any of these conditions may be considerable, but two or more acting together may have a cumulative effect.

Priestley, (9) who for many years conducted the student counselling office at the University of Melbourne, has referred to the spiralling interaction between high failure rates and high anxiety. Over a period of three years one thousand students voluntarily sought the help of the student-counselling service. Of these, 6 per cent were experiencing disturbance severe enough to disrupt their university life, such as depression, sexual problems, and psychotic conditions and family conflict. Ten per cent were suffering the handicaps of anxiety states, less serious depression, social isolation, or family conflict, which, though severe, were not crippling. More than 25 per cent had doubts and worries about vocational aims, and almost as many were having difficulties in settling to study, reading, and learning.

Vocational aims and career prospects are thus important for university students, even for those engaged in studies that have very little direct link with any specific vocation. But such aims and prospects are probably much more important in the achievement of students on vocational courses. Venables (10)

30

interviewed part-time technical college engineering students who had failed. Fifty per cent gave lack of interest as one of the main causes of failure. It was clear that very few firms made study worth while in terms of money or status. Wages go up according to the calendar and are generally unaffected by success at college. It is unrealistic when external incentives are so lacking to rely upon intrinsic interest in the subject of study for the continuance of training.

While it may not be clear to what extent these factors, individually or collectively, would affect performance, there can be little doubt that some would have a crippling influence, while others, if managed well, might even have a facilitating effect. It is not true that students automatically fail because they are having problems. Problems as seen by students must be considered in relation to their abilities, interests, personalities, and motives, including incentives of status and remuneration. Clearly we must move away from the oversimplified view of equating ability with academic promise.

The Reasons Students give

When students are interviewed about the circumstances which have led to failure it cannot be assumed their answers are entirely objective, because, consciously or unconsciously, they employ ego defence mechanisms, and, of these, rationalization is probably the chief. After this has been allowed for it is useful to note the reasons they give. Olsen (11) interviewed 80 failing students of all faculties. Only 9 thought they knew the reason for failure. Of these, serious illness causing absence from lectures and impossible study conditions were among the reasons given; these were probably not rationalizations. Of the other 71 failing students only 22 blamed faulty lecturing. Twelve felt they understood too little of the standards likely to be required, and 15 felt they could not budget their time properly because no detailed syllabus was available to help them in the early part of the year to plan their time and work ahead. Although there is possibly more than an element of rationalization here, it is unreasonable to deny credence to the reasons students give. Supplementary explanations advanced by students included loss of interest, home worries, excessive travelling, financial worries, love affairs, and too much sport.

Flecker (12) studied 157 first-year mathematics students, and

50 per cent of the failing students admitted they had not worked consistently over the whole year, but had left their most regular effort until the final term. A large proportion of the failure group claimed they had had personal worries which had interfered with their studies. The main sources of anxiety resemble closely those which Priestley found most frequently in the counselling setting, although the students in his case were not necessarily failing students. Difficulties at home were frequently cited, including strained relations with parents, ill-health, and poor study facilities. Less frequently cited were romance problems, financial worries, and difficulty in settling down; these were cited almost equally.

Of the students studied by Schonell (13) 58.8 per cent blamed themselves for their learning difficulties in not working hard enough, 48.8 per cent maintained that the subject in which they had difficulty was not relevant to their major course of study, was too wide in scope or too difficult. Only 11.2 per cent blamed lecturers for bad presentation and otherwise poor communications with faculty. Students who dropped out or transferred gave as reasons loss of interest in their original courses, which had often been undertaken in response to family pressures or inducements that were later withdrawn, sometimes following a failure. Often two or more of these reasons were given by the one student. Students from country towns often claimed that their failure was related to loneliness and to emotional problems on being away from home for the first time; others thought social distractions and development of new interests limited their academic effort. The findings of Olsen, Schonell, Priestley, and Flecker bear a striking resemblance to one another and also to English and American findings.

For example, Malleson (14) invited students to state what criticisms or difficulties they had experienced as undergraduates. The major ones given were, in order of frequency, social isolation, 15.4 per cent; inadequacy or remoteness of teaching staff, 14.3 per cent; difficulty in budgeting between work and social interests, 13.4 per cent; too much travelling, 12.1 per cent; study difficulties, including inefficient concentration and poor memory, 10 per cent; financial difficulties, 10 per cent; living at home with parents, 8.3 per cent; poor lodging, 3 per cent. Less frequently cited were wrong choice of subject and lack of interest or incentive. Howell (15) in his evidence to the Robbins Committee on Higher Education found that 40 per cent of students mentioned environmental and health factors. Physical illness, nervous strain, and psychological troubles made up 20 per cent of these, and were mentioned more frequently by women than by men. This proportion is high compared with findings in other studies, yet Howell regarded it as a conservative estimate because it referred only to definite crises, taking little account of incipient conditions whose presence was suggested only by lack of self-confidence and worry about work, but which in some cases would develop into more severe states.

This view is supported by Lipset and Altbach, (16) who reported a clinical study of young people aged 13 to 24 years, in which the proportion giving educational stresses as their primary problem jumped from 37 per cent in 1953–54 to 74 per cent in 1960–61. The authors attributed the steadily increasing academic pressures to the proportionately lower numbers of educational places available for increased numbers of candidates for places at each age level. Watson (17) supports this. Students of the City University of New York who were requesting leave of absence were interviewed to determine the precise reasons for their request, and to offer possible alternatives, in an effort to prevent withdrawals. They were all potential or actual drop-outs. The most frequent reason they gave for leaving was the pressure of a severe personal or emotional problem (28 per cent). Twenty-two per cent left because of a home emergency such as death of a parent and for financial reasons. For men financial problems were dominant, and the majority hoped to resume college, presumably after they had saved enough money to continue. Twenty per cent of women left because of pregnancy and the need to support children, and 12 per cent because of accidents and other health reasons. In addition, almost as many were transferring to other colleges as were leaving for health reasons. These were mostly men, and were voluntarily changing their plans, very often in first term.

Astin's (18) findings showed a different emphasis. In his sample, male students most often dropped out because of unsureness about what to study, unsatisfactory grades, and tiredness of being a student, while women gave up studies most often for financial reasons, or family responsibilities, or because they were tired of the student life.

Differences in research design and sampling would account

33

for some of the difference in emphasis between findings, but similar factors were shown to be operating in almost all the studies. The reasons students give must be treated with respect, while allowing for some inevitable rationalization of failure. The most prominent reasons students gave were lack of vocational aim, tiredness of being a student, difficulties in achieving a balance between academic and social life, social isolation, and social and psychological disturbance. Many, but certainly not all, of these seem to add up to lack of motivation. Some of the attendant circumstances are clearly susceptible to modification. These possibilities will be studied in Chapter 3.

Least Influential Variables

It has been demonstrated in a small number of studies that several variables have little correlation with academic achievement. Age, size of family, social class, place of residence while a student, and peer relations are examples of such variables. Though some of these appear to be highly relevant to academic performance, studies by Hopkins, Malleson, and Sarnoff, (19) and Himmelweit and Summerfield (20) in Great Britain and by Astin (21) in the United States have found only marginal relationships.

Hopkins, Malleson, and Sarnoff in their study of students who left University College, London, without obtaining a degree found no significant differences between graduate and failure groups in age, nationality, religion, whether or not they were evacuated away from their homes to the country or abroad during the War, whether or not they had done National Service training, number of siblings, place of residence while at university, estimated time spent on games, sport, or union activities, questions relating to childhood happiness, parental harmony or discord, and childhood discipline. Himmelweit and Summerfield studied 40 over-achievers and 40 under-achievers, who were selected from a larger sample on the criterion of their being plus or minus at least one standard deviation from the mean discrepancy score—*i.e.*, the discrepancy between I.Q. scores and attainment. The two groups did not differ significantly in age, intelligence, social class, family size, whether or not from a broken home, type of school, parents' education, or in personality test scores.

These two studies share some similar findings. The students

in both studies were highly selected samples; it follows that because of the small range of ability of the subjects there would be some shrinkage in the correlation between ability and attainment. It might have been expected that the other variables cited would assume greater importance than ability in this narrow ability range, and it is therefore of great interest that they had no influence.

The reasons which students themselves give for terminating studies are somewhat different from those variables studied by Hopkins, Malleson, and Sarnoff, or Himmelweit and Summerfield, and are not directly comparable. In Astin's study of dropping out students gave the following reasons least frequently: few of their friends being at college, discouragement from faculty; lack of confidence in ability and termination of grant (women); college not relevant to students' goals, and family ties (men).

It is not suggested that definitive generalizations can be made from three studies or, on the other hand, that these variables are of no account; before they can be dismissed more investigations are required.

Ability

It is perfectly clear that students cannot achieve at any level without the necessary ability, but necessary ability does not need to be as high as is generally believed. It is possible for students with an I.Q. of 130 plus to fail in their studies, and it is possible for other students with I.Q.'s as low as 105 to gain degrees, provided that they possess other attributes which enable effective study and provided students have the opportunity to exercise those attributes. Gibson has found that even university scientists sometimes have unexpectedly low I.Q.'s. (22) Sir James Learmonth (23) once said a good 'beta' is capable of completing a medical training (granted certain conditions and personal attributes), and Schonell has found that students of low measured ability sometimes complete their university studies while some of the most promising fall by the wayside.

Comparisons made by Schwartzman (24) between a group of failing medical students and a successful group showed a marked contrast between the substantial scholastic disparity between the two groups and their approximately equal intellectual similarity, suggesting that other factors were contributing to the students'

35

academic performance. Watson (25) also discovered that of students who were dropping out of courses 33 per cent were in the upper half of their class in ability. In general, of the men who withdrew slightly more were above the class median in ability than were below. Twenty per cent of the students who left were in the top tenth of ability in this highly selected group. Watson showed that scholastic aptitude was at any rate not the only factor in leaving college because the ability distribution of leavers was much the same as those who stayed in college. A report recently published by the Transvaal Education Bureau (26) reaffirms that at university a high I.Q. does not guarantee success. One-fifth of all failures at South African universities are students who are normally classed as 'very gifted', having an I.Q. of 130 plus. Venables, (27) in her study of engineering apprentices in England, also found little evidence that lack of ability was responsible for high failure rates in technical colleges.

From these varied studies of medical school, several faculties in universities in Australia, the United States, and South Africa, and a technical college in England, the point must readily be taken that ability is not the only important variable in attainment.

Advocates of the 'more means worse' thesis may require a little further convincing, but there is scarcely any need to labour the point, except to note that Eysenck, (28) selecting 34 well-designed studies out of several hundred, found an average correlation of 0.58 between ability-test results and various academic criteria. McKeachie, (29) referring to this order of correlation between ability measures and grades, fairly high though it is, explains that even the best measures of ability leave over half the variance in grades unaccounted for. Even a correlation of 0.70 between ability and academic achievement would scarcely account for 50 per cent of the variance. In the studies reviewed by Eysenck the average 0.58 correlation would account for barely 35 per cent, leaving 65 per cent to be accounted for by other variables. Moreover, correlations are not always so high. Vernon (30) has put the correlation between measured intelligence and university attainment as low as at 0.20. This is a statistically significant correlation for a sample of 250 subjects, but it accounts for only 4 per cent of the variance in attainment at the university. Other factors thus assume importance far beyond what is customarily thought.

Social Class and Other Social Factors
The literature contains a great number of findings relating social class to academic attainment. It is true that at every stage of education middle-class pupils and students are over-represented among the high achievers. Middle-class children find their way early into upper streams of British primary schools (31) —that is, where streaming still prevails—and they are usually over-represented in grammar schools. (32) In the United States, even among veterans who qualify for Government grants in higher education, a larger proportion of soldiers having middle-class origins take advantage of it than those of working-class origin. (33)

Social class *per se* does not in itself account for the differences. Correlations between social class and attainment are generally of the order of 0.30 to 0.35. (34, 35) Though statistically this is highly significant for a modest sample, it allows for a large number of exceptions to the general trend, and, furthermore, what matters is not the social class from which the person originates, but rather it is the characteristics of the person and his social environment which influence his attainment. Recent research is beginning to clarify the point. The Plowden Report on Primary Education (36) made it clear that, so far as children are concerned, home circumstances, including physical amenities of the home or lack of them, the occupation and income of the father, the size of the family, the length of the parents' education and the qualifications they had obtained, which are all indices of 'social class', accounted for only 9 per cent of the variance in educational performance of primary-school children. Parents' attitudes, on the other hand, accounted for 20 per cent of variance. The criteria of parents' attitudes included age at which they wished their children to leave school, their initiative in visiting the school, in talking to heads and class teachers, interest in children's homework, time spent with children in evenings and general literacy of the home as assessed by the kinds and amount of reading, and library membership.

In another study Miller (37) found that two factors which together correlated 0.66 with school achievement and accounted for 44 per cent of variance in achievement were correlated only 0.19 and 0.23 with social class. The greatest possible multiple correlation of these two factors with social class could be no higher than 0.40, probably much less, and could account for

37

no more than 16 per cent of variance in social class. Such a discrepancy between the sizes of the correlations of these factors with achievement and with social class confirms that social class in itself is relatively unimportant. It might be concluded also that the factors which promote achievement in the higher social-class families are present in some lower social-class families to a far greater degree than had earlier been believed. Conversely, this would also mean that factors which promote academic success are not always present in middle-class families, or are present to a lesser degree than had formerly been taken for granted.

When examining the effects of social class, or any other variable, on student performance in higher education we must take into reckoning the fact that we are considering a select group. Not only are they generally of superior ability, but they are also of a comparatively restricted range of social class. This means that we should not expect social class to have such an overall influence in higher education as for the whole range of population, because the standard deviation, or spread, will have shrunk, as for other variables already discussed. Thus, for instance, Malleson (38) found that social-class grouping appeared to have very little influence on the failure rate and academic performance generally of students in arts, science, law, engineering, and political economy. Of those students from the highest social-class grouping 35 per cent failed to graduate, compared with only 10 per cent from the next lower social-class groups. This might be explained in a point made by Marris (39) that working-class students are sometimes superior academically, perhaps because they are more highly selected. They would be less likely to go to university unless they were of exceptional ability; their education most often involves sacrifices for their parents, which they feel they should justify by doing well. They may also feel less at ease with the university culture, and so have fewer distractions outside work, though the latter point could be argued in the opposite direction because it has been found in some studies that social isolation does not promote academic success. (40, 41)

The educational and vocational aspirations of the family, and its expectations that the children will undertake an arduous educational career and eventually enter high-level jobs, and the material and moral support the family give, are, in Vernon's view, of central importance. (42) Rowlands (43) showed that the cultural level of the homes of secondary-school boys was much more closely related than economic level to the tendency of boys to enter university, and Lovell and White (44) found that children are often influenced by their parents, even to the point of choosing particular subjects.

Fathers' occupation, parents' prior connection with university, and degree of family support are persistently referred to throughout the literature. Hughes (45) cites several Australian studies that emphasize the importance of these and also others related to cultural values of the home, and whether they are similar to those traditionally associated with higher education, such as respect for learning as an end in itself. This is linked with the question of whether student performance is affected by parents having themselves had any experience of higher education. The Robbins Committee on Higher Education (46) found no evidence that more 'first generation' university students leave without success than other students. Table 7, reproduced from the Robbins Report, shows wastage by sex and social class.

TABLE 7

Percentage of Undergraduate Entrants in 1955 (excluding Medical Students) who left without Success by Spring 1958: by Sex and Social Class

		Men		Women	
		Percentage who left without success	Number of entrants (=100%)	Percentage who left without success	Number of entrants (=100%)
University Group	Father's Occupation				
Oxford and	Non-manual	4	2,780	6	450
Cambridge	Manual	3	386	6	32
London	Non-manual	13	1,260	13	830
	Manual	12	486	10	166
Civic	Non-manual	12	3,335	8	1,730
	Manual	10	1,844	11	564
Wales	Non-manual	11	410	12	255
	Manual	10	348	8	126
Scotland	Non-manual	13	950	8	645
	Manual	18	400	14	132

Source: Robbins Report, Appendix II A, p. 135, from Sociological Research Unit Survey, London School of Economics.

The Report makes the point that a quarter of undergraduate students in 1955 had fathers in manual occupations, the proportion being slightly higher for men and lower for women. Except in Scotland, there was little difference in wastage rates between those whose fathers were in non-manual and those whose fathers were in manual occupations. In Scotland wastage was rather higher among students who were children of manual workers than among other students. The situation was almost the same across all faculties. Marris's point should be remembered, that the working-class students who came into higher education are to some extent atypical; at 25 per cent in Britain the working class is still under-represented, though well ahead of any other country, with the possible exception of the United States.

Researchers in other countries, even those with a less clearly defined social-class system than Britain, find that the homes of working-class students can be very unsupportive. Gray and Short (47) and Maclaine (48) in Australia have referred to the 'hiatus that exists between home and university'. Only one in five students had fathers who had attended university, and one in fifteen had mothers who had done so. One in twenty parents of students and one in ten other close relations of students were indifferent or opposed to the students' attendance at university. Unfavourable family attitudes towards university courses and the university itself created conflicts which sometimes resulted in failure and withdrawal of students from university. Five or 10 per cent may not seem very significant, but in a university population of 10,000 this represents 500 or 1000 students. Schonell (49) too has taken up this point. He found that working-class students do not do as well as students from homes of parents in professional, semi-professional, and administrative groups, of whom a good number would presumably have had university or college education of some kind. Problems of adjustment, both academic and social, may be greater for some of them, particularly where parental attitudes to higher education and even the general amenities of the home may not be helpful to the student in developing effective study methods. Hammond's study (50) of 954 first-year students from faculties of science, engineering, medicine, dentistry, law, and arts confirmed this. He concluded, 'It would seem that even where intellectual training and attainments are equalized [at entry], the student with the better social background performs better than his intellectual equal. Prior connection of the family with university study assists adaptation from school to university as judged by examination results.' Sanders (51) takes the point farther, suggesting that the prior connection of parents with university is important not so much in itself, but rather because a culturally deprived home with poor study facilities, and even a materially better home given to frequent entertainment, is a deterrent to academic success. Although results conflict and individual students, despite handicaps, do succeed, the trend is in this direction.

The difference between the apparently greater success of students from working-class families in English than Australian universities may be partly accounted for by the fact that 31 per cent of the men and 19 per cent of the women admitted to universities other than Oxford and Cambridge had fathers in manual occupations, (52) compared with Queensland, for example, where only 3.5 per cent of students are sons of working males in semi-skilled and unskilled jobs. (53) Exact comparative statistics are not obtainable, but if those available reflect the true situation it may be that in English universities students from working-class homes experience less of the stress of being the odd man out. In England two and a half times as many students with parents in manual occupations entered universities in the first five years after the War (54) as did so in the ten years before the War. This trend has not continued, however.

A point made by Furneaux (55) following his research on selection is as relevant to higher education as it is to schools. He commented that the reasons for the marked academic superiority of the average child in school whose father is in a profession (and presumably has had some form of higher education), as compared with one whose father is an unskilled worker, are still matters for controversy.

There can be little doubt that sheer physical handicaps are important, such as lack of a quiet place in which to work, but some of the difference is caused by the differing attitudes and traditions of the various social groups. . . . If we knew more about . . . the atypical students [that is, those in sixth forms and universities and colleges] and the ways in which qualities and circumstances conspire to produce these very atypical students, then we might begin to understand how to reduce the tremendous waste of talent, which almost certainly occurs at present within the less fortunate socio-economic groups . . . the children of semi-skilled and unskilled workers, who, by the time they enter sixth form have displayed an educational history so unusual for members of their group as to suggest that either they themselves or perhaps they and their parents must possess qualities of a quite exceptional kind.

What we have already been discussing in relation to the academic performance of undergraduates also applies to such diverse groups as engineering apprentices in a technical college (56, 57, 58) and eminent scientists long after they have left university. It is not a simple question of social class *per se,* but rather a question of early inculcation of interest by parents by some process, the nature of which is not yet fully understood. Venables found that scores on attainment tests obtained by engineering students in four technical colleges were correlated with (i) whether the student had a father or near relative in the engineering industry, and (ii) a father doing a skilled or managerial job. That cultural or subcultural differences are stronger than social class is suggested by Venables' further finding that youths whose fathers were in unskilled or semi-skilled jobs fared at least as well as, and often better than, those from professional families. These students were not representative of their social class; those from professional and managerial backgrounds tended to be intellectually inferior members of their social-class, while those from semi-skilled and unskilled backgrounds tended to be the more intelligent members of theirs. Venables considered how social factors and attitudes affect achievement in the technical college. The secondary-modern school leaver and the child of the semi-skilled and unskilled manual worker appear to take their chance of further education at a local technical college more seriously than their classmates from grammar school or from a superior social class. There is, of course, a further possibility that the former sees his training as a means of upward social mobility while the latter would not, and, on that account, might view his technical studies with some indifference.

The study of eminent scientists by Anne Roe (59) produced very different data which supported the same thesis, that it is not social class *per se* which matters so much as a cultural impetus deriving from the students' social origin. Of 64 eminent scientists none came from extremely wealthy families, and few were sons of working-class families. The occupations of the fathers of these scientists were very unlike the population of the

U.S. as a whole. According to census reports of 1910, only 3 per cent of employed men in the United States were professional men, whereas in Roe's group of eminent scientists the proportion ranged from 38 per cent for fathers of anthropologists to 84 per cent for fathers of theoretical physicists and 53 per cent for fathers of the group in general. This confirms a study by Cattell and Brimball, cited by Roe. They found that 51 per cent of the fathers of leading scientists were professional men. Roe hypothesized from these findings that the reasons middle-class membership encourages academic achievement are (i) inherited intelligence, and (ii) the middle-class value of learning for its own sake. Corresponding values in working-class families seem to have exerted the same influence on Venables' students in the technical colleges. In so far as this argument is true, as the evidence suggests, it seems that cultural values, pressures, and interests of different groups influence choice and success in occupations and professions, and are the key; rather than socio-economic status itself, which at best offers only a convenient system of classification, but not an explanation of differential achievement.

The studies and conclusions already described are supported by the literature reviewed by Harris (60) in 1940 and also by the previously mentioned studies of Astin (61) as well as studies by Sinha in India. (62) Astin found a highly significant relationship ($p < .001$) between the tendency to drop out of college and low level of mothers' and fathers' education, and fathers' occupation; Sinha found that low-achieving Indian undergraduates had less well-educated parents than those who graduated. In studying social factors in performance we must look beyond social class, to interests and values which may reflect the level of parents' education. But first there are other different social factors which also need to be discussed.

Birth Rank and Family Size

These are factors that have been investigated very little, certainly in higher-education research, though the possibility of a relationship with achievement has exercised some people's minds.

Douglas (63) cites two Scottish studies (64) which showed that children aged 11 did not vary consistently in ability according to birth rank, but found in his own national survey reported in *The*

Home and the School that elder children did slightly better on
11-plus tests for secondary selection than only children. Douglas
suggested that lack of competition at home may lead to lack of
competition at school. Although his findings on this point were
not conclusive, it seemed from his data that eldest children may
receive a stimulus which the younger children lack, and the
stimulus seemed to be the presence of a younger child in the
family, rather than the fact of being first born. Douglas's data
for family size were more conclusive. They showed that, even
after allowing for environmental differences among families
of differing size, children from large families did not generally
score as highly in tests of ability as children from smaller
families.

Turning to a later stage of development, post-school, Douglas
made the interesting observations that in later life the eldest
child seems to stand out as superior in achievement, and cited
Galton, (65) who, in 1874 had noted that distinguished men of
science were more often eldest or only sons than younger sons.
Galton qualified this by saying that eldest sons were more likely to
become possessors of independent means and able to follow their
interests more freely than younger sons, but he also thought they
were more likely to be treated as companions by their parents
and to have earlier responsibility, both of which would develop
independence of character, and that "probably also the first born
of families not so well-to-do in the world would generally have
more attention in infancy, more breathing space and better nour-
ishment than his younger brothers and sisters". This Victorian
observation has been confirmed more recently. Douglas cited
American and Italian studies and the *Dictionary of National
Biography,* (66) which support Galton's observations—particularly that scientists and university professors are more often
eldest sons than younger.

Harris (67) reported conflicting findings on family size and
birth rank in relation to academic performance up to 1940, but
in 1953 Roe (68) discovered that of a sample of 64 eminent
scientists no less than 39 were eldest children. Of the remainder
most were first-born sons, and the rest were born after a long
gap since the older sibling was born. There was an age gap of
five years between them and their next elder brothers. Roe hypothesized the same as Galton eighty years before, that the reason
for supremacy of eldest sons is that they develop independence

more than younger siblings, Roe suggesting additionally that they do not suffer from baffling failure to do things which their older siblings can do, and that "when there are enough years between them competition is not acute in the same way, and it is much more easily taken for granted that the older brother is stronger or can do things the younger brother cannot."

These are only hypotheses, and we have not progressed far on this question since Galton, but on the evidence cited there seems to be some link between birth rank and attainment. A clearer understanding of this link might also add to our understanding of personality differences in academic performance.

Home Location and Cultural and Ethnic Differences

In several studies it has been found that the home location of students has some association with academic performance. Of course, it is not simply the location of his home that matters, but what this implies. The implications vary in different studies. For example, it may coincide that the student has rural origins, that he has to travel a long distance from his home each day to attend lectures, or that he has to live in unsatisfactory housing, or that he comes from a province or country having cultural characteristics which differ markedly from the place where he is having his higher education. The latter might also imply ethnic origins different from those of fellow-students.

Forster (69) at Queen's University, Belfast, Priestley (70) at the University of Melbourne, Sinha (71) at the University of Allahabad, and Summerskill (72) and Astin (73) in the United States have all referred to home location of the student as a variable which appears to influence academic achievement, Forster finding that students at Belfast who did not live there did not perform as well as those whose homes were in Belfast. He offered the possible explanation that the majority of students who had come from schools outside Belfast had necessarily to live in lodgings or to travel long distances between home and university during term-time. Priestley made a similar statement about Melbourne students from rural regions. Country students have been shown to have had greater difficulty in their studies than suburban students whose homes were nearer the campus. It was not necessarily a problem of commuting over long distances. Students' private accommodation, in contrast with student residence and students' own homes, often left much to be

45

desired. But Priestley's main explanations were that the families of rural students very often failed to see the relevance of university study for their children, and did not wholeheartedly support them. At the beginnings of their undergraduate careers, and often later, they have little in common socially with their urban colleagues at university, often forming a very small group with other students from country high schools.

The findings of Forster and Priestley are supported by Sinha. Although it is impressive that similar findings have been made in India, Australia, and Northern Ireland, all the findings are not entirely consistent. Summerskill reviewed much American research up to 1961, and found that attrition, or dropping out, was often higher among rural students than among those from cities and towns, but this is not always confirmed. Astin found a significant difference between the tendency of commuting female students to drop out compared with those in residence, but for males the finding was insignificant. The effects of intervening variables must again be considered. One possible explanation is that some schools in rural regions may fall short in the amount of intellectual and cultural stimulation they give their pupils.

Ethnic differences sometimes intrude in discussion of student origin by region, and how important this factor might be is obscure. In Australian universities in 1953 a study was made of more than 3000 Asian students from Singapore, India, China, Ceylon, Indonesia, Thailand, Pakistan, Burma, and the Pacific Islands. (74) Tests showed that although they had a mean I.Q. of 100, 'passing' Asians having a mean of 102, and 'failing' Asians 95, low scores which must be expected when cultural and linguistic differences are considered, yet studies of pass rates indicated that in certain universities Asians were as successful as Australian students. Since they were obliged to use a foreign language in their studies and had to become accustomed to some social isolation by living in a country with cultural characteristics different from those with which they had grown up, their performance is remarkable, and the question of the effect of home location on students' academic performance becomes complicated. Ethnic differences in the values, abilities, and in the drive to achieve should also be considered. There is a possible link between this study and that in which Rosen (75) examined the educational aspirations and motivations of groups of Greeks, Jews, White Protestants, Italians, French Canadians, and

Negroes. Some of the differences could be accounted for by social class, which is significantly correlated with achievement, but some differences remained even when social class was controlled. Within each social class, Protestants, Jews, Negroes, and Greeks in his sample were found to have higher educational aspirations than Italians and French Canadians.

Although some positive findings have been made there remains considerable obscurity about the importance of home location, cultural and ethnic differences. The indications are that cultural and ethnic differences are the most important of the three, and these differences can possibly best be interpreted as differences in values held by the differing cultural and ethnic groups.

Family Characteristics

More has been written about school-children's family characteristics than about the characteristics of students' families. Apart from social class and family size, there are grounds for believing that for both groups family characteristics are influential in educational attainment, as the following studies suggest.

Merrill, (76) using a sample of 296 male students, studied the relation of non-intellectual factors to persistence of low-ability students and lack of persistence of high-ability students at Berkeley campus of the University of California, and found a clear distinction between the family relationships they had experienced. High-ability persisters had had a history of harmonious family relations, and low-ability persisters had experienced more stable family relations than the non-persisters. By contrast the non-persisters of high ability had experienced less stable and more dissident family relations, tended to be less flexible in their studies, and were less likely to seek help from adults who might have been able to help them when they were having academic difficulty. The Report of the Select Committee on Education in *Education at Berkeley*, (77) discussing a similar study, added that capable non-persisters tended to be isolated from their peers and to have had difficulty in finding their place in the world.

Turning to another aspect, that of family relations of individuals who seek education beyond the compulsory age, Elder (78) found that of 1000 people of all ages in Great Britain, the United States, Italy, Mexico, and Western Germany, who were interviewed about the type of family in which they were brought

47

up, there was a strong tendency for individuals who stayed on at school after 15 years of age to have come from families which were democratic and egalitarian. In these families the mother and the father tended to play equal roles and to encourage self-reliance and initiative in their children.

One of Douglas's main findings (79) was that parental interest in their children's school life was the most important single factor in children's primary-school achievement. Bernstein (80) suggests that the quality of communication that exists between parents and children also plays an important role. Miller, in his research with primary-school children, found family characteristics which correlated highly with the school performance of children across the whole range of social class. Those were what might be called: punitive autocracy as shown in parents' strictness and corporal punishment of the child and not allowing the child to make decisions, a combination of several kinds of parental dominance in association with submissive attitudes in the child; and differences between parental and school attitudes as seen by the child ($r = -0.48$, p<.001); independence and freedom of thought in the family ($r = +0.30$, p<.001); general impoverishment—cultural, intellectual, social, and emotional ($r = -0.41$, p<.001). (81)

Considering the small number of studies of the family relationships of students as related to academic achievement which seem to have been performed, there is a remarkable amount of agreement between them. The studies generally show that achieving scholars, both at school and in higher education, tend to come from families where there is freedom of thought and communication between members, where there is minimal autocracy and something rather more like democracy in the distribution of authority in the home, in which parents are harmonious and stable rather than dissident or contentious, and where parents are interested in the academic careers of their children. These findings suggest promising areas of further inquiry into ways of understanding academic failure and success at each level.

Financial

For some students finance, or lack of it, is crucial to their being able to continue in their studies. Obviously higher education is open only to those who can afford it: this bald consideration does not take into account differences between students in the degree of financial deprivation they are able or willing to tolerate, or the possibilities of certain students being able to continue their studies piecemeal.

In British universities it is comparatively rare for a student to take a year or several years off from studies in order to replenish his finances for a later continuation. To lose a grant at the end of three years after failure in the final examination and to have no credits in sections of the course allowed for in the event of later resumption of studies heralds the end of many an academic career; it almost certainly entails dropping out. Transfer is difficult, if not impossible, and it may be that the student, if he still has the stamina, will have to start again from base in one of the few institutions which will allow him to study part time. Slim resources of money and pressures to earn more from the age of 22-plus will more than likely prevent the student from taking such a decision.

By comparison, in the United States, Australia, and numerous Continental countries it is possible for students in financial straits to continue their studies, by taking leave for a year or two from the institution in which they started, and resuming later with credits in some or all subjects in which passes have been achieved. The problem is then one of persistence and determination to overcome financial difficulties, and not one of having doors shut for want of a grant, and no chance to resume with legitimate credits allowed. Howell (82) found that, for British students, loss of a grant was nearly always followed by withdrawal.

It is highly likely that one of the reasons why middle-class students generally do better than working-class students is because the latter are less able to stretch budgets to any effect. Though Merrill (83) found in his sample that persisters and non-persisters did not differ significantly regarding yearly income and father's occupation, Australian studies (84) indicate the contrary. Though the correlation between income and success in university or college studies may be non-significant for the whole range of students, this general correlation does not focus sufficiently on those individual students who are in difficult circumstances, and why some of them find it necessary to drop out and others manage to continue.

Summerskill (85) found that, in the main, findings were equivocal regarding financial difficulty and tendency to drop out. Of the studies he reviewed the most pertinent findings include the following. Iffert's sample of students (86, 87) ranked financial difficulties third in importance, and in sixteen of twenty-one other studies cited by Summerskill financial difficulty was ranked first, second, or third in importance. Iffert also found that drop-outs' families had significantly less income than graduating students' families. Summerskill points out that in a study of the financial difficulty of students it is also necessary to control for academic ability, because high-ability students generally have scholarship funds available which less able students do not have, and some students may say they have financial difficulties as a face-saver rather than admitting to poor motivation or lack of ability. Three studies actually showed that self-support enhances chances of graduation, (88, 89, 90). However, self-support is not practical in any but the most flexible circumstances of home, work, and course structure. Such flexibility does not exist for most British students because of the rigidity of course structures geared to a fairly inflexible three-year period in most faculties. Encouraging some degree of self-support could provide a crude test of motivation.

Age and Maturity

A number of studies have reported differences in academic performance according to age. It is sometimes noticed that younger students seem to be more able. Sanders (91) has cited six studies (92-97) which indicate that younger candidates tend to obtain better degree results. Flecker (98) in Australia, Howell (99) in Great Britain, and Harris (100) in the United States have made similar findings.

Several important qualifications need to be made. First, in Howell's study of 9550 students the percentage of failure was the same for all age groups, and the tendency for younger students to get better degrees was only marginal. This was a general finding not broken down by subjects studied. It may be, for example, that greatest differences occur in science or mathematics or language studies, and that by contrast there is some advantage in being older for study in humanities and the social sciences, which are more closely related to life experience. Confirming this possibility, Sanders cites evidence that maturity associated with increasing age and experience seems to be a positive predictor of success in English, philosophy, law, psychology, history, and economics.

Secondly, there is evidence from earlier post-War studies (101) that ex-servicemen with a median age of 23 years and 6 months performed better than civilian students direct from school. It is possible that maturity gave some advantage and also that ex-servicemen were more highly motivated to make up for lost time and to obtain degrees in minimum time than the younger civilians.

The most important qualification is that any superior academic performance of younger students is probably not so much a function of age as of intelligence. Students who enter university earlier than their peers are most likely of superior ability. In the studies cited by Harris in which intelligence was controlled there was no difference between age groups.

Since it is known that mature students can perform as well as, or better than, younger ones, it is possible that maturity is an important factor—at least in certain subjects. In a study conducted by the Derbyshire Education Committee (102) it was suggested that wastage was in part accounted for by the immaturity of students. Common causes of failure were considered to be inability to make satisfactory adjustments to living away from home in new surroundings and to assume the responsibilities of independence. For some students it was thought that the transition from school and home to university or college was too abrupt. For them the report suggested that it might be better if it were common for students who intended to follow full-time courses to spend perhaps a year in employment before embarking on a course.

Such a policy, involving a break in studies, might have several effects. It would give students a break from a lifetime of continuous study. Astin (103) found that many of the most gifted students in the United States, National Merit Scholars, drop out because they are "tired of being students". It would also eliminate the less strongly motivated students, and perhaps raise the motivation of those who would find that the work they were able to obtain on leaving school was largely routine and not as interesting as a carefully selected field of learning. For intending teachers it would give an opportunity to break the life cycle of school-college-school, and enable them to gain experience in life that would help them in their future work with children and their parents. Lastly, such a policy would give candidates time to become more self-directed than they could be on leaving

51

school, an attribute of distinct advantage in any form of higher education.

Extra-curricular Interests, Need for Affiliation, Sociability

Furneaux's well-known general finding (104) that high-drive introverts are superior in academic work has been confirmed in recent studies in the United States of 'sociability' or the 'need for affiliation', which seeks to take into account students' needs and pressures which sometimes conflict with institutional goals. A prime institutional goal, to encourage students to learn, probably meets with more co-operation from an introverted, and comparatively unsociable, person than from one high in need to affiliate. Although Furneaux's finding is related to personality attributes which are discussed in a later section, it is relevant under the present heading because introversion and extroversion are clearly related to need for affiliation, and high drive to need for achievement.

Boyer (105) studied three social variables, attraction to the group, norms, and social support, in relation to three performance criteria, grade point average, over- and under-achievement, and improvement. The sample were also examined on the two personality variables, need for affiliation and need for achievement. Students allocated randomly to suites in groups of six were interviewed. The personality variables were treated as intervening variables having mediating effects between social and performance variables. Boyer found that pressures for achievement in the school were frequently in conflict with students' sociability and needs for affiliation. Students low on need for affiliation and peer acceptance and high on need for achievement performed better than students who were high on need for affiliation. While they may initially have felt that they need meet only the academic demands of the school, they soon discovered they were in a social environment where fellow-students also placed demands upon them.

The extent to which participation in extra-curricular activities *per se* affects academic performance is obscure. There is no simple relationship. Conflicting findings are reported in the literature. Harris (106) reviewed many studies and found there is no general relationship, though some studies report to the contrary. For example, Lucas, Kelvin, and Ojha (107) found that unsuccessful students participated less in social activities than successful students, and Himmelweit (108) obtained a similar result, but a group of engineers in Gray and Short's (109) sample who took part a great deal in extra-curricular matters performed least well, as did the student teachers in the Derbyshire report. (110) In a technological university Marris (111) also found that students who were active in union affairs, societies, or sports were notorious for their academic failure. Malleson (112) found that students who isolated themselves socially achieved more first-class degrees and fewer poor degrees than those who took a great part in union affairs.

In the studies reviewed by Summerskill, (113) however, there was little evidence to support the notion that drop-outs are frequently caused by over-participation; on the contrary, some studies showed a positive correlation, and Gray and Short found that, for their sample generally, extra-curricular activities made no significant difference to academic performance.

What most of these studies suggest is that the way in which participation by students in non-academic affairs affects their academic performance depends a great deal on several other factors. It depends first on how far students can budget their time carefully between the two. Malleson's study showed that over three years there was little difference between graduates who were socially oriented and those who were socially isolated in the time they spent in actual study. 'Unioneers' tended to work longer hours in their final year, while 'social isolates' were, by comparison, tending to relax a little. Secondly, the students' ability must be taken into account. Perhaps students who are active socially and who do better than others are also the more intelligent and able. The failure rate in the institution or department also plays a part. Where the failure rate is high in the first year it would involve considerable risk to neglect studies in first year, and to do so intending to make up for lost time later would be useless since by then the opportunity would have passed. The need to achieve is a further factor intervening between academic and other interests, acting as a counterpoise to need for affiliation, as already remarked.

From the few studies reviewed in this section it appears to be of great importance for students to exercise careful judgment about their allocation of time to academic and extra-curricular affairs. It is this judgment which is important, not the extra-curricular interests themselves.

53

Study Habits of High and Low Achievers

It is suggested that the way students divide their time between academic effort and extra-curricular activities is crucial. Whether students spend a great deal of time on outside affairs is less important than the time they spend in study. Malleson's (114) finding, already discussed, that 'unioneers' often spent as much time on study as more isolated students and Flecker's (115) that those who failed spent less time on study than those who passed, suggest this.

Time spent is a fairly useful index of motivation; but the more motivated and interested students not only spend more time, they probably study more effectively. On the other hand, there are possibly ineffective students who spend too much time in study. Harris (116) reported mixed findings in several studies of the time students spend in study. In one of these there was a correlation of 0.32 between the time spent and the grades achieved, but no relationship was shown in other studies.

Sinha (117) found that the high achievers in his sample got down to serious study earlier in the year than the low achievers, but probably more important was his finding that high achievers were also more regular and systematic. Only a small amount of research has been done in this field, but what exists is convincing, that students' habits of study are of greater importance for success than the time spent. Himmelweit (118) cites a number of studies which confirm Sinha's finding. The systematic person who distributes his time evenly does not usually get rushed, works consistently, and generally does better than the person who is erratic. Roe (119) believed that while ability is important, achievement is more a function of how hard the student works.

If we accept that method is more important than time spent it is still not so clear what the best methods are. Harris (120) again found that studies were not consistent in their findings. Malleson (121) discovered that the great majority of students who fail to graduate do not appear to do fewer hours of work than those who are successful. He points out that problems of learning technique at the higher educational levels have as yet received little attention, and we do not know what constitutes the optimum conditions or the best techniques.

It is possible that no particular technique suits all individuals, yet Pond's (122) study revealed some general differences in study *habits* between high- and low-achieving students. High achievers read more required references, did more preliminary reading, and read more in preparation for tutorials, attended more lectures and tutorials, and were less inclined to neglect subjects in which they thought they might fail. High achievers had better understanding of library facilities and followed regular study programmes, revised lectures on the same day, and attended to pressing tasks more readily, while low achievers were more random in their study methods, and unable to find ways of improving their methods and habits.

Hammond (123) made findings very similar to those of Pond, the most important aspects of study being amount of study time, amount of use of library, attendance at tutorials, even distribution of study time, and, possibly of great importance, participation in small informal discussion groups. Little research appears to have been done to assess the comparative effectiveness of each study method, but Hammond's last suggestion seems well worth further exploration. Participation in informal discussion has several advantages that others lack. Students learn to elucidate and verbalize their most serious problems; they have a chance to study other people's modes of thinking and to work out solutions. In so doing they elaborate the studied material in their own and other's terms, then more sophisticated problems emerge, and in turn these are solved and elaborated further.

This process has something in common with Piaget's (124) theory of the growth of intelligence in children. Adaptation and mastery of the environment proceeds by way of assimilation and accommodation, assimilation being the process by which new stimuli and experiences are comprehended in the context of current knowledge, cognitive structure or schemata; and accommodation being the development or elaboration of existing schemata into more highly organized and sophisticated forms demanding further elaboration. This, of course, is what should take place whatever method of study is used. When three or four informed and motivated people meet of their own initiative to share their problems and to develop solutions in a co-operative, non-competitive mood, stimulation can be experienced that is rarely to be found in the library or in solitary study, and not always in the seminar; ideas can flow and become crystallized more readily, requiring only verification.

The differences between high and low achievers' study habits and methods are clearly important. From this discussion it will

55

be realized that effective methods presuppose high levels of motivation, curiosity, persistence, incentive, and intrinsic interest in the subject-matter. But it does not follow that the highly motivated person will necessarily find the best study method, and methods of study and motivation therefore merit separate discussion and research.

There is an apparent contradiction here. The distinctions between motivation, time spent in study, and effectiveness of methods are to some extent blurred. There has been no real attempt to estimate their relative importance. Brown and Holtzman's (125) work on study habits and study attitudes shows that attitudes to study might be more important than the methods used, the one tending to promote the other. They found that attitude items in their Survey of Study Habits and Attitudes (S.S.H.A.) differentiated between high and low achievers in college better than items about methods. In his study of primary-school children Miller (126) did not make such a distinction, but found a factor of academic aspiration and enjoyment of school combined with parental support which was positively correlated with achievement, 0.45 for boys and 0.30 for girls, a mean correlation of 0.37. In so far as study attitudes and academic aspiration have elements in common, which it would seem they do, these two studies of two very different samples, English primary-school children and American college students, are in considerable agreement. Attitudes, personalities, and motivation which are associated with effective study habits are discussed in the next section.

Personality and Motivation

In considering personality and motivation in relation to achievement we soon find that there are a large number of more specific aspects which merit attention. Some of these are curiosity, persistence, intrinsic interest in learning generally and in specific subjects, external incentives, vocational orientation, and creativity. These are the main areas to be found in the literature. Although quite a large amount of work has been done in most of these areas, they have not been mapped out in any definitive sense, and overlap between them must still be assumed, although it will be seen that some appear more important than others.

The standard of student intake has been rising in quality since the War, and, as demand for higher education increases, will continue to rise unless enormous increases in places can be found. Personality and other factors will thus become more critical. Students entering higher education tend as time passes to have higher I.Q.'s, and the standard deviation will contract as selection by ability and school performance becomes more rigorous. Lipset and Altbach (127) at the Harvard University Center for International Affairs have referred to the growing difficulty in getting into college without extremely high test marks, and earlier reference was made to Sanders, (128) who has noted the rising standard of student intake at two Australian universities. In British universities students are coming forward with higher Advanced-level results in their General Certificate of Education examinations, and selection becomes increasingly rigorous in spite of increases in the number of university and college places that are available.

Motivation is not easy to study because, as Summerskill (129) has pointed out, it is not a static concept, because the interests, needs, and goals of young men and women shift and evolve. Changes in family situation, love affairs, financial support, and illness and emergency can affect motivation, yet, according to Summerskill, attrition studies show that these factors account for a relatively small number of drop-outs, though it is still possible for them to affect performance generally. Howell (130) has noted that withdrawal and delay may represent different responses to similar obstacles, but Dale's (131) work has strongly suggested that the principal reason for failure in university examinations is lack of application to work. The Report of the Select Committee on Education, *Education at Berkeley*, (132) suggested that there was some similarity between 'uncommitted' students who were studied by Keniston (133) and those students who drop out when confronted with academic or personal difficulty. According to the Berkeley Report, both these groups seem to have some difficulty in adjusting to the world. They seek to escape or to avoid the past, and they ignore the future. Douglas (134) referred to a similar group of students at the London School of Economics. These uncommitted students are not ready to commit themselves to any particular discipline, and, according to Douglas, many view their undergraduate years as a moratorium during which they gradually 'find themselves' and their relation to the world, and this enables them to postpone decisions about their place in it.

In some universities undergraduates are encouraged not to see their studies as being directly instrumental to some specified future career, rather that study should be pursued as an end in itself, and that postponing vocational decision for as long as possible is desirable. Powerful traditional arguments support this idea. For example, this is said to encourage liberal-mindedness, tolerance of complexity, a healthy objective cynicism, to prevent unconscious acquiescence in current assumptions and prejudices, to encourage challenge to the specious, and to "awaken critical sympathy for men's diverse convictions that is the stuff of civilized life." (135) There is no occasion to elaborate these and other far more extensive arguments. They are widely accepted.

But, however energetically these and similar arguments are applied, they do not offer support to the uncommitted students who are not only uncommitted to learning, but who are just 'uncommitted'. University places are expensive, and it would perhaps be better to admit only those students who are committed to learning, even if only vocationally, and to allow the uncommitted to assess their own objectives during a period in industry, commerce, or social service until they find themselves able to make realistic and suitable choices regarding their education. They may find that higher education is, for them, an unsuitable goal. There seems little point in parents and teachers pressing them to take up places, which so often is the case.

Many of the students who drop out seem to need this break from studies following the pressure of the years up to and including sixth form. The Berkeley Report stated that often these students drop out "to think over what they are doing" and "to re-evaluate things", and that many of them return to university or some other institution to continue their education, often emerging ultimately as superior students. The Derbyshire study (136) agreed that the transition to university might be better accomplished if students more often first gained new experience outside education.

A break in studies at the end of the school years might have several effects, among them being to weed out those who leave because in Astin's (137) words they are "tired of being a student". Even National Merit Scholars, the most gifted students in the United States, give this as a reason for dropping out. The break would eliminate some of the least motivated, raise the motivation of those who would have to take jobs below their ability, and provide the less mature with an opportunity to become more mature and self-directed in their choice of studies than they might otherwise have been. Intending teachers would have an opportunity to learn something of the world which they might never have the opportunity otherwise to learn, to become acquainted with life in the factory, shop, or office which would help them to understand a little more of the social background of those they would teach, and also the parents whom they should at some time meet.

Where it is weak motivation may not survive, and there seems little point in encouraging weakly motivated students to take up costly university and college places. By contrast, strong motivation appears, from a growing number of studies, to have great powers of survival. Kendall (138) at University College, London, found that of students who failed their degrees 70 per cent tried for other degrees or diplomas, and, of these, 66 per cent eventually gained them. Knoell (139) and Eckland (140) in the United States made similar findings. The truism that strong motivation has great powers of survival might be borne in mind when doubts arise that students may not take up available places if allowed to have a period away from learning before proceeding to higher education. These considerations have particular relevance in Britain, where the system of providing grants to students for a three-year period is under scrutiny.

Extrinsic Motivation and Incentives
According to some researchers, the vocational or professional aims of students are an important ingredient in academic success. Intrinsic interest on the part of the student and the inward drive to learn are not the only keys to motivation. External incentives in the form of high professional and socio-economic status are also important. Because of the wide consensus of opinion that the aims of higher education are not exclusively related to vocational or career goals, but rather the contrary. that education is an end in itself, there is considerable reluctance to view education as a means to a vocational or professional end, and courses which are tied to a particular vocation are sometimes referred to as 'training' rather than 'education'. Teaching, social work, and engineering seem to be regarded in this way, though, strangely, law and medicine are not, and some other professions

59

such as psychologist and sociologist seem not to be, possibly because they are closely identified with arts faculties.

Sinha (141) studied 185 high achievers and 190 low achievers. The high achievers were generally ten points higher in I.Q. and more persistent, and also had clearer vocational or professional aims. Astin (142) also found significant differences between drop-outs and persisters in the degree to which they were satisfied with their career choice; the persisters being well satisfied with their choice while the drop-outs had reservations. This finding applied only to men. For women there were no significant differences. Vocational or occupational aims seem to loom quite large in the minds of a high proportion of different kinds of undergraduates. The Robbins Committee (143) on Higher Education in Great Britain reported the following finding regarding students in various stages of their undergraduate careers, other than medical students. Twenty-five per cent of the students in the sample were in their final year. They were asked if at the time of going to university they had "fairly clearly in mind an occupation (either a general type of occupation or a specific occupation) they thought they would like to take up". Fifty-four per cent of students replied 'Yes', the proportions being 56 per cent of the men and 52 per cent of the women. Students in applied science were, as expected, the most vocationally oriented (75 per cent), as doctors and lawyers might also be expected to be, but 49 per cent of students in humanities, social studies, and science were also vocationally oriented. (See Table 8, p. 61.)

Nor was there much difference in the vocational orientation of students in widely differing universities, as Table 9 shows.

In *Education at Berkeley* (144) there is some discussion of the role vocational orientation plays in academic performance, and how both at the undergraduate and graduate levels the academically strongest students have fixed upon careers and are seizing opportunities offered by the university to educate themselves for a lifetime of work and advancement in their fields. In discussing such college-student sub-cultures Clark and Trow (145) link together the vocational and the academic. They say with regard to these students:

> Their attachment . . . is to the institution which supports intellectual values and opportunities for learning. . . . The products of this culture are typically aiming at graduate

TABLE 8

Percentage of Students with an Occupation in Mind on going to University: by Faculty

	Percentage of students who had an occupation in mind	Sample numbers (=100%)
Faculty		
Humanities	50	1,192
Social Studies	51	407
Science	46	985
Applied Science	75	582
All Faculties	54	3,166

Source: Undergraduate Survey (cited from Robbins Report, Appendix II B, p. 168).

TABLE 9

Percentage of Students with an Occupation in Mind on going to University: by University Group

	Percentage of students who had an occupation in mind	Sample numbers (=100%)
University group		
Oxford and Cambridge	43	584
London	52	408
Larger civic	57	1,023
Smaller civic	54	384
Wales	58	230
Scotland	60	537
All Universities	54	3,166

Source: Undergraduate Survey (cited from Robbins Report, Appendix II B, p. 168).

and professional schools; it is not surprising that they identify so strongly with the faculty, and internalize the scholarly and scientific habits of mind and work as part of their antici-patory socialization to future professional roles.

And the Berkeley Report notes that there appears to be a relation-ship between the probability that an academically capable student will drop out and the variety of student to which he belongs, women for example being more likely to leave than men (perhaps) because they lack as strong a vocational orientation.

Hunter and Schwartzman (146) present clinical evidence to support this hypothesis as it applies to medical students. They reviewed the case material of seventy consecutively counselled medical students who consulted the counselling service which had been made available to McGill medical undergraduates. Students having difficulties were self-referred or referred by the Dean of the faculty. Those having "intrinsic study problems" included some who had negative or uncertain motivation for the study and practice of medicine as a career or way of life. For some this was rebellion against parental wishes that they should study medicine. Vocational aims can be affected by emotional reactions to the subject material. Some students' ability to learn certain parts of the medical curriculum was impaired in this way, a few reacting by hysterical repression of information relating to sexual and other organs. Although nothing quite so exotic would be likely to emerge in non-medical fields, it seems possible that equivalent emotional reactions can affect other students' vocational orientations and, thus indirectly, their academic performance. These motivations might be difficult or impossible to interpret outside the counselling room, but there can be little doubt that they influence the learning behaviour of at least a small number of students.

Exactly how much importance can be placed on vocational orientation and other external incentives as opposed to intrinsic interest is unknown. Himmelweit and Summerfield (147) found that a group of under-achievers contained a higher proportion of students who considered material reward more important than opportunities for research and helping and advising people. In a review of research Himmelweit found a number of studies which showed that students who remained undecided about their future vocation throughout all the years of their courses tended to work poorly. The research evidence, though not extensive, and somewhat conflicting, suggests some link. Himmelweit suggested that any relationship might be connected with the degree of vocational orientation of the particular fields of study—for example, chemistry, medicine, and engineering as opposed to social science and humanities, in which the connection between vocational orientation and external incentives is generally more tenuous. Some support for this view is contained in the findings of Beard, Levy, and Maddox, (148) that one of the characteristics of over-achievers in electrical and mechanical-engineering courses is their tendency to read less material outside their field of study than under-achievers. Though wide reading may increase the understanding of humanities and social-science students and enable them to produce more sophisticated and informed answers in examinations, it seems that in a specialized field like engineering or medicine a more concentrated effort confined largely to the subject material produces better examination performance. This is not to say that high fliers according to examination criteria necessarily make the most imaginative and creative engineers, doctors, or chemists. It may be that by conforming so thoroughly to the rigid discipline of their studies they are less flexible in their later professional lives. There is no evidence for this possibility or its opposite, and perhaps some of the current research in creativity could profitably focus on this aspect of the education of professionals.

Other extrinsic motivations require consideration besides those of material reward, occupational aims, and socio-economic status. This is suggested in a study by Thistlethwaite (149) of a large sample of highly talented American students who were winners of the Certificate of Merit award. Some of these students had been accorded wide publicity and social recognition for their high-school achievement; and others, although they had been commended and were of similar ability, had received less publicity. Thistlethwaite found that social recognition was accompanied by more favourable attitudes to intellectualism, and by larger numbers seeking higher degrees, and planning to become college teachers and researchers.

The attractive theory that students who are activated to study by non-instrumental motives achieve highly is not well supported. There is evidence that in some fields vocational aims play no small part in students' success in academic study. It appears that for professions like medicine, engineering, law, and teaching instrumental or vocational motives are of greater importance than for less professionally oriented courses having a larger component of general education. Even for a wide cross-section of extremely able youth Thistlethwaite's finding showed that social recognition, which must be regarded as an instrumental motivation, inspired students to academic and intellectual ambition.

Intrinsic Interest and Curiosity

A distinction can be made between intrinsic interest and external incentives. Presser, Boyd, and Lea (150) give an instance to illustrate the distinction.

> If a child 'wants' to learn more about Magna Carta because he is interested, because his previous studies have left him with the promise of further exciting reading or discovery or because he wants the answer to some questions which have occurred to him, he is motivated. If he 'wants' to learn because he wishes to please his parents or teacher, or show off to his fellows, or gain marks, punishment, praise, rivalry and reward are said to be incentives. Incentives are administered by external causes; motivations arise within the person when a need has been created.

Schonell (151) pointed out that in practice incentives and motivations merge, and for most students external incentives are important factors in success, but Miller (152) found small but significant correlations between the academic success of primary-school children and their view that there was no importance in school marks for future success in life. Children who saw no link between the two actually tended to do better school-work. Children who expressed increased interest in learning when it presented some difficulty, apparently when their curiosity was thereby aroused, also tended to perform better than other children. These were not strong factors nor high correlations, but together they do suggest the greater importance of intrinsic interest in learning when compared with interest in learning as means to a future extrinsic goal.

In work with 1450 drop-outs in the United States Iffert (153) has shown that lack of interest in studies was given by 48 per cent as a reason for dropping out. Freedman (154) considered that frequently drop-outs come to college for reasons other than interest in study or the gaining of a degree, preferring to acquire a smattering of liberal education for its usefulness in social situations. A proportion are resistant to real intellectual development; some come in order to make a good marriage.

Hopkins, Malleson, and Sarnoff (155) found that more students who failed had decided on their careers earlier in childhood than had other students, though probably lacked real interest in their subjects, their choice having been made in response to strong parental aspirations rather than being genuinely free. Himmelweit (156) cited studies showing positive correlations between interest in chosen courses and examination results, and Astin (157) found significant differences between drop-outs and persisters in connection with whether they intended to proceed to higher degrees in their subjects or only to Bachelors' degrees. Men and women who intended to take higher degrees were both more likely to stay on in college than to drop out. This might be indicative of ambition or some other drive, but intrinsic interest in their subjects cannot be ruled out. The work of Heist and Williams, (158) who reported significant differences in intellectual disposition among three achievement levels, using the Strong Vocational Interest Blank profiles supports this hypothesis. Heist and Williams found that high achievers were more strongly oriented to inquiry and to speculative and creative thought than were lower achievers. For a homogeneous sample of science students of high ability this was the most influential factor. Most other differences were slight.

Further support for the thesis that intrinsic interest in learning generally is related to academic performance comes from Himmelweit and Summerfield, (159) who studied 232 students at the London School of Economics. Comparing two sub-samples of over- and under-achievers, they discovered that under-achievers did significantly less well than over-achievers in a test of information in fields not directly related to their university studies. As in Heist and Williams's study, these two contrasting groups did not differ on other variables which were hypothesized as being important but only on a variable indicative of interest in knowledge. The two groups did not differ on personality-test scores, social class, age, intelligence, type of school, and parents' education. Hopkins, Malleson, and Sarnoff (160) discovered a distinction between a failing group of students and a passing group. The failing students tended to give vocational reasons for choosing their subject. They said it was a "means to a profession", or that they had chosen the subject following parental pressure. The passing students, on the other hand, more often said they had chosen their subject because of their interest or aptitude. In the same way significantly more of those graduated who chose their college "because it was the best college for my subject" than those who chose the college for extraneous reasons such as "because my friends were there" or "because it gave access to London".

In research on creativity and research performance Pelz and Andrews (161) have studied American scientists, and Chaney (162) has studied British scientists working in America. Both found that items which measure the extent to which scientists feel their work to be exciting, interesting, and important provided significant correlations with research performance. Although the British scientists were partly a product of their new American environment, the similar findings with the two groups from differing cultural and national origins suggest that Chaney's results can be generalized across cultural and national boundaries.

The degree of importance which should be attributed to any one variable in its relation to academic performance in general is not known. Students need to be studied as individuals or groups of individuals, and research needs to be aimed at the study of homogeneous groups of students rather than students in general.

Though the findings reported are valuable and encouraging, it remains true, as Summerskill (163) has said, that some excellent students are not motivated in the ideal sense. Some come to university or college to assert their independence, to gain security and status, to learn how to make money, and for a host of other reasons. However true this may be we need (as a means of furthering our understanding of variance in academic performance) to study more closely the student who is motivated by lively and sustained interest in a subject and learning generally.

A possible near relation of the variable intrinsic motivation and keenness to know more about a subject or about learning generally is the factor of 'conservatism vs. radicalism', from Cattell's 16 P.F. Inventory. Flecker (164) studied the characteristics of 157 passing and failing students in a first-year mathematics course at an Australian university. Using Cattell's inventory, he found that, of the 16 personality factors, only conservatism versus radicalism differentiated between the passing and failing groups. Failing students generally lacked an experimental or critical approach. This finding is the more striking because the two groups were homogeneous in mathematical ability, 60 per cent of the failing group having distinctions in mathematics at school. The students who passed in mathematics also passed most of their other examinations, compared with the failing group, who also failed in their other examinations.

66

It would be useful to know how far Cattell's factor,* conservatism versus radicalism, is correlated with openness and flexibility of mind and interest in learning, as opposed to rigidity and convergent thinking, or if they all constitute the same essential factor. Basic studies in these and associated fields might bring to light a syndrome indicative of academic achievers.

Other personality variables are associated with academic achievement, and, as indicated earlier, these appear to be related to specific subjects. Roe, (165) for example, found that eminent biologists and physicists tended to keep clear of intense emotional situations, whereas social scientists were much concerned with them. It might be that these personality characteristics were instrumental in the academic choices that were made and that once a choice was made these characteristics were what led to the eminence of the persons in Roe's sample. Heist, McConnell, Matsler, and Williams (166) have shown that personality characteristics are associated with choice of college. Whether choice of subject is also involved is not clear. Heist *et al.* found that students who chose more productive colleges were significantly higher scorers than those who went to institutions of lower productivity. Those who chose institutions of higher productivity scored more highly on originality, complexity of outlook, social introversion, thinking introversion, and authoritarianism. Women were higher on ego strength and were especially higher on authoritarianism.

Two very different researches have shown that higher achievers are enthusiastic and less subject to despondency and depression. Vernon (167) in 1939 studied a large group of graduate students at a Scottish university and found that the best students, those with the highest marks over a four-year period, although more tense, were less liable to depression and instability, were more dependable, and could concentrate better. Sinha (168) in 1966 also found that Indian high achievers were more enthusiastic than low achievers, and less despondent in the face of failure in a game-type situation.

Other personality characteristics have been found by Holland (169) to predict academic success. Using the California Psychological Inventory with a sample of students of high ability, he found that the best predictors were, for males, sociability and masculinity, and, for females, responsibility, achievement via

* R. B. Cattell, *The Scientific Analysis of Personality* (Pelican, 1965).

conformance, self-control, and femininity. Psychological variables generally showed greater predictive value than scholastic aptitude for this high ability group, though their effectiveness varied between colleges; in multiple correlations the psychological variables boosted prediction to two and three times as great as the scholastic tests alone.

Holland (170) has made a careful distinction between two kinds of academic achievement, thus challenging the use of grades as the only criterion. In a study of talented adolescents and young adults he distinguished between high-school grades, on the one hand, and creative performance which had merited public recognition through prizes, awards and publications, inventions, or other notable performances in arts or science.

Holland found that students who had merely attained high grades were persevering, responsible, and sociable, and often came from families in which the parents held authoritarian values and attitudes. By comparison the students who had published or had received some award or prize were more frequently asocial, independent, and more expressive than the high academic achievers. They were also more consciously original and had higher aspirations for future achievement. However, although Holland discovered that creative students were more independent and asocial compared with high academic achievers who were more responsible, Grace (171) found that the more persistent and effective students, and therefore those who ultimately gained most degrees, had the characteristics of both the creative and the formal achievers. They were independent and responsible. Grace used the dominance scale of the Minnesota Multiphasic Personality Inventory as a measure of independence, and this is not necessarily the same as Holland's measure of independence. This may explain in part the conflicting character of the findings. There is probably a need for a more accurate elucidation of the terms 'independent' and 'responsible', and this could perhaps be best done by factor analytic studies.

These conclusions call for further research and replication in different fields of learning. The notion that creativity is fostered in a free, democratic, liberal milieu, and that students from such environments are more creative is an attractive one, but in the enthusiasm that research into creativity has generated other research should not be overlooked. There is evidence from earlier than 1940 (172) suggesting some relation between formal grades and liberal or radical views held by students. Miller's (173) finding of a correlation between primary-school children's academic performance and a factor suggesting free and liberal expression and interchange of ideas between children and parents of the same magnitude as that between social class and achievement and Elder's (174) finding in several countries of a consistent correlation between democratic homes and formal academic achievement both suggest some confirmation of the early evidence noted by Harris. It seems highly likely that independence and originality, liberalism, democracy, and radicalism do encourage creativity. However, they also seem to encourage formal learning, and from Getzells and Jackson's (175) evidence it seems that creativity is related to the concept of 'over-achieving', or higher performance than ability tests predict. Though 'over-achieving' is now sometimes considered a nonsense term,* (176) because, it is said, a student cannot perform more highly than his ability will allow, and although when several tests have been used the achievement quotient may be partly a product of test error and regression to the mean, it is interesting to consider Getzells and Jackson's findings in the light of the concept of 'over- and under-achieving'. The authors compared two groups of children. The mean I.Q. of one group was 150, but they were comparatively low in creativity as measured by Guilford's creativity tests. (177) The second group had a mean I.Q. of 127, but were in the top 20 per cent in creativity. Results showed that the 'lower I.Q./high creativity' group were superior in formal school achievement. High creativity appears to enable children to perform more highly than their measured intelligence predicts. Getzells and Jackson suggest as an explanation that creativity is a cognitive style that is not sampled by ordinary I.Q. tests. This cognitive style may include an intensive interest in learning for its own sake, and an ability to make effective associations between a problem and a wider range of possible solutions than the uncreative person can appreciate and which he rejects as irrelevant and having no connection with the problem.

Students under Stress

Anxiety, maladjustment, neuroticism, and introversion are

---

* For a thorough statement on the concepts 'over-achiever' and 'under-achiever' see R. L. Thorndike, *The Concepts of Over- and Under-Achievement* (Columbia University, New York, 1963).

other personality characteristics that have been studied in relation to academic performance, but the findings are inconsistent. Several studies reviewed by Harris (178) showed that under-achievers, those performing lower than their I.Q.'s would predict, had more anxiety than high achievers, those performing higher than their I.Q.'s would predict, and Grace (179) found that drop-outs tended to show greater anxiety than persisters. Sinha (180) found that low achievers were more anxious than high achievers, and Hallworth found that secondary modern school children tended to be more anxious than their more academically successful contemporaries in grammar schools. The literature on anxiety is in some disarray. Though the findings are often significant, there are many inconsistencies. Reed (181) has called anxiety "the ambivalent variable". Inconsistencies are revealed in studies reviewed by Lavin. (182) One possible explanation is that nobody has yet succeeded in operationally defining anxiety. It is a highly complex variable, as a perusal of Rollo May's book* demonstrates. Freud (183) called it "a nodal point, linking up all kinds of most important questions: a riddle, of which the solution must cast a flood of light upon our mental life." It is no wonder that the literature on anxiety and academic performance is practically chaotic. Apart from the recognition that anxiety is one of the most complex variables and has been defined differently in almost every study, confusion has occurred also because of the variety of learning tasks that have been studied inside and outside the laboratory, from reflex learning, such as the eye blink, to university performance in first year through to finals. Controlling for intelligence sometimes produces more clear-cut findings, but the relationship between anxiety and student performance may be non-linear. No attempt is made here to discuss the problem of anxiety in detail. A fairly comprehensive review has been made in another place; (184) and this has led to the conclusions already stated. The reader is referred to the authors discussed earlier, May and Reed.

A considerable amount of work has been done in Britain by Eysenck on dimensions of personality. His dimensions of intro-version-extroversion and neuroticism-stability were used by Furneaux, (185) who found that neurotic introverts had 79 per cent academic success in first-year examination. Stable introverts

---

* Rollo May, *The Meaning of Anxiety* (New York, Ronald Press, 1950).

had 74 per cent success. Neurotic extroverts had only 64 per cent success, and the poorest performance of all was shown by stable extroverts, of whom only 39 per cent were successful, 61 per cent having failed, compared with only 21 per cent of unstable introverts. These findings confirm the findings of several studies which were reviewed by Harris (186) in 1940, and which showed that introversion is often associated with better grades. In one of these there were correlations of different size for students in different studies. A variable of 'studiousness' which may in some way resemble introversion was found to predict college grades with correlations of 0.19 to 0.29 for technical and business students and up to 0.55 for arts students. Neurotic introverts are sensitive people and stable extroverts are not.

The work of Furneaux using Eysenck's dimensions of personality is of considerable significance. In so far as introversion and instability can be accepted as aspects of neuroticism and anxiety we may say that anxiety appears to promote academic success. But this thinking is probably too loose; the terms are not necessarily synonymous, and it is possible for extroverts to be anxious along with introverts. The work of Eysenck and Furneaux is with personality, not with anxiety specifically, and if the role of anxiety in academic performance is to be clarified it should be studied more directly.

A promising clue to this problem has been suggested by Lavin (187) and supported by Miller (188). Both suggest that anxiety may be specific to situations, and anxiety or worry about specific matters rather than general anxiety may be more related to student performance. Miller found almost zero correlations between general worries and the performance of primary-school children, but when specific worries were grouped into areas, worries about school and the future produced significant negative correlations with the achievement criterion, leaving all other areas non-significant. This is only a start; it would be agreed with Lavin that further studies are needed on the dimensions of anxiety. This should be the next step towards elucidating the relation of further specific anxieties to academic performance. Later we may find that we must study the influence of specific anxiety to individual fields of academic learning.

Students are often under stress. Attainment of a place in university or college is a high point in their achievement and the culmination of years of academic effort. Once in a place, all that has been striven for is at stake, and pressures begin to make themselves felt from several sides. The student, if he is conscientious, may feel he has to justify himself in the sight of his parents, teachers, and peers in a new environment that is not structured for him in the same way as school has been. He must find his own way through what may seem an amorphous body of information and try to synthesize where synthesis is not apparent.

The student may be away from home for the first time, having to come to terms with a new set of peers and a new kind of student-teacher relationship. If he is in a hall of residence his entry into higher education may be cushioned for him, but he may equally rebel against regulations that may be deemed necessary by the warden but which to him may appear redundant. If he comes from a rural home and has found himself in uncongenial accommodation he may feel isolated and unable to cope with the necessary organization for living and working. Against this will be felt the pressure to keep up with studies, and if he has been crammed at school he may lack the inner direction that would otherwise give him confidence and ability to work in the self-directed manner that university work demands. If he is the first of the family to have entered higher education his isolation may be increased by a sense of growing away from his parents and family, and he may feel himself to be suspended between two cultures, especially if his family is hostile or indifferent to the idea of education into adulthood.

Most students are able to cope with these stresses, but some are not able, and for them anxiety may develop beyond their tolerance level. Lipset and Altbach (189) have discussed the increasing competition for places in education in the United States and the accompanying pressure to attain good grades at all levels. They report that the suicide rate among young people of high-school and college age has risen rapidly, while that of older-age cohorts has been declining. In the decade to 1962 suicides by young people increased 48 per cent among 15–19-year-olds and 26 per cent among the 20–24-year-age group, compared with 4 per cent generally; the suicide rate for the 55-year-plus group actually declined. Young people aged 13–24 who sought private psychiatric help mentioned stresses associated with education twice as often as in 1953.

The incidence of stress and its influence on academic performance seems to vary between institutions. Clinical and other research reports are inconsistent, probably because different criteria of stress are taken in each study. There can be no doubt that it is a serious problem, but precise measurement of student stress has not yet been achieved. First it is necessary to define the nature of stress. Parnell (190) studied 145 Oxford undergraduates who had missed a term or more. Of these 76, or 52.5 per cent, were away because of mental illness or 'nervous breakdown'. Parnell asserts that as a measure of morbidity this is a misleadingly low figure, and Malleson (191) agrees. Students reporting to their college that they are away sick are not likely to volunteer a diagnosis of mental rather than physical illness. In addition there were 9 suicides in the period of Parnell's study and an unspecified number of cases with such conditions as duodenal ulcer and asthma in whose aetiology mental strain might have played a part. There are probably further cases whose breakdown follows summer examinations and whose period of incapacity is over by October, so that they are able to start term punctually. Nor does this reckoning take into account the severely disturbed cases who do not miss a term but who are just able to hold off a breakdown.

Priestley (192) reported on 1000 students who voluntarily sought the help of the student counselling office at Melbourne over a three-year period. Of these 60 (6 per cent) were suffering from personal disturbances involving serious disruption to their student careers; they included cases of psychosis, pronounced depression, serious family conflict, severe sex problems. One hundred others (10 per cent) were suffering similar difficulties and lesser anxiety not severe enough to disrupt their lives critically. In addition there were 800 students who needed counsel about difficulties that might generate anxiety unless ameliorated.

Gray and Short (193) in another study judged that 20 per cent of the annual intake to another university were in need of counselling. Worries about wrong choice of subject, serious home conflicts, and loneliness and despair, especially among overseas students, were the main reasons for their anxiety. Though only a minority of these would be suffering from serious stress requiring psychiatric treatment an element of stress must be assumed.

Granted that quite large numbers of students need counselling or treatment, there remains the question—to what extent does stress adversely affect their academic performance? For some

73

students it is incapacitating, for others not. This depends to some extent upon the student's personality. Weiss, Segal, and Sokol (194) studied for six years the male undergraduate population of a liberal-arts college with a student body of 2900 men, using the Minnesota Multiphasic Personality Inventory. Of 4839 cases more than 11 per cent showed clinically significant emotional impairment. Students who dropped out tended to come from that group of students of high verbal aptitude but having some emotional impairment. Students with mathematical aptitude were least likely to drop out.

Spencer's (195) study of 100 Oxford undergraduates under care at the Warneford and Park hospitals also showed that personality played a part in illness and performance. Most of these students were in the hysterical neurotic group, fat and muscular in physique, extroverted in personality and more than averagely unstable. It will be remembered that Furneaux (196) also found that unstable extroverts had a high rate of failure. Of Spencer's sample 42 seemed to have triggered their illness by academic revoke—that is, running away from academic work or examinations.

Spielberger's work (197) suggests that ability is an intervening variable between anxiety and performance. In a study of 248 students at Duke University he found that students with high anxiety of low and middle ability failed more frequently in their studies than students of the same ability with low anxiety. By contrast anxiety appeared to enhance the performance of students of very high ability, having A.C.E. scores above 150.

In general it has been found that psychiatric disturbance hinders academic performance. Lucas, Kelvin, and Ojha (198) studied 198 students of University College, London. Students whose progress had been delayed or who had dropped out of their courses were found to have a higher incidence of psychiatric morbidity. Two-thirds of these students were disturbed, but Lucas et al. say that although the wastage group included this high proportion of disturbed students, other students suffering from very serious and socially crippling disturbance were able to succeed in their studies. There is some suggestion that the students who failed were also less sociable, of lower social class, and lower in ability. The authors also noted that the unsuccessful group were relatively more reluctant than the successful group to complete questionnaires, which the authors thought indicated another personality characteristic associated with inferior performance. If this indicates lack of involvement, as Lucas considers it may, their study may offer some confirmation of Spencer's finding that academic revoke by students, or avoidance of study, appeared to precipitate worry. If students of whatever personality avoid study it is little wonder that they become anxious and disturbed as the examination date draws near. For extroverts who probably settle less well to study this must be a special problem.

Still (199) plotted the frequencies of students' consultations with university medical officers for psychological reasons month by month over four years. His graph showed a sharp peak each year in the month of May—the examination period. The symptoms varied. There were mild and severe anxiety, panic, examination phobia, psychasthenia, poor concentration, and a rich variety of other manifestations, including psychosomatic changes. Still estimated that of 224 students having psychological illnesses in one Summer Term, the nearness of examinations appeared to have played the major role in precipitating symptoms in 135 cases. The other cases had some antecedent components, and the examinations precipitated the nervous conditions. It would be wrong, therefore, to make a gross generalization that the only failures are those extroverted students who do not work during term and who react to the day of reckoning with panic, even though the few studies cited do suggest that for some students this is true. Still distinguishes between the student whose anxiety is the result of the knowledge that he has not worked and the conscientious and able student who has been disappointed in his performance in the first paper.

We may have here a further partial explanation of the inconsistencies in the literature on anxiety. On the one hand neurotic introverts, who probably have some anxiety, do better than extroverts as students; on the other, extroverts who have not worked because of their outgoing social life are also anxious when examinations loom ahead, and they do poorly—two anxious groups, one performing well, the other poorly. The difference between them lies not in the fact that they are anxious, but in their personalities and in the way they approach academic tasks. This might also help to explain the difference between those students with psychiatric illness who fail and those who graduate. Malleson (200) found that of 551 students 10 had

75

major psychiatric illness, yet 5 graduated, and of 101 students with minor psychiatric disturbance only 16 failed to graduate, almost the same percentage of wastage as for the whole sample.

The research suggests that the presence of psychiatric disturbance, although important in relation to academic performance, is less important than the personality of the student and whether the disturbance arose before examinations for want of timely effort. Clinical studies might be more conclusive if Still's distinction between anxiety of the procrastinating student who is anxious because of poor preparation and the anxiety of the over-conscientious, hard-working, introverted student were taken fully into account. This is an extension of the idea of situation-specific anxiety discussed earlier.

Summary and Conclusions

The large number of student variables which influence the academic performance of students can be classified in the following manner:

(i) Variables of least influence in academic performance,

(ii) Variables producing inconsistent findings,

(iii) Variables producing consistent findings.

STUDENT VARIABLES OF LEAST INFLUENCE IN
ACADEMIC PERFORMANCE

Within this first group there is a wide range. Among these are age, peer relationships, place of residence while a student, nationality, religion, whether evacuated from town to the country or abroad in war-time, time spent in the armed services, estimated time spent on games, sport, or union activities, childhood happiness, childhood discipline, ability, and social class. All of these seem to have less effect than might be expected on student performance. In the case of a few individual students any of these variables, if severe enough, could individually or collectively have a profound effect on achievement, but the few researches concentrating on those variables which have been reviewed do not suggest they are influential, and students in the studies cited have not suggested that they have influenced their performance.

Of all the variables in this group, age, peer relations, time spent on games and other extra-curricular activities, ability, and social class require a little further elucidation. None of these is very influential on its own, but only when acting jointly with others. For example, it is often observed that some of the youngest students are outstanding, but age itself is not necessarily the crucial variable. It is much more likely that the young person coming to the university is of higher ability and better motivated than his peers. His early arrival at the university usually follows an outstanding school career. If his motivation remains high he should in theory do just as well at university or college as he did at school, but if it flags he will grow into a more ordinary student. This may happen if new social activities take too high a precedence over academic work or if he becomes tired of being a student. Malleson (201) found that failure increases with age at entry, but considered that this was due to the greater social responsibilities of older students and greater calls upon their time.

Peer relations and time spent on extra-curricular activities are not of importance on their own. Astin (202) has described how need for affiliation with peers affects performance only in so far as the values held by peers and the pressures they exert on the student are in conflict with the pursuit of academic work. Similarly, time spent on extra-curricular pursuits is of no consequence unless there is actual neglect of studies. Malleson's (203) finding is important here. Over a three-year period there was little difference between the time spent on study by students who were active in union activities and those who were not. Clearly if both the socially active and the more isolated students spend similar time on their studies it is doubtful if the amount of involvement in extra-curricular activities affects academic performance, and we must look to other variables for explanations of any differences. It may be found that students who engage in extra-curricular affairs plan their studies well. This would then be another factor to consider.

Ability and social class are probably the most controversial to list among the least influential variables. It is true that both play a large part in whether a student finds a place in higher education, but once there the influence is less marked. One reason why social class is less important may be that of a vast number of potential working-class students only a small percentage of the most able and most highly motivated proceed to higher education. By contrast, among middle-class potential students a much higher proportion actually become students, and these are of more mixed ability. Unlike working-class youth, of whom many able ones do not even proceed to sixth form, middle-class youth and their families appear over a long period to place a higher value on education, and consequently a greater number in the middle range will aspire to a university or college place. In this situation one would thus be comparing high-ability working-class students with students coming from middle-class families and public schools whose intake covers a wider range of ability than grammar schools. It seems likely then that while social class operates as a selector at every school level, it is not such a powerful determinant of academic success or failure once a university or college place is attained.

Ability is of fundamental importance for entry to university or college, but at university the spread of ability is not so great. If we consider that the mean I.Q. of any year's intake of students is about 126 and rising, and that the standard deviation is contracting, it can be readily appreciated that we are admitting an increasingly homogeneous group. Studies of extreme groups show even more clearly that differences in ability are not so crucial. In those studies reviewed earlier it was noted that students of extremely high ability fail or drop out inordinately. Students of I.Q. 130-plus, the top 4 per cent in ability, account for 20 per cent of the wastage in one university, while students of only high average ability, I.Q. 105, at about the 55th percentile, who have managed to gain entrance to university, sometimes attain degrees. (204) If we are to account for differences between their performance, clearly we must study factors other than ability. Ability is best regarded as a threshold variable. A certain level is required but, given that, it is not absolutely critical: other intervening variables supplant it in importance.

STUDENT VARIABLES PRODUCING INCONSISTENT FINDINGS

Inconsistent findings regarding the variables in this category suggest not that they can be discarded as having no effect on academic performance, but rather that we are not yet able to understand them with certainty. There is little doubt that they have some influence, but the reasons are obscure, and the research methods used have not yet elucidated their precise roles.

Anxiety presents the greatest difficulty of all. Findings conflict because of the different measures of anxiety which have been used and the variety of kinds of learning which have been studied. For most students it appears that anxiety makes academic learning difficult in school and university, yet for students of higher ability it seems to be facilitating, and some students actually do well while undergoing severe stress. There is some suggestion in recent literature that studies which consider anxiety concerning specific situations may yield more consistent findings. Intense general anxiety can be crippling to a student's academic effort, but it seems more likely that anxiety that is specifically related to the academic life will prove even more important.

Birth rank and family size have attracted the attention of some researchers. Though Harris (205) in 1940 reported many conflicting findings in the literature, the discovery of Douglas (206) that children from large families tend to perform less well in school than those from smaller families, and the discovery of Roe, (207) that nearly two-thirds of her sample of eminent scientists were eldest children and most of the remainder either eldest sons or without an elder sibling of approximately the same age, point to the need for further inquiry with new samples.

It is also important to consider the location of students' homes, because this has implications for policies of student residence. We have seen that the location of the home appears to influence academic performance for a number of reasons differing according to the type of student. Home location seemed to matter little for men commuters in Astin's (208) study, but for women it made a significant difference to their performance. Quite apart from whether commuting is entailed, the location of the students' home may be less important than if the student sub-culture is very different from the one surrounding his home, and whether he can come to terms with it. Students from rural areas who have come to a university or college in a large city where most students live at home and have already established friendships of their own can suffer seriously from loneliness, especially if they are in poor accommodation on a shoe-string budget. When they are in residence with kindred students who are also cut off from their old friends, home location probably assumes a lesser importance. But even in England, where it is accepted that students will leave their homes to study, there are student residences where a large number of students live within easy distance of home. These students may not have severed links with former peer groups, and might go home each week-end. In such situations students who are a long way from home may be at a disadvantage when compared with students whose homes are close to the college. If their homes are so distant that cultural or ethnic differences between themselves and other students are involved their problem may be serious.

However, it is doubtful how far home location can affect students' graduation, except where it implies other problems, such as loneliness, poor preparation for university or college in inferior rural schools, cultural problems, excessive time commuting, or other concomitant factors.

In some studies parental discord and broken homes seem to have had no effect on grades, but in a study of student persistence, Merrill (209) provides evidence that students who have had experience of unstable and discordant family relations were more likely to drop out. This tendency might be connected with finance, discordant and unstable homes producing a higher incidence of uncertain financial arrangements which lead to enforced dropping out.

Given a certain minimum finance which allows him to live, the financial status of the student seems to have little influence on his achievement. In the research so far reviewed students complained little that finance problems had affected their studies, and it was found in three American studies (210) that students who were working their way through college actually performed better than their contemporaries. This presupposes unusually high motivation on the part of the student and also a great deal of flexibility in the curriculum whereby students can take a job to replenish finances and return to university at a later time with credits allowed. It could not be expected to work in a rigid curriculum bound to a three-year study in which no provision is made for the accumulation of transferable credits. However strong the motivation of the student and his tolerance of poverty, for most British students the end of a grant means almost certain termination of the course, in part, no doubt, because of the rarity of opportunity to study a course by units with credit given for each as part of the degree, and the British commitment to the idea of a fixed period for all students to complete a degree course. Apart from that, for the student, finance, like ability, is a threshold variable. With neither, it is impossible to achieve success, but, given a minimal amount of each, success is possible if the student has certain other attributes.

Of all the factors discussed in the literature those now to be summarized have probably the greatest implications for institutional and departmental policy, school teaching, university selection and guidance, and certainly for future research. However, some of the variables discussed in the two preceding sections —for example, ability and finance—should not be entirely left out. If we were to take ability and circumstances for granted at a prerequisite level, the simplest possible way to summarize the remaining variables affecting academic performance would be to say that success depended on the effort students were prepared to expend on their studies. Academic performance might be said to depend on ability, circumstances, and effort. This in turn leads to the consideration of a seemingly small number of more subtle variables without which effort is scarcely feasible.

The question is, what induces or enables a student to expend efficient effort on learning. In studies reviewed the variables which most consistently stand out are interest, curiosity, aspirations, and study attitudes. These are influenced by purpose, drive, and persistence, which according to fairly strong evidence are enhanced or inhibited by the social interaction to which the individual has been accustomed, particularly in his family. The studies of Iffert, Freedman, Astin, Heist and Williams, Pelz and Andrews, Chaney, Flecker, and Miller confirm the hypothesis that wide-ranging interest and curiosity rather than narrowness and depth are most important. Parkyn's finding of a higher correlation between school results in general subjects and university results than between specific school subjects and university results is indirect evidence of this. These studies indicate numerous aspects of interest in learning that point towards our overall conclusion. For example, it was found in these studies that high achievers score highly in tests of information not related to university studies, and in tests of accuracy, arithmetic, and vocabulary; that drop-outs frequently say they are not interested or are tired of being students, and that interest in chosen courses is positively correlated with favourable examination results.

Significant differences have been found between drop-outs and persisters in their interest in study beyond the bachelor's degree, while high achievers have been found to differ significantly from low achievers in the extent of their orientation to inquiry and speculative and creative thought. Comparable groups of students, some failing and others passing, have been found to be differentiated in the extent to which they found their chosen subject intrinsically interesting or merely a means to a vocation, and whether they chose a particular college for its status in their chosen subject or because their friends went there or some other extraneous reason. Productive and creative scientists have been found to differ from lesser scientists in the extent to which they found their work interesting and exciting and important, and in primary schools high achievers differed from low achievers in becoming more rather than less interested in material that presented some difficulty.

Likewise it has been found that of mathematics students who had gained distinctions at school, those who failed at university lacked an experimental or critical approach. Study habits and attitudes to study have been found to differentiate between high and low achievers in college even more than methods of study, and positive correlations exist between school performance and academic aspiration and enjoyment of school. Eminent scientists in a wide range of fields have similarly reported that from an early age they had derived enjoyment in discovering knowledge.

Earlier in this summary brief mention was made of the social interaction an individual has experienced from childhood. What seems most to influence his ability or willingness to learn is the type of interaction within his family, though school variables are also important. Although there is not a vast mass of evidence, what there is points in the same direction. Children from homes that are democratically run, where decision-making is not concentrated in one person and where initiative and self-reliance are encouraged tend to stay on longer at school. Punitive, autocratic, dominating parents who make their children accept an over-submissive role tend to produce non-inquiring minds that fit them poorly for learning and discovery. Achieving scholars and persisters generally seem to come from families which are harmonious and stable, where freedom of thought, inquiry, and communication has been encouraged and where there has been support for academic aspiration.

These factors may not be amenable to manipulation by university and college faculty who are trying to select the best students, but change can probably be affected by parents and schools. In the present context they suggest explanations why some students are industrious, persistent, curious, purposeful, aspiring, and with a drive to achieve, while others are not. For it is ultimately these qualities which make a good student. From the literature it seems that few other variables intervene apart from extreme anxiety and social disorganization. Social class is subordinate to the qualities listed above, and even ability and finance are relatively unimportant provided there is a certain requisite level of each.

The present discussion of student variables may be completed by reference to Vernon (211) and Schonell. (212) Vernon considered that some of the main factors in the supply of suitable students were the educational aspirations of the family and the material and moral support it gives, the cultural level rather than the economic level of the home; also the individual's own drives, ideals, and interests, the traditions and current attitudes in the school he attends, and the effectiveness of teachers in developing favourable attitudes to education. Schonell summarized his views as follows:

> The student who has a good measure of persistence, industry, organising ability, thoroughness, who is well adjusted and motivated, is excellently armed to overcome such handicaps as average intelligence, poor home environment or university shortcomings in arrangement of courses, in lecturing, or in tutorials. Indeed a personality which will go on grappling with problems and overcoming difficulties is the most priceless asset to any university student. Conversely, a student who appears to possess every advantage of both intelligence and environment [and might we add high A-levels or other prerequisites?] may lack personality strengths of these kinds and become a failure in university studies.

In the course of this discussion it has become clear that there are a large number of implications for institutions and their policies. While students' motivations and personality are clearly crucial, they cannot be considered properly in isolation. The way a student approaches his university or college work will depend upon how he has been taught and the manner in which he has been expected to study at school in the sixth form *and earlier*.

Students who encounter difficulties in study and those who undergo psychological, social, or financial stress can be helped by student counsellors and psychiatrists. Students who have chosen the wrong subjects to study or who need to take leave of their studies for financial and other reasons need not be wasted if academic and administrative policies are flexible. Selection can be improved if factors other than A levels or other entry requirements are fully considered. In the next chapters topics in these and other areas are studied and some of the many implications for schools, colleges, and universities are examined.

REFERENCES

1. D. Harris, "Factors affecting College Grades: A Review of the Literature", *Psychology Bulletin,* 37, 1940.
2. Sir Alexander Carr-Saunders, in *Proceedings of Home Universities Conference,* 1952.
3. W. D. Furneaux, "The Psychologist and the University", *Universities Quarterly,* 17, 1962.
4. J. J. Broe, "Failure Rates and Quotas: A Note", *Vestes,* 7, 1964.
5. T. H. Matthews, "Academic Failures", in C. Bissell (ed.), *Canada's Crisis in Higher Education* (University of Toronto Press, 1957).
6. Michael Forster, *An Audit of Academic Performance* (Queen's University, Belfast, 1959).
7. Sir Fred J. Schonell, Ernest Roe, and Ivor G. Meddleton, *Promise and Performance—A Study of Student Progress at University Level* (University of Queensland Press and University of London Press, 1962).
8. Sir Fred J. Schonell, The Problems of Teaching, *Conference of Australian Universities,* 1963. (Cited by A. G. Maclaine, "A Programme for improving Teaching and Learning in Australian Universities", *The Australian University,* 3, 3, 1965.)
9. R. R. Priestley, "The Mental Health of University Students", *Melbourne Studies in Education,* 1957–58 (University of Melbourne Press).
10. Ethel Venables, "Placement Problems among Engineering Apprentices in Part-time Technical College Courses: Part II", *British Journal of Educational Psychology,* 31, Part 1, 1961.
11. F. J. Olsen, "Failure in First Year University Examinations", *Australian Journal of Education,* 1, 3, 1957.
12. R. Flecker, "Characteristics of Passing and Failing Students in First Year University Mathematics", *The Educand,* 3, 3, 1959.

13. Sir Fred J. Schonell, 1962, *op. cit.*
14. N. B. Malleson, "University Student, I, Profile, 1953, A Study of One Year's Entry to University College, London", *Universities Quarterly*, **13**, 3, 1959.
15. D. A. Howell, "A Study of the 1955 Entry to British Universities", Evidence to Robbins Committee on Higher Education (Mimeo), (University of London, 1962).
16. S. M. Lipset and P. Altbach, "U.S. Campus Alienation", *New Society*, September 8th, 1966.
17. Gladys Watson, "Happy College Years", A Report on the Specialized Counselling Program (Mimeo), (Brooklyn College of City University of New York, 1963).
18. Alexander W. Astin, "Personal and Environmental Factors associated with College Dropouts among High Aptitude Students", *Journal of Educational Psychology*, **55**, 4, 1964.
19. J. Hopkins, N. B. Malleson, and I. Sarnoff, "Some Non-Intellectual Correlates of Success and Failure among University Students", *British Journal of Educational Psychology*, **28**, *Part I*, 1958.
20. Hilde Himmelweit and Arthur Summerfield, "Student Selection—An Experimental Investigation: III", *British Journal of Sociology*, **2**, 4, 1951.
21. A. W. Astin, *op. cit.*
22. Sir Fred J. Schonell, 1962, *op. cit.*; and John Gibson and Phyllis Light, "Intelligence among University Scientists", *Nature*, **213**, 5057, 1967.
23. Sir James Learmonth in *Proceedings of Home Universities Conference*, 1952.
24. A. E. Schwartzman, R. C. A. Hunter, and R. H. Prince, "Intellectual Factors and Academic Performance in Medical Undergraduates", *Journal of Medical Education*, 36, 353, 1961.
25. Gladys Watson, *op. cit.*
26. "Gifted Failures", *The Times Educational Supplement*, February 17th, 1967.
27. Ethel Venables, 1961, *op. cit.*
28. H. J. Eysenck, "Student Selection", *British Journal of Educational Psychology*, **17**, 1947.
29. W. J. McKeachie, Lin Yi Guang, J. Millholland, and R. Isaacson, "Student Affiliation Motives, Teacher Warmth and Academic Achievement", *Journal of Personality and Social Psychology*, **4**, 4, 1966.
30. P. E. Vernon, "The Pool of Ability", in P. Halmos (ed.),

The Sociological Review Monograph, No. 7 (University of Keele, 1963).

31. J. W. B. Douglas, *The Home and the School* (London, MacGibbon and Kee, 1964).

32. Jean Floud and A. H. Halsey, "Social Class, Intelligence Tests and Selection for Secondary Schools", in A. H. Halsey, Jean Floud, and C. Arnold Anderson (eds.), *Education, Economy and Society* (New York, Macmillan, 1961). Hilde Himmelweit: "Social Status and Secondary Education since the 1944 Act: Some Data for London", in D. V. Glass (ed.), *Social Mobility in Britain* (London, Routledge and Kegan Paul, 1954).

33. R. J. Havighurst, *Growing up in River City* (New York, Wiley, 1962).

34. P. E. Vernon, 1963, *op. cit.*

35. G. W. Miller, "Social and Emotional Correlates of Academic Achievement in Primary School Children", Ph.D. thesis, London, 1967.

36. *Children and their Primary Schools,* Plowden Report, paras. 89–91, Table 1, (London, H.M.S.O., 1967).

37. G. W. Miller, *Educational Opportunity and the Home* (in preparation).

38. N. B. Malleson, 1959, *op. cit.*

39. P. Marris, *The Experience of Higher Education* (London, Routledge and Kegan Paul, 1964).

40. N. B. Malleson, "Student Performance at University College, London, 1948–51", *Universities Quarterly,* **12**, 1958.

41. C. J. Lucas, R. P. Kelvin, and A. B. Ojha, "Mental Health and Student Wastage", *British Journal of Psychiatry,* **112**, 484, 1966.

42. P. E. Vernon, 1963, *op. cit.*

43. R. G. Rowlands, "Some Differences between Prospective Scientists, Non-Scientists, and Early Leavers in a Representative Sample of English Grammar School Boys", *British Journal of Educational Psychology,* **31**, 1961.

44. K. Lovell and G. E. White, "Some Influences affecting Choice of Subjects in School and Training College", *British Journal of Educational Psychology,* **28**, 1958.

45. P. W. Hughes, "Academic Achievement at the University: An Analysis of Factors related to Success" (Mimeo), (University of Tasmania, 1960).

46. *Higher Education,* Robbins Report. Appendix II A, p. 135. Cmnd. 2154 (London, H.M.S.O., 1963).

47. G. A. Gray and L. N. Short, "Student Progress in the University" (Mimeo), (University of New South Wales, 1961).
48. A. G. Maclaine, "A Programme for improving Teaching and Learning in Australian Universities", *The Australian University*, **3**, 3, 1965.
49. Sir Fred J. Schonell, 1963, *op. cit.*
50. S. B. Hammond, "Draft Report of a First Year Student Survey 1955–56" (Mimeo), (University of Melbourne, 1957).
51. C. Sanders, "Australian Universities and their Educational Problems", *The Australian University*, **1**, 2, 1963.
52. R. K. Kelsall, "University Student Selection in Relation to Subsequent Academic Performance: A Critical Appraisal of the British Evidence", in P. Halmos (ed.), 1963, *op. cit.*
53. Sir Fred J. Schonell, 1962, *op. cit.*
54. *Ability and Educational Opportunity*, Organization for Economic Co-operation and Development, London, 1961.
55. W. D. Furneaux, *The Chosen Few* (Oxford University Press, 1961).
56. Ethel Venables, "Placement Problems among Engineering Apprentices in Part-time Technical College Courses, Part I", *British Journal of Educational Psychology*, **30**, 3, 1960.
57. Ethel Venables, 1961, *op. cit.*
58. Ethel Venables, "Social Differences among Day-Release Students in Relation to their Recruitment and Examination Success", *British Journal of Sociological and Clinical Psychology*, **2**, 1963.
59. Anne Roe, *The Making of a Scientist* (New York, Dodd, Mead, 1953).
60. D. Harris, 1940, *op. cit.*
61. A. W. Astin, 1964, *op. cit.*
62. Durganand Sinha, "A Psychological Analysis of some Factors associated with Success and Failure in University Education", *Indian Educational Review*, **1**, 1, 1966.
63. J. W. B. Douglas, 1964, *op. cit.*
64. *Scottish Mental Survey 1947*, Scottish Council for Research in Education, 1949; J. Maxwell, *The Level and Trend of National Intelligence* (University of London Press, 1961).
65. Francis Galton, *English Men of Science* (London, Macmillan, 1874).
66. *Dictionary of National Biography* (Oxford University Press).

67. D. Harris, 1940, *op. cit.*
68. Anne Roe, 1953, op. cit.
69. Michael Forster, 1959, *op. cit.*
70. R. R. Priestley (Private Communication), 1965.
71. D. Sinha, 1966, *op. cit.*
72. John Summerskill, "Dropouts from College", chapter in N. Sanford (ed.), *The American College*, (New York, Wiley, 1962).
73. A. W. Astin, 1964, *op. cit.*
74. C. Sanders, "Asian Students in Australian Universities" (Mimeo), (University of Western Australia, 1954).
75. B. C. Rosen, "Race, Ethnicity and Achievement", *American Sociological Review*, 24, 1, 1959.
76. K. E. Merrill, "The Relationship of Certain Non-Intellective Factors to Lack of Persistence of Higher Ability Students and Persistence of Lower Ability Students at the University of California, Berkeley." Ph.D. thesis, University of California, Berkeley, 1964. Cited in *Dissertation Abstracts*, **25**, p. 3939.
77. *Education at Berkeley: Report of Select Committee on Education*, 1966.
78. Glen H. Elder, "Family Structure and Educational Attainment: A Cross-National Analysis", *American Sociological Review*, 30, No. 1, 1965.
79. J. W. B. Douglas, 1964, *op. cit.*
80. Basil B. Bernstein, The Sociological Conditions for, and Consequences of, Two Linguistic Codes with Special Reference to Socialisation (9 published papers), Ph.D. thesis, London, 1963.
81. G. W. Miller, 1967, *op. cit.*
82. D. A. Howell, 1962, *op. cit.*
83. K. E. Merrill, 1964, *op. cit.*
84. P. W. Hughes, 1960, *op. cit.*
85. J. Summerskill, 1962, *op. cit.*
86. R. E. Iffert, "Dropouts: Nature and Causes; Effects on Students, Family and Society", Association for Higher Education, Current Issues in Higher Education, 1956, 94–102; Washington: National Education Association, 1956; cited in N. Sanford, 1962, *op. cit.*
87. R. E. Iffert, *Retention and Withdrawal of College Students*, U.S. Department of Health Education and Welfare, Bulletin 1958, No. 1. (Washington: Government Printing Office, 1957).

88. Margaret Mercer, "A Study of Student Mortality in the Home Economics College", *Journal of Educational Research*, 34, 1941.

89. Martha Thompson, "Admission Information as Predictors for Graduation", M.A. thesis, Cornell, 1953. Cited in N. Sanford, 1962, *op. cit.*

90. G. Weigand, "Motivational Factors associated with Success and Failure of Probational Students", Ph.D. thesis, University of Maryland, 1951. Cited in N. Sanford, 1962, *op. cit.*

91. C. Sanders, 1963, *op. cit.*

92. C. Sanders, *Student Selection and Academic Success in Australian Universities* (Sydney, Government Printer, 1948).

93. H. Philp and A. Cullen, "A Further Study of Age and Academic Success", *Forum of Education*, 14, 1955.

94. W. G. Fleming, *Personal and Academic Factors as Predictors of First Year Success in Ontario Universities* (Atkinson Study Report No. 5), University of Toronto, Department of Educational Research, 1959. Cited in C. Sanders, 1963, *op. cit.*

95. Sir Fred J. Schonell, 1962, *op. cit.*

96. C. Sanders *Psychological and Educational Bases of Academic Performance* (Melbourne, A.C.E.R., 1961).

97. V. D. Barnett and T. Lewis, "A Study of Factors affecting the Relation between G.C.E. and Degree Results" (Mimeo). Paper to Royal Statistical Society, London, January 1963.

98. R. Flecker, 1959, *op. cit.*

99. D. A. Howell, 1962, *op. cit.*

100. D. Harris, 1940, *op. cit.*

101. C. Sanders, *Aspects of Scholastic Intelligence* (Mimeo), Australian and New Zealand Association for the Advancement of Science, Section J, Brisbane, Queensland, May 25th, 1951.

102. Derbyshire Education Committee, Awards to Students (Mimeo), 1966.

103. A. W. Astin, 1964, *op. cit.*

104. W. D. Furneaux, 1961, *op. cit.*

105. R. K. Boyer, *The Student Peer Group: Its Effect on College Performance* (Mimeo), (Case Institute of Technology, 1966).

106. D. Harris, 1940, *op. cit.*

107. C. J. Lucas *et al.*, 1966, *op. cit.*

108. H. Himmelweit and A. Summerfield, 1951, *op. cit.*
109. G. A. Gray and L. N. Short, 1961, *op. cit.*
110. Derbyshire Education Committee, 1966, *op. cit.*
111. P. Marris, 1964, *op. cit.*
112. N. B. Malleson, "University Students, 1953", *Universities Quarterly*, **15**, 1, 1960.
113. J. Summerskill, 1962, *op. cit.*
114. N. B. Malleson, 1953, *op. cit.*
115. R. Flecker, 1959, *op. cit.*
116. D. Harris, 1940, *op. cit.*
117. D. Sinha, 1966, *op. cit.*
118. Hilde Himmelweit, "Student Selection—An Experimental Investigation", *British Journal of Sociology*, **1**, 4, 1950.
119. A. Roe, 1953, *op. cit.*
120. D. Harris, *op. cit.*
121. N. B. Malleson, 1958, *op. cit.*
122. L. Pond, "A Study of High Achieving and Low Achieving Freshmen", *Australian Journal of Higher Education*, **2**, 1, 1964.
123. S. B. Hammond, 1957, *op. cit.*
124. J. Piaget, *The Psychology of Intelligence* (London, Routledge and Kegan Paul, 1950).
125. W. F. Brown and W. H. Holtzman, "A Study Attitudes Questionnaire for predicting Academic Success", *Journal of Educational Psychology*, **46**, 1955.
126. G. W. Miller, *op. cit.*
127. S. M. Lipset and P. Altbach, 1966, *op. cit.*
128. C. Sanders, 1963, *op. cit.*
129. J. Summerskill, 1962, *op. cit.*
130. D. A. Howell, *op. cit.*
131. R. R. Dale, "Psychological Tests in University Selection", *Educational Review*, **4**, 1951.
132. *Education at Berkeley*, op. cit.
133. K. Keniston, *The Uncommitted: Alienated Youth in American Society* (New York, Harcourt Brace, 1965).
134. Lawrence F. Douglas, "Types of Students and their Outlook on University Education: A Comparative Study of Students in the Physical and Social Sciences", Ph.D. thesis, London, 1964.
135. J. P. Corbett, "Opening the Mind", in D. Daiches (ed.), *The Idea of a New University* (London, Deutsch, 1964).
136. Derbyshire Education Committee, *op. cit.*
137. A. W. Astin, *op. cit.*

138. Michael Kendall, "Those Who Failed I: The Further Education of Former Students", *Universities Quarterly,* **18,** 4, 1964.
139. Dorothy M. Knoell, "Undergraduate Attrition: Mortality or Mobility?" (Mimeo), paper presented at Princeton University Conference on the College Dropout and the Utilisation of Talent, October 8th–9th, 1964.
140. B. K. Eckland, "College Dropouts Who Come Back", *Harvard Educational Review,* **34,** 1964.
141. D. Sinha, *op. cit.*
142. A. W. Astin, *op. cit.*
143. *Higher Education,* Robbins Report, Appendix II B, p. 167, para. 65, (London, H.M.S.O.), Cmnd. 2154, 1963.
144. *Education at Berkeley,* op. cit.
145. B. R. Clark and M. Trow, "Determinants of College Student Sub-Cultures", (Mimeo). Cited in *Education at Berkeley,* op. cit.
146. R. C. A. Hunter and A. E. Schwartzman, "A Clinical View of Study Difficulties in a Group of Counselled Medical Students", *J. Medical Education,* **36,** 1295, 1961.
147. H. Himmelweit and A. Summerfield, *op. cit.*; H. Himmelweit, 1950, *op. cit.*
148. Ruth M. Beard, P. M. Levy, and H. Maddox, "Academic Performance at University", *Educational Review,* **16,** 1964.
149. D. L. Thistlethwaite, "Effects of Social Recognition upon the Educational Motivation of Talented Youth", *Journal of Educational Psychology,* **50,** 1959.
150. H. A. Presser, G. W. D. Boyd, and R. C. G. Lea, "The Social Conditions for Successful Learning", in O. A. Oeser (ed.), *Teacher, Pupil and Task* (London, Tavistock, 1955).
151. Sir Fred J. Schonell, 1963, *op. cit.*
152. G. W. Miller, *op. cit.*
153. R. E. Iffert, 1954, 1956, *op. cit.*
154. N. B. Freedman, "The Passage through College", *Journal of Social Issues,* **12,** 1956.
155. J. Hopkins *et al.,* op. cit.
156. H. Himmelweit, 1950, *op. cit.*
157. A. W. Astin, *op. cit.*
158. P. A. Heist and P. A. Williams, "Variation of Achievement within a Select and Homogeneous Student Body", *Journal of College Student Personnel,* **3,** 1961. Cited in G. D. Yonge, "Students", *Review of Educational Research,* **25,** 1965.

159. H. Himmelweit *et al.*, 1951, *op. cit.*
160. J. Hopkins *et al.*, op. cit.
161. D. C. Pelz and F. M. Andrews, "Organizational Atmosphere, Motivation and Research Contribution", *The American Behavioural Scientist*, 6, 1962.
162. F. B. Chaney, "A Cross-Cultural Study of Industrial Research Performance", *Journal of Applied Psychology*, 50, 3, 1966.
163. J. Summerskill, *op. cit.*
164. R. Flecker, *op. cit.*
165. A. Roe, *op. cit.*
166. P. A. Heist, T. R. McConnell, F. Matsler, and Phoebe Williams, "Personality and Scholarship", *Science*, 133, 1961.
167. P. E. Vernon, "Educational Abilities of Training College Students", *British Journal of Educational Psychology*, 9, 1939.
168. D. Sinha, *op. cit.*
169. J. L. Holland, "The Prediction of College Grades from the California Psychological Inventory and the Scholastic Aptitude Test", *Journal of Educational Psychology*, 50, 1959.
170. J. L. Holland, "Creative and Academic Performance among Talented Adolescents", *Journal of Educational Psychology*, 52, 1961.
171. H. A. Grace, "Personality Factors and College Attrition", *Peabody Journal of Education*, 35, 1, 1957.
172. D. Harris, *op. cit.*
173. G. W. Miller, *op. cit.*
174. Glen H. Elder, *op. cit.*
175. J. W. Getzells and P. W. Jackson, *Creativity and Intelligence* (London and New York, Wiley, 1962).
176. R. L. Thorndike, *The Concepts of Over- and Under-Achievement* (New York, Teacher's College, 1963).
177. J. P. Guilford, "Creativity", *The American Psychologist*, 5, 1950; and "Progress in the Discovery of Intellectual Factors", in C. W. Taylor (ed.), *Widening Horizons in Creativity* (New York, Wiley, 1964).
178. D. Harris, *op. cit.*
179. H. A. Grace, *op. cit.*
180. D. Sinha, *op. cit.*
181. H. B. Reed, "Anxiety—The Ambivalent Variable", *Harvard Educational Review*, 30, 2, 1960.

182. David E. Lavin, *The Prediction of Academic Performance* (Russell Sage Foundation, and New York, Wiley, 1967).

183. Sigmund Freud, *General Introduction to Psychoanalysis* (New York, Washington Square, and Liveright Publishing Corporation, 1935).

184. G. W. Miller, *op. cit.*

185. H. J. Eysenck, *Dimensions of Personality* (London, Routledge and Kegan Paul, 1947); W. D. Furneaux, *op. cit.*

186. D. Harris, *op. cit.*

187. David E. Lavin, *op. cit.*

188. G. W. Miller, *op. cit.*

189. S. M. Lipset and P. Altbach, *op. cit.*

190. R. W. Parnell, "Mortality and Prolonged Illness among Oxford Undergraduates", *The Lancet,* March 31st, 1961.

191. N. B. Malleson, *A Handbook on British Student Health Services* (London, Pitman Medical, 1966).

192. R. R. Priestley, *op. cit.*

193. G. A. Gray and L. N. Short, *op. cit.*

194. R. J. Weiss, B. E. Segal, and R. Sokol, "Epidemiology of Emotional Disturbance in a Men's College", *Journal of Nervous and Mental Diseases,* 141, 2, 1965.

195. S. J. G. Spencer, "Academic Revoke and Failure among Oxford Undergraduates", *The Lancet,* August 30th, 1958.

196. W. D. Furneaux, *op. cit.*

197. C. D. Spielberger, "The Effects of Manifest Anxiety on the Academic Achievements of College Students", *Mental Hygiene, (N.Y.),* 46, 1962.

198. C. J. Lucas *et al.,* op. cit.

199. R. J. Still, "Psychological Illness among Students in the Examination Period" (Mimeo), Department of Student Health, University of Leeds, 1963.

200. N. B. Malleson, 1959, *op. cit.*

201. N. B. Malleson, 1959, *op. cit.*

202. A. W. Astin, *op. cit.*

203. N. B. Malleson, 1964, *op. cit.*

204. Sir Fred J. Schonell *et al.,* op. cit.

205. D. Harris, *op. cit.*

206. J. W. B. Douglas, *op. cit.*

207. A. Roe, *op. cit.*

208. A. W. Astin, *op. cit.*

209. K. E. Merrill, *op. cit.*

210. Margaret Mercer, "Personal Factors in College Adjustment", *Journal of Educational Research, 36,* 1943; Martha Thompson, *op. cit.*; and G. Weigand, *op. cit.*

211. P. E. Vernon, 1963, *op. cit.*

212. Sir Fred J. Schonell, 1962, *op. cit.*

CHAPTER 3

STUDENT SELECTION

O F the many institutional variables which can affect student attrition or wastage that which has received the most attention of administrators and researchers has been selection. This variable is complementary to those student variables which have been discussed earlier and which make possible some degree of prediction. It is a persistent hope among selecting tutors that there is some further possibility of refining selection, and it may be that further research will yield some slight improvement. Before examining the research it is apposite to consider some pertinent questions about the extent to which continued effort in improving selection may or may not prove to be justified in lessening wastage and achieving higher productivity in terms of greater proportions of students attaining degrees.

It should be clear that selection and prediction are by no means always synonymous. To assume that they are is a fallacy, because it implies a stability in the policies and practices of institutions which does not exist. To the extent that such stability is lacking, prediction must be inaccurate, and hence a source of error in selecting students is built in. Some of the sources of such error are the subject of extended discussion in this and subsequent chapters. If one could imagine a point in time when selection has been perfected, the probability would still remain that some students, all 'perfectly selected', would still drop out or be failed in their finals.

The quality of student intake has been rising generally in most countries for many years, if we take previous academic success at school as the criterion. This rise in quality is occurring in several ways. Pupils are being encouraged to stay on at school longer, higher education is becoming more popular and fashionable and a requisite qualification for an increasingly wide range of occupations. It follows that institutions can choose their intakes from a large number of qualified applicants. In Britain what were thought to be inflated projections of the demand for higher education when the Robbins Report was published in 1963 (though it should be noted that the Committee itself thought them conservative) have already been dramatically exceeded. Improved student intake, using matriculation or A levels as the criterion, and imposition of quotas in some fields must lead to diminishing returns in the improvement of selection procedures. In spite of the care with which selection to British universities is made, using the methods available to the present, Woodhall and Blaug (1) were still able to claim in 1965 that productivity in universities has declined since 1938 and that there has been a deterioration in recent years.

It seems obvious that in order to find ways of lessening wastage, and hence improving the productivity of institutions, other devices will have to be considered. Structural changes in the system, availability of ancillary services, aspects of teaching and examining, and flexibility and rigidity of courses are examples and are the subject of later discussion. Meanwhile, selection itself will be examined.

First there is a key question—what are we selecting for? Are we to disregard every other consideration save whether the student will successfully pass his examinations? Is examination ability more important than the question whether the student will make a good architect, doctor, engineer, teacher, social worker, or lawyer? If not, should the examination be the only criterion of whether the student will succeed in his chosen profession? If success in the chosen profession is not of central importance, what is important? Are we trying to select candidates who will develop a certain mandarin ability to apply their minds effectively to any problem? There is some evidence that students who succeed in examinations are not necessarily the best professionals. If we accept that we are simply seeking to select candidates who will pass their examinations let us refer to the findings of Furneaux (2) that neurotic introverts are the most successful students. We can then ask should we select neurotic introverts where possible? But do we want most graduates to be neurotic and introverted? Is it not a good thing to have some extroverts too? If we find that the best student engineers and doctors are those who specialize in their subjects to the exclusion of any interest in the humanities and the arts, then, before we select them or encourage their development accordingly, we must ask if we want the majority of graduate engineers and doctors to be

Philistines. Would it not be better for them to have some philosophical or aesthetic interests as well?

In one American study (3) it was shown that sociability scores were negatively correlated with success in engineering. If we agree that we do not want unsociable engineers only, and that it is desirable to have people with a range of personality and interests in every field, then we ought not to limit our selection of candidates to those who satisfy such criteria, however effective these criteria might be in predicting academic success. It is certainly doubtful if we would be content at the present time to enrol only middle-class students on the basis that there is a positive correlation between social class and academic achievement in school.

Some other predictive criteria are less ridiculous. For example, it is possible to hypothesize that people with a respect for the personalities of children make good teachers, or that students who have a great deal of curiosity and are strongly motivated in their subjects will make good researchers and so on. It should be possible to take for granted that university students should be curious, creative, industrious, tolerant, and liberal. These would surely be admissible attributes to use in selection of students and to inculcate in them. It will depend on the kind of university population selectors are trying to choose. The Franks Report (4) stated, "The search for a balanced academic community is often held to involve some sacrifice of efficiency in selection for academic promise" (para. 139), and such a liberal view will find wide acceptance. But, in the absence of stronger scientific evidence than is at the moment available to support these sentiments, selectors will continue to rely on examinations as the main criterion.

Locke (5) has noted that an important but frequently neglected aspect of evaluation of educational achievement is the meaningfulness of the criteria by which such achievement is judged; grades may often be merely reflections of an ability to memorize and reproduce facts rather than an ability to use facts creatively. At the present time a growing number of writers are raising an old question by challenging the use of grades as the only measure of academic progress, and if there is any validity in their queries we may be compelled to query the use of students' school grades as the main criterion in selection. In what little research has been done on this subject so far there is some suggestion that academic

97

and non-academic accomplishment are relatively independent of each other. Holland and Richards' (6) study of 7262 college freshmen in 24 colleges and universities produced a median correlation of .04, between measures of academic achievement and measures of art, music, literature, drama, and independent scientific activity. This is an arresting finding. The early zero correlation questions assumptions that academic progress and general cultural interests automatically go together. For this large sample there was no association between the two. Replication of the study in different universities and colleges and within each discipline should attract a high priority.

These questions having been posed and some of the more obvious points at issue briefly mentioned, discussion of selection is now focused on the problem of selecting students who will perform best in their examinations, this being the most widely accepted criterion of academic success at the present time. The Franks Report (7) raised several points that frequently escape the notice of writers dealing with student selection. Having referred to the paucity of research on selection in the United Kingdom, the report then outlined some limitations of existing techniques. The Franks Report states,

> It is often supposed that their efficiency may be judged by the accuracy with which they enable the probable performance of candidates in the final examination to be predicted: the better the tests the higher the probability of an accurate forecast. The truth is not so simple for some important factors . . . cannot be determined by tests [at present in existence], but remain beyond the reach of any improvement in forecasting devices.
> . . . within the broad groups marks are an uncertain guide to the forecasting of individual performance : yet selectors have to make positive choices. Preference for a candidate who obtained x marks on one particular set of questions over a candidate who obtained x—1 marks has no merit beyond that of simplicity. In selection for a university place, the choice between such candidates must hinge on other considerations, since on purely intellectual grounds they are indistinguishable. Weight can properly be given to evidence about their motivation, their background, the nature of their schooling, or their non-academic interests and activities. [Paras. 137–138]

The Report does not go into which particular non-academic

interests and activities should be considered relevant or the manner in which weight should be given to them, but it makes the very important point raised at the beginning of this chapter.

> . . . The rigorous application of the principle of competitive examination must always be tempered by the feeling [common to all British universities] that undergraduates are being admitted as individuals to a society or community of scholars. From this follows the desire to admit a variety of types and avoid a situation in which those admitted are all cast more or less in the same mould. [Para. 139]

Here there is support for the suggestion made earlier that it might be desirable to have different types of people in various disciplines—for example, the clever and vigorous Philistine, the pragmatist, and the academic who is able to suspend judgment and tolerate complexity and ambiguity while considering all possible evidence, even if he is unable to make effective, clear-cut decisions. A spread of personality and interest in persons of each calling would help to ensure a continual injection of different ideas and thought into those fields. If we accept this suggestion, certain variables which it is thought would assist prediction of academic performance will have to be critically examined before being used for student selection, because in applying them we would at the same time be vitiating the possibility of having a range of personalities in each discipline.

However this may be, universities and colleges are presumably in business to produce graduates, and, as Sir James Mountford (8) proposed, when more than 10 per cent of a class fails, there is something seriously wrong with selection or other policy in the particular department. Selection is not a simple task, and it is subject to serious error. Llewellyn (9) has voiced what must be in the minds of many, "Because he [the student] has been so carefully selected, his teachers have a vested interest in his success, otherwise their methods and criteria of selection come into question." Furneaux (10) has shown that substantial differences of opinion exist among selectors as to the worth of a large proportion of applicants, and that the actual performance elsewhere of qualified students rejected by one university is indistinguishable from that of those who are accepted. Furneaux held that within the group of qualified candidates, selection procedures which are generally applied can have only moderate validity. As the quality of student intake rises, if the best students are to be selected, other criteria of selection need to be extended. Darley (11) found that, between 1952 and 1959, in 167 United States institutions the mean ability score rose in spite of the 50 per cent increase in enrolment in that period. From 1951 to 1963 the proportion of higher-ability students planning to go to college in Minnesota increased almost three times as fast as the general proportion of high-school graduates planning to do so. (12) From this it is clear that there has been an improvement in the measured ability of college students over that period. To the extent that these findings apply to other countries there need be no fear that 'more will mean worse'. The concern should be not so much about whether we shall get better students, but, perhaps, how we shall treat those we select.

In England Furneaux (13) has shown that more qualified applicants wish to enter universities than can be accommodated, and this becomes more acutely obvious each year. Some of those who gain a place without difficulty make very poor students, while others admitted with some hesitation do well, and however improved are the candidates each year the evidence from different countries over many years is that graduation rates remain stable. (14) [The Robbins Report also cited evidence that wastage rates have remained nearly constant in faculties whose entrance standards are known to have risen.] It seems likely that improved selection is not the only answer to this problem; nevertheless some of the advantages and disadvantages of present selection procedures should be examined.

School Performance as Selection Criteria

The current way of selecting candidates for higher education according to their standard of performance in school would seem to provide the most accurate method, especially when the subject to be studied at the tertiary level is the same as that studied to A level. This has proved to be the case in a number of researches. Matriculation or A-level standard is to date the best single predictor, (15) but it is dangerous to ignore a large number of important qualifications.

Firstly the correlations between secondary and tertiary academic results are not very impressive. For example, Parkyn

(16) studied 4000 students with a mean I.Q. of 123. The correlation between School Certificate marks and university performance varied for different groups between .36 and .15. These correlations are highly significant, and we might well expect them to be, but they only account for between 3 and 12 per cent of the variance in university performance. This leaves a great deal to be explained by other variables.

It will now be asked if so little a correlation applies to subjects taken at university or college which were also taken up to university-entrance standard. Here, as expected, better prediction is possible, and correlations can be quite high. Harris (17) found that for physical sciences, languages, music, history, and social sciences experience of these subjects had some bearing on success at college. For history correlations of .67 were found, and for social sciences .56. But correlations of this order are certainly not typical. Himmelweit conducted two studies (18) of student selection at the London School of Economics, with 337 B.Sc.(Econ.), B.Comm., Social Science, and Medical students in 1951, and 593 B.Sc.(Econ.) and Sociology students in 1959. One of her findings was that A-level success in subjects relevant to the university subject offered no better prediction of success at university than success in any other A-level subject. Only in economics did a poor A-level mark predict low university performance.

A number of other studies have shown that matriculation or A-level marks predict as well as in those studies reviewed by Harris. For example, Williams (19) found correlations of .77 between school marks in biology and first year M.B. biology. Correlations were generally higher between school science results and university science results; but for English and physics it was only .33. Katz, Katz, and Olphert (20) found overall predictions of .5 to .57 in their studies, extending from only .37 for science subjects generally to .91, a remarkable correlation, for agricultural economics. Himmelweit (21) reviewed a number of American studies showing correlations of about .50 to .55 between some high-school and university results.

Although some of the above results are encouraging, when we bear in mind the variation between the findings for different subjects, we are on quite shaky ground if we depend too heavily on A-level or matriculation results. Even though they appear to be the best single predictors, the inconsistency of the relationship casts enormous doubt on their reliability, and hence their predictive validity.

What happens if selection is made more rigorous merely on the basis of matriculation or A-level results or other tests of ability is shown in several studies. Anderson (22) studied 132 students who had completed the prerequisite subjects for a science course, being 62 per cent of a year's intake into the science faculty in the University of Western Australia. He compared the efficacy of selection by I.Q. level and matriculation level. He found that failure was distributed over the whole range of I.Q., some students with I.Q.'s of 130 plus failing badly. His findings showed that if selectors accepted only those candidates with I.Q.'s of 125 and more, 27 per cent of the failure group would have been excluded from studies. This might seem satisfactory if it were not that 24 per cent of those who later passed would also have been prevented from taking up places. Even more interesting is that if selection had been made more rigorous so that only students of I.Q. 130 plus had been selected, 68 per cent of the failing group would have been excluded, but 52 per cent of the passing group would also have been prevented from taking up studies at the university.

Selection by matriculation results was more accurate, but was still too blunt an instrument to be used on its own. In selecting students according to their matriculation marks, if those with average marks of less than 65 per cent were excluded, half the failing group and 14 per cent of the passing group would have been selected out. A loss of 14 per cent of promising students is quite serious, but if the average matriculation marks required were raised to 70 per cent nearly one-third of the passing group would then have been denied places. The superiority of matriculation marks over I.Q. rating has been clearly demonstrated. The students with lower I.Q. but good matriculation results were better than those with high I.Q. and low matriculation marks. The problem that remains with us is, how can we select the best without excluding a large percentage of apparently not very promising candidates who would in fact turn out to be good students?

Sanders (23) makes a distinction between scholarship-winners selected on school results and other students. Scholarship-winners tend to produce a higher proportion of students who graduate in minimum time. In the first year they show somewhat higher overall pass rates than the total population of students, gain more credits and distinctions, and less often need supplementary examinations. By raising the matriculation standard, departments hope to eliminate students who will require more than one attempt to pass their examinations, but Sanders points out that this is difficult to accomplish. While some very weak matriculants fail in their first year, others are successful; and ultimately, Sanders believes, although the poorer matriculants generally tend to require more than minimum time to pass their exams, there is in reality not a great difference between them and the better matriculants in the time they take to graduate.

Anderson (24) found too that the relation between matriculation marks and academic success is not sufficiently strong to justify demands for more stringent selection, since it does not lead to substantial increases in university pass rates. He cites a study which shows that to achieve a 10 per cent increase in pass rate, from 64 per cent to 74 per cent, by more rigorous selection, would have required the rejection of 30 per cent of applicants, of whom 43 per cent in fact passed. Once over the first-year hurdle, the drop-out and failure rates decline markedly, and students of all abilities and matriculation standard finish their studies in comparable time. Anderson cites Schonell, (25) who found in Queensland that the price of excluding from the university about 30 students who would have failed to graduate was the rejection of 44 who would have been successful. The proportion of total enrolment making satisfactory progress would have been 71.8 per cent as against 68.5 per cent, which is not an impressive gain. Using matriculation levels as a device to raise pass rates therefore holds little promise.

Several writers in different countries have made this point repeatedly. (26) Himmelweit (27) has explained that from her research it was clear that whether a student got an A or a B mark in G.C.E. examinations made no difference to the quality of his degree, and claimed that universities should accept that there was a ceiling to prediction and that individuals developed at different rates. The report of the Transvaal Education Bureau in Johannesburg stated that the problem of first-year failures is not to be overcome by raising entrance standards and that a higher university entrance examination has the effect of depriving the country of a number of potentially capable persons by excluding them from the university.

The table from Sanders (28) which follows gives a clear idea of how little can be gained by raising entry requirements.

TABLE 10

Variability in Academic Performance and Matriculation Levels

Performance in University First-year Exam	Leaving Certificate			Total
	Upper Third	Middle Third	Lower Third	
Clear Distinction	2	1	1	4
Borderline Distinction	3	—	—	3
Clear Pass	16	11	6	33
Borderline Pass	5	11	9	25
Clear Failure	1	3	11	15
Total	27	26	27	80

Source: C. Sanders (1958).

It can be seen that only 2 in the upper third in leaving examination results achieved clear distinction in their first-year examinations, while 7 in the lower third leaving examination did better than 6 of those in the upper third, and better than 20 in the middle and upper levels. Sanders reports that, in later university examinations, while the upper third in leaving certificate marks weakened slightly, the originally less promising students in the middle and lower thirds improved their performance.

Nisbet's table for Scottish students, ten years later, shows the same trend. As Nisbet and Welsh (29) point out, the group with only the minimum entrance qualifications had the highest failure rate and the lowest proportion of honours, yet, if that group had been excluded from studies, the failure rate would only have been reduced from 16 to 13 per cent. That would be a useful but unimpressive saving in university resources, but the significant matter is that in doing this, no less that 89 students would have been disqualified from study who turned out in the event to be successful students, 36 achieving honours. This rejection of good students would scarcely be justified by the small decrease of 3 per cent in the failure rate.

TABLE 11

Combined Results (Scottish Students only: Percentages in Brackets)

| Result | Scottish Certificate of Education Number of Higher Passes | | | | | | | | Totals | |
	6+		5		4		3			
Honours degree students	34	(56)	83	(43)	87	(32)	36	(27)	240	(36)
Ordinary: minimum period	23	(38)	72	(37)	103	(37)	40	(31)	238	(36)
Ordinary: extra year	2	(3)	11	(6)	21	(8)	13	(10)	47	(7)
Failed to graduate —voluntary withdrawal	2	(3)	6	(3)	12	(5)	5	(4)	25	(4)
Failed to graduate —unsatisfactory	—		21	(11)	50	(18)	37	(28)	108	(16)
Totals	61	(100)	193	(100)	273	(100)	131	(100)	658	(100)

Source: J. Nisbet and J. Welsh (1966).

Scholastic Aptitude Tests and Creativity Tests

Examination gradings are notoriously unreliable, as a small acquaintance with the research literature on examinations will show. This will be discussed under a later heading; for the present it is sufficient to ask if there are alternatives to such an unreliable instrument which can be used to predict university and college success and hence improve student selection.

The comparative unreliability of matriculation marks and the fact that students vary between regions and examiners, as Jackson (30) and others have shown, have led to a growing demand for standardized scholastic aptitude tests in England. (31) The Robbins Report (32) received evidence that they promised greater accuracy in selecting students; and research is now being conducted in preparation for their design and development. (33) In the United States they have been in use for a long time, and have been more readily accepted as an accurate selection instrument compared with high-school grades than they have in England. In Australia also there has been some suggestion that they should be used, (34) and they are being developed by the Australian Council for Educational Research. They are seen as augmenting formal academic qualifications rather than replacing them.

The traditional role of university teachers in selecting students is thought by some to be a role for which many are inadequate. Himmelweit's studies have shown that traditional methods are not efficient, partly because the data on which selection is based are not sufficiently valid as predictors. It is being questioned if interviews serve any purpose in the selection process. In Britain the Committee of Vice-Chancellors and Principals, the Department of Education and Science, and the Schools Council are sponsoring a project on predictive tests, and the universities have set up a Standing Conference on University Entrance. It is believed that selection techniques can be improved. However, in Australia Sanders (35) has warned against placing too blind a faith in scholastic aptitude tests. He considered that they might enhance the accuracy of prediction in some subjects, in arts and social science, but that in other fields negligible improvement would result.

Interest in creativity tests and their usefulness in selecting students is running parallel with interest in scholastic aptitude tests. With interest in creativity, questions regarding the criteria of academic success and failure are raised. Since the outcome of higher education is not meant to be merely 'grades', interest in other criteria of performance and therefore interest in other criteria of selection, become relevant; and, indeed, some highly selective American institutions have begun to pay more attention to non-academic criteria—for example, Radcliffe and Williams. Some of the criteria of selection are congruent with criteria of creativity; for example, aesthetic values, ability to synthesize, association, flexibility, the divergent as opposed to the convergent mind, creative set, originality, sensitivity to problems, fluency, curiosity, and elaboration of ideas. Taylor and Williams (36) list almost two hundred works in this rapidly growing field. Getzells and Jackson (37) show that people who score highly in tests of creativity perform more highly than their I.Q.'s alone would predict. There is as yet no evidence that creativity tests added to school grades improve the prediction of success and failure in higher education. Although this is no new field— J. P. Guilford (38) was one of the early researchers twenty years ago—it is now more fashionable on both sides of the Atlantic, and greater attention is being paid to it by researchers, (39) though sometimes with inadequate definition of the concept.

Personality, Motivation, Interests, Ambition

Research into the personality, motivation, and interests of students to achieve has become more extensive in recent years. We have already referred to the lessening differentiation in achievement which ability can predict as student intake continues to rise in quality as it has done in the last twenty years. Although grades and other measures of scholastic ability will continue to be widely used, the diversity of psychological tests can be expected to increase, and this field seems to offer considerable promise. Weintraub and Salley (40) in 1945 anticipated that this approach might open the way for a radical reduction in the percentage of academic mortality, but in 1962, after reviewing prediction studies, Fishman (41) concluded that prediction of academic success over the preceding fifteen years from personality and biographical inventories had been disappointing, and even suggested that we should forget about prediction until we knew more about students' characteristics other than ability and about the institutional environments in which they learn and are examined.

Other writers are more enthusiastic. Himmelweit and Summerfield (42) concluded from their investigation that the use of psychological tests would lead to an 80 per cent reduction of the failure rate in the final examination, but to this they added an important rider, as Fishman probably would have, that this improvement could be made *"provided the standard of marking examinations remained constant"*. Herein lies the fallacy of assuming that in improved selection we can find the solution to academic wastage and failure. Clearly if standard of marking varies the most perfect selection procedures will fail in their purpose. This point is the subject of later discussion. Meanwhile at present we still pursue the possibility of improving selection as a separate, though related, question.

Astin (43) in the United States has suggested that potential drop-outs could be identified better if more data were collected from each student on enrolment. Astin has made extensive studies of more than six thousand National Merit Scholars and recipients of similar awards who are generally in the top 6 per cent in ability, and if the students are affected by the variables he suggests it seems possible that they will affect students of lesser ability even more. Among those Astin suggests could be considered in selection, and which could be included in intake data, are expectations about college, standard of degree to which the student aspires, father's educational level, mother's educational level, whether the student's peers plan to enter college, anticipated financial difficulties, and future marriage plans, the latter especially for girl students. It may be questionable if students should be selected, and others excluded, on any of those grounds, but if perfect prediction is being sought those variables cannot be ignored, because statistically significant relationships were found between each one and the drop-out rate among gifted students. Astin also considered that measures of impulsivity, dependence, and egocentricity showed some promise as predictors of persistence in college or dropping out.

Prediger (44) studied 1469 male students in the University of Missouri using the Missouri Biographical Data Inventory, and his findings support those of Astin. This instrument contains sixty items about parents' occupation, students' health, marital state, home location (type, size, and distance from campus), financial state, social and cultural activities, school subjects taken, and time spent away from parents. Prediger found a distinction between ability groups in the power of these biographical data to differentiate between drop-outs and persisters. He compared low-, medium-, and high-ability groups. For students of low ability the bio-data did not contribute to prediction, but for students of medium and high ability statistically significant differences were found between persisting students and drop-outs. Because of this link with ability Prediger concluded that ability acts as a moderator variable. These results are of particular interest because, while Fishman's finding that bio-data do not discriminate across the whole range of ability is not contradicted, Prediger has found they do discriminate *within* ability groups. Since there is a steady climb in the ability of student intakes over the years, it seems that personality and bio-data can serve as useful predictors of academic achievement for the narrowing ability groups entering universities and colleges—that is, assuming that we continue to insist on more accurate initial selection techniques.

However, enthusiasm has to be tempered with caution, because of the unreliability of other factors which intervene. Hogben's (45) study of 376 first-year medical students over a five-year period emphasizes this point. The bio-data he collected were different from those of Prediger, but the argument remains the same. Hogben found no significant differences between students of each year's intake on age at entry, reading ability, intelligence, matriculation performance, yet the pass rates in each year varied from 58 per cent to 78 per cent, fluctuating up and down in alternate years.

Researches by Furneaux (46) and Lynn (47) give further support for the use of bio-data and psychological data in predicting academic success. Lynn found that good students were more often neurotic and introverted than poor students, and also that university students of both sexes were more often neurotic than apprentices and non-students. This supported Furneaux's earlier finding, and Lynn concluded that neuroticism has two effects on academic attainment of university students. In stress situations it can be disorganizing, but it also has a facilitating effect in motivating sustained work. At the sixth form and university Lynn concluded that its disorganizing effects seem more than compensated by its motivating effects. Furneaux found with engineering, science, and arts students that certain other bio-data predicted university performance. Students with well-educated professional parents tended to find places in university more often than others, especially if they came from small families. Vocational aims affected students differently according to faculty. For example, students in professional courses of applied science, engineering, and medicine, who had clear career objectives, had superior academic performance; but for students in arts and pure science vocational orientation made less difference. These findings have implications for selection policy, but they are perhaps more interesting for the reason that any benefits of selection based on these criteria would differ between faculties.

Other studies have produced significant results using personality measures. (48) Martha Maxwell (49) studied four hundred male students in arts and sciences, business, public administration, and engineering, and compared those who graduated with those who did not. Using the California Psychological Inventory and the American Council on Education psychological test, she found that students in different faculties who graduated or failed to graduate differed in ways that varied with the discipline studied. She compared the predictive power of C.P.I. tests with the predictive power of A.C.E. tests of academic aptitude, and found that C.P.I. tests were marginally better. Arts and science students' graduation was best predicted by the C.P.I. scales of dominance, responsibility, socialization, tolerance, intellectual efficiency, and achievement via conformance. For students of business administration "achievement via conformance" and socialization were the best predictors. For engineering students, responsibility and "achievement via conformance" also predicted well, but sociability was a negative predictor.

Maxwell's conclusions were that these motivational variables were as effective in predicting graduation as were tests of scholastic aptitude, that some were significantly more predictive, and that these motivational characteristics operate differentially according to the discipline studied. Her main conclusions were that the California Psychological Inventory profile merits greater use in selection of students for university and college studies and in helping students to formulate educational and vocational career plans. She claimed that in selection these data should be weighted as heavily as intellectual ability and achievement scores. Maxwell's study strongly supports similar recommendations made by Himmelweit (50) following her studies at the London School of Economics in the 1950's, when she suggested the use of psychological tests as means of selection.

Sanders (51) has taken up the question of selecting mature students for more places in higher education. There seems no reason why students should be expected to go into university or college straight from school. Astin's finding (52) about study fatigue in new undergraduates is pertinent here. It might do no harm to allot larger numbers of places to people who have worked perhaps for a year or more before entering university. The Report to the Derbyshire Education Committee (53) suggests such a possibility. Sanders noted that since the Second World War and the unexpected academic success of mature students who had spent several years in the armed services there have been suggestions that students should spend a period in employment between leaving school and going to university to gain the necessary maturity for academic studies.* Sanders cites research evidence which indicates that such delays may do no damage to arts students—and, indeed, it may profit them in certain arts courses.

* See also A. M. Iliffe, "Are sixth-formers old enough for university?" *The Times Educational Supplement,* July 11th, 1969.

For intending science students there would perhaps be some temporary retardation of mathematical and scientific skills which might handicap them in their initial university work, though that has yet to be demonstrated. On the other hand the gain in maturity might offset any temporary falling back. Sanders cites other evidence showing that retention of capacity in the social sciences and literature continues well after middle age, though there are doubts if this is true for the physical and biological sciences. The suggestion that scientists do in fact suffer a decrement appears slight, and may possibly be based merely on impressions.

Harris (54) cited research in 1940 which found that boys out of school for two years before entering college, and girls out of school for one year or more, do superior college work, though Hughes (55) found a clear tendency for younger students to achieve superior results, probably because they are brighter and have skipped a year at school. Findings are clearly conflicting on this question, but it is possible that a year in industry or other work would be a good test of students' motivations to pursue an academic discipline. If potential students were to lose their academic motivations during this period it would certainly seem that they would not have been among the most serious and motivated students had they gone on to university. It would also seem that those whose motivation had survived this period would be less likely to drop out, and would make best use of their grants and places. With university and college places in such short supply, and likely to become more so as demand increases, research into this question would have very practical implications.

Need for achievement (n Ach) is an aspect of motivation that has been studied by McClelland (56) and others over the past twenty years. The need to achieve is claimed by McClelland to motivate the individual to perform tasks as excellently as possible consistent with the individual's abilities, so that a person of inferior ability may perform more highly than an abler person who lacks achievement motivation. McClelland's method is to present subjects with a series of pictures about each of which the subject tells a story. These stories are scored for themes which suggest achievement motivation. It is, in fact, a projective technique similar to the Thematic Apperception Test described by Murray, (57) although questionnaire techniques have also been used employing the same concept. A high score on need for achievement seems to be a useful indicator of future academic performance. McClelland and his associates have found correlations as high as 0.39 between academic achievement and n Ach as measured in Thematic Apperception Tests. Lavin (58) cites twelve studies of achievement motivation and its relation to academic performance in high school, college, and graduate school. Of nine studies which were controlled for ability four showed a consistent relationship between the two variables, but five showed projective measures of n Ach to be unrelated to achievement. In spite of the negative findings it would seem premature and ill-advised to regard this as an unimportant variable. As Lavin pointed out, studies using questionnaires produced more consistent findings, but if need for achievement is to be used as a selector variable more work would seem necessary to devise adequate scales and to eliminate the effects of intervening variables. To do this would require probably a factor analytic approach to discover how far elements of need for achievement cohere with elements of possible intervening variables, such as level of aspiration, authoritarianism, conscience, and anxiety. There might well be many other variables which intervene or overlap with need for achievement. Projective techniques do not always have high reliability, and since they are the ones most used in studies of this kind, this could account for the inconsistencies of the findings reviewed by Lavin.

Some reference was made earlier about students' interest in academic aims. There is evidence to suggest that it is a good predictor to the extent that it is closely related to achievement. Summerskill (59) has stated that there is a need to distinguish between motivation with respect to entering college and motivation with respect to graduation from college. He cited a study (60) which indicated that 62 per cent of drop-outs felt satisfied with their careers in college. If a student enters college without the resolve to attain a degree it must be, to some extent, accidental if he decides to complete the studies he has undertaken. Summerskill suggests that in motivational studies it would be advisable to exclude or to treat separately those who have intentions which would conflict with degree requirements if these could be isolated. In selecting students it would be possible to make useful, though imperfect, assessments of the students' academic level of aspiration. As early as 1943 Mercer (61) found that drop-outs had less satisfaction with, and presumably less interest in, school than successful students, and ratings of students' intellectual and working characteristics had greater predictive power than ratings by school principals of other personality characteristics.

This section on personality, interests, motivation, and ambition can probably best be summarized by reference to statements by Sanders, (62) Summerskill, (63) and Dale, (64) all of which are relevant to student selection. From long experience and research in education, Sanders wrote that character and personality as well as intellectual ability and a good educational grounding enter into student success. He cited a study of borderline matriculants, some with relatively low I.Q.'s, some of whom succeeded in graduating in minimum time—a feat achieved by only about 35–40 per cent of students in most Australian universities. He also referred to the academic high fliers who achieve high honours and sometimes go on to higher degrees—saying that these are very often persistent students of high aspiration, intensely devoted, healthy, and capable of long periods of effective effort and concentration.

Dale agreed that there were strong indications that the principal reason for failure in university exams was not lack of ability, but rather lack of application to work, and suggested construction of a reliable measure of candidates' industry to be used in student selection. Though this is undoubtedly an important factor it leaves unanswered the question of what motivates or makes it possible for a student to be industrious. Industry in academic work must have many roots, including those stated by Sanders. Summerskill elaborated further and considered that we need to know more about the capability of students for the job of scholarship with its demands on curiosity, initiative, and intellectual energy, and warned that research in this area has only scratched the surface.

We shall now leave the criteria which may be applied to selection of students and turn to measures of a more administrative nature, evaluating some of those now used, and suggesting possible indications for modification.

Sixth Form and University First Year

In Britain it is customary for at least two years to be spent in the sixth form—the lower and upper sixth. At this time it is usual for students to sit for the General Certificate of Education Advanced-level examinations. British universities generally require a minimum of two good A-level passes; some require three; some departments have their own particular subject requirements, occasionally requiring unusually high marks in particular subjects.

This procedure has caused a 'backwash effect' in the schools, and one frequently hears the criticism that pupils are coached to attain high marks in their A-level examinations, instead of being educated more broadly in chosen subjects. Early specialization is sometimes forced on children to enable them to attain the highest marks possible so as to qualify for university places against heavy competition.

It is not uncommon to spend longer than two years in the sixth. The third-year sixth is associated partly with competition for places in Oxford and Cambridge, because it was at the seventh term in the sixth form that students were required to sit for examinations for entry to these universities. Another reason for the third-year sixth is associated with age, where pupils have been placed earlier in 'express streams' because of their outstanding ability and are, perhaps, considered too young for university life.

There is a further, perhaps less valid reason for the third- and fourth-year sixth form, and this reason has very wide application. The Report of Commission of Inquiry, University of Oxford, (65) states that, although 69 per cent of applicants and 71 per cent of admissions sat for entrance examinations in the seventh term of sixth form (the third-year sixth),

quite a large proportion (28 per cent) of students from independent boarding schools entered the competition after three complete years and a term [from the fourth-year sixth]. From maintained schools only was there a substantial proportion (28 per cent) of applicants from the second-year sixth. Among admissions, compared with all applicants, there was a lower proportion from the second-year sixth, and a higher proportion from the fourth-year sixth, and 34 per cent of all admissions from independent boarding schools were from the fourth-year sixth. [Franks Report, vol. 2, para. 114.]

This situation suggested two things. First, that students who can spend only one full year in the sixth, usually from maintained schools, are at a disadvantage in selection to those whose parents can afford to keep them at school longer, especially in independent boarding-schools. This is a question of social or financial inequality. Second, and of greater relevance to this study, it suggests that students are often kept on at school for a longer time in order for them to maximize their A-level marks. It is sometimes said that there are good intellectual reasons for prolonging experience in the sixth form, as opposed to going straight on to university, but these are not explicit. Lord Butler (66) has expressed regret that one of the major problems facing Cambridge colleges was that of the "vanishing third-year sixth former", because the supply of sixth-form teaching staff is expected to shrink by 25 per cent in the next few years. As school pupils are generally being encouraged to stay on at school longer than up to the present, it therefore seems that the staffing position will be exacerbated more than shrinkage in staff supply alone suggests.

We must therefore question the wisdom of providing scarce sixth-form resources to enable prospective candidates for university and college places to raise their A-level results by the few points necessary to gain a university place. Lauwerys (67) has said :

> The demand from universities for high A level marks often puts pupils under the necessity of spending a third year in the sixth form, and although this is often intellectually desirable, it is extremely doubtful whether time is well spent in repeating A level syllabuses.

And also,

> the Oxford and Cambridge scholarship examinations exert . . . pressure, and their effects are pervasive. . . . Schools are willing to devote effort to the pursuit of scholarships and places at Oxford and Cambridge, even when the yield is low, because success does much for their reputations. . . . All this increases the pressure on schools to use express routes, and results in small third- and even fourth-year groups staying on in the sixth form in the hope of gaining a place or scholarship at Oxford or Cambridge.

Numerous other writers have referred to the practice of staying on in the sixth to boost A-level or matriculation marks by a few points (68) which is clearly a prime purpose of the third- and fourth-year sixth. Lauwerys has written:

> Such is the competition for university places generally [in the U.K.] that, particularly in boys' schools, efforts are made to spend three years in the sixth form. . . . In their third year they either compete for Oxford and Cambridge scholarships and places, or attempt to improve their A level performance of the previous year in order to secure a university place.

Some of these candidates will have failed at the first attempt, but others may well have passed all the subjects taken at the first attempt and be formally qualified for admission, but they stay on to take A levels in the same subjects again in expectation or hope of a higher mark.

What are the possible advantages in student selection of prolonging the sixth form by one, two, or more years? Apart from the prospect for the individual of improving his chances of a place in higher education and some possibility of study in depth or other intellectual gain, the advantages are hard to discern. The Crowther Committee Report (69) recognized that study in depth at sixth-form level is admirable because it could lead the pupil beyond his own subject to search for a wider synthesis, but Lauwerys pointed out that in practice "the competitive need to teach for maximum marks defeated the object of study in depth," and the Crowther Report (para. 436) stated, "It sets a premium on the kind of teaching which never strays from the syllabus, which is relentless in its rejection of side issues." The Crowther Committee believed that advanced teaching of a subject that made possible a comprehension of the subject in its wider and proper context was possible "only if attention has not to be riveted firmly on the need for securing every attainable mark." (70)

If students are prepared in this rigid manner it is questionable how valid high marks in A-level or matriculation examinations can be regarded as a principal criterion for selection to higher education. The rigidity to which the Crowther Report referred seems hardly likely to be a proper preparation for the more flexible and self-disciplined intellectual requirements of university studies. To extend such preparation beyond one or two years is highly questionable in terms of the true educational gain achieved, except, possibly, in highly specialized subjects which the student proposes to continue to study at university, and only then when they are studied beyond the syllabus requirements.

Besides level of marks in sixth-form subjects we must consider, as a separate though related question, the time students require to satisfy entry requirements. Three Australian and two British researches have shown that the students who require longer time to achieve requisite matriculation marks for university are not the best in university studies. Hogben (71) studied 376 first-year medical students and found that students who had experienced some failure at school or required more than one matriculation attempt generally fared less well in first year of medical studies than those who had no previous history of failure. Theobald (72) made a similar finding. Of 407 first-year students, in non-medical subjects, those who had taken two years instead of one to satisfy matriculation requirements had a failure rate of 62 per cent, compared with a 22 per cent failure rate among those who had matriculated at the first attempt. Schonell, (73) Gray and Short, (74) and Sanders (75) found the same with different samples.

Since these studies were done Anderson (76) has developed a formula which takes into account the length of time a student has *needed* to satisfy matriculation requirements. This formula includes a reduction factor which is applied to matriculation marks achieved in more than one attempt. This has the effect of making those marks equivalent to a formula score from a single attempt. Another aspect of the formula is to give 'bonus marks' to candidates repeating the matriculation year, but who have studied additional other subjects successfully during their second year in sixth form.

In England Dale (77) drew attention to the same question and suggested that one of the most likely causes of error in selection of university students was the placing of insufficient emphasis on the previous failure of those taking the examination a second time, or even not noticing that the same examinations had been taken twice. Nisbet and Welsh (78) in a study of science and arts students at the University of Aberdeen have found that students who qualified for university entrance after a fifth year of secondary education performed better in first year at the university than those who required six years to qualify. The differences were even more striking than those found by Theobald. Students who required the extra year to qualify had failure rates from one and a half to six times as high as those who did not.

The consistency of these findings in English, Scottish, and Australian universities is highly significant in any consideration of student selection. It seems repugnant to suggest we should deny candidates a second try, and rigid application of these findings would be deplorable, for there can be little doubt that injustices might be done to borderline candidates who, for any number of reasons, might fail in the initial attempt. Ill-health, nervousness, and inferior examination ability could easily lead to the exclusion of perfectly acceptable candidates.

These researches are very relevant to the question of how we should employ our scarce resources, including those of sixth-form teachers and accommodation. The findings suggest clearly that when candidates are selected because they have slightly higher A-level or other matriculation marks, but who have required repeated attempts to gain them, some poor prospects are thus being selected, while some superior students are at the same time being excluded. Other things being equal, the principle is suggested that students who satisfy requirements at the first attempt should be preferred.

If we continue to select candidates on their A-level results without considering whether they needed a second try, we may in fact be not only encouraging cramming of the kind which the Crowther Report condemned, but also positively encouraging the squandering of sixth-form resources, especially teaching staff, and in so doing excluding superior potential students who have perhaps slightly lower marks but have required only one attempt in the selection examination. The argument is capable of further extension. It seems likely that university places, and grants, are being allocated less wisely than they might be. It seems socially unjust to favour with places and grants those candidates who can achieve high A-level marks only after a long sixth-form career and only because their parents can afford to keep them at school. Policies which allow this must be indefensible when research indicates that their university work is likely to be inferior to that of students requiring only a first attempt. The caution is repeated that rigid application of the proposed procedure may impose injustice in certain cases. However, as a general principle it appears sound.

The research into time required to satisfy entrance requirements may partly explain the limitations of matriculation levels as predictors of university performance, and the failure of very promising students (in terms of matriculation and A levels) to perform at university as well as their A levels would seem to predict—a curious thing which has so often been noted.

While it would be wrong to deny genuinely aspiring students a second attempt at university entrance, the implications for selection policy and the sixth form are clear. Spoon-feeding and intensive coaching in sixth form over an extended period appear to achieve little if anything in terms of university and college education, and high results so obtained can be positively misleading to selectors of university candidates who place too much importance on matriculation results alone, without regard to the time expended in achieving them. As has already been noted, present selection procedures when based essentially on high A levels have a damaging 'backwash effect' in schools.

Lauwerys (79) reminds us that "in the past university selection procedures have been operated with little consciousness of their effects on the preparation of students." He cites the Sub-committee on Entrance Requirements Report (80) as a major step forward

> because it openly accepted the universities' responsibility for the pattern of education in the schools. The proposals of the sub-committee . . . are designed to prevent premature and excessive specialization, [and include], for example, the substitution of a general paper after January of the second year in sixth form . . . and incorporation of complementary elements for scientists and arts candidates in the general paper.

Objections to a scheme embodying a general paper include the possibility that a pedestrian standard might be set, it being argued that students require careful preparation in depth at A level to be able to cope with university subjects. In view of the limited predictive power of A levels, (81) it is questionable how far this argument is valid except possibly in highly specialized subjects to be taken at university. Although it is recognized again that matriculation results are the best single predictor, as has already been shown there is still a very great amount of error in selection owing to other variables, some of which have already been discussed.

I am obliged to Lord Penney for informing me of some studies he has made of the academic progress of several classes of science students through their three-year degree courses at the Imperial College of Science and Technology. There are variations in practice between different departments, but each department has records of marks obtained by various entry classes in four to six examinations through the three years of an honours degree course in science and mathematics. Students have a (test) examination at the end of the first term, a (test) examination at the end of two terms, a (college) examination at the end of three terms, and (degree) examinations at the end of the second and third years.

The diagram overleaf is illustrative of the general results.

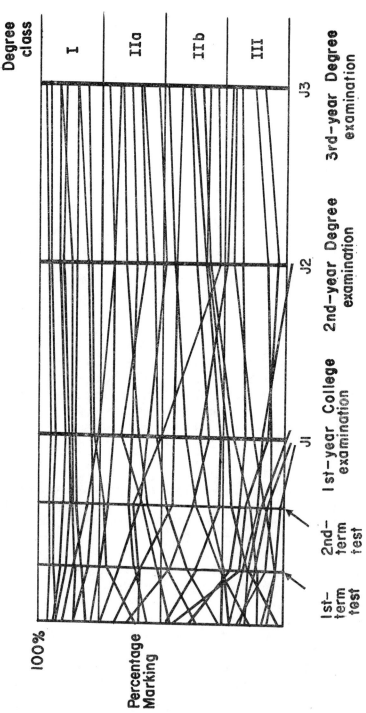

Academic Progress through Three-year Course of Physics, Mathematics, and Chemistry Students at Imperial College of Science and Technology. N = 200.

If the students are put into groups, selected by bands of, say, five marks per cent in the first test or examination, the results obtained are as follows:

(1) Most of the students near the top remain consistently near the top, but a small proportion fall more or less steadily.

(2) Most of the students near the bottom stay near the bottom, but some drop out, and, very exceptionally, a few per cent show a big and progressive improvement.

(3) The middle groups crisscross a great deal, but exceptionally a few per cent improve substantially and a few per cent fall substantially.

If students with the same marks in the first test or examination are followed through later examinations, their distribution about the mean mark in later examinations is roughly Gaussian, except that an occasional student starting near the top or the bottom has moved substantially. The standard deviation (assuming a Gaussian distribution) about the mean mark for the group in any later test or examination is about 7 per cent. Grouping the students by their marks in their last examination and coming backwards in time, we find that the dispersion increases the farther back in time we go. The standard deviations are roughly like a physical diffusion process from a point source.

The opinion of the staff concerned with the test examinations at Imperial College is that the first test or examination held after entry gives a good indication for most students as to how they will perform in later examinations. The consistency is very much better than estimates made on the basis of A-level performance plus an interview.

Studies are continuing of the correlation of examination performance of classes of engineering students throughout their degree courses, especially as regards the correlation between first-year tests in science and mathematics with examinations in engineering subjects in the second and third years.

The argument which this implies is that if selection is to be improved it can best be done on the basis of the first-year results of a larger first-year entry. A further advantage in this would be that some of the less promising students, as inadequately assessed by A levels, would be given a chance to attempt degrees which they are now denied, and some of these may well be superior students. There would need to be much larger intakes in first year, but the expense involved would possibly be justified in better graduates and a worth-while number of people who had had the benefit of at least one year in higher education, in itself a social, educational, and economic gain.

Research may be needed to determine if the first gain, that of improved selection and an improved graduate body, should it accrue, would be economic. This could perhaps be explored in advance by actuarial studies of theoretical groups of students by computer, showing the proportion of students it would be economically sound to admit in order to achieve the optimal gain.

The second gain is obvious. Those who failed in first year could be transferred to other less exacting courses, as the Robbins Report advocated: even one year at university without the benefit of further study would qualify these students for a large range of other occupations, which they would not have been able otherwise to manage successfully. This procedure of having a larger intake of a greater ability range combined with selection on first-year results thus seems academically, economically, and socially sound.

A further point which arises from our study is related to the subject material. If the progress of science students, highly selected by A-level results and interviews, is, except for the high fliers, so very little capable of prediction, how much less prediction is possible in subjects which can be less objectively assessed? If it is so far from perfect in science, does it make sense to rely on A levels in selecting for the arts, social sciences, and humanities, and then being content with the ones so selected on what is, at best, a very inaccurate predictor?

Would it then not be economical of talent, second- and third-year places, and dons' time to select by first-year results rather than by A levels or matriculation results, which, though at present the best single predictor, leave much to be desired? The case for such a procedure is strong in science, as we have shown, but in arts, humanities, and social sciences the argument would seem even stronger, because of the greater possible error in assessing students at A level than can be expected in the more objective science subjects.

Viewing the progress of students in reverse time is even more striking. As we go back from third to first year and the initial test, the students' examination records spread out more randomly. If we extrapolate further to A levels and then to O levels, and take account of the discontinuity between school and college, it requires little imagination to visualize the poor predictive value of school performance, except, perhaps for the most exceptionally motivated. For the arts and humanities and for the social sciences, except for the extremely weak pupils, the predictive power of school performance is almost non-existent. Specialization at school in those subjects then becomes more difficult than ever to justify.

The broadening of general education at secondary level seems desirable educationally in preference to rigid specialization from the age of fifteen years, which implies enforced commitment to subjects which pupils may later find unsuitable. One of the advantages of accepting for higher education students with the highest ratings in a range of subjects would be to leave students room for flexibility of choice. There is evidence that this procedure would lead to better university performance. Sanders (82) found that students whose school programme had not been prematurely narrowed overtook their contemporaries who had specialized intensively, and then stayed in the lead, and Parkyn has found that correlations between a total of marks in several school subjects and university examinations in almost any subject are higher than correlations between results in a subject taken at school and in the same subject taken at university. (83)

Another possible gain in discouraging highly specialized sixth-form work extending over more than two years is the rationalization of sixth-form resources. It is well known that some third- and fourth-year sixth forms are extremely small, yet they do not always produce the best university students, because, as we have seen, the best students do not require to repeat sixth-form work.

Dancy (84) said:

When I talk of "vital resources in short supply" I mean, of course, sixth form masters. To meet this shortage we shall have to make sacrifices of various kinds. . . . We may even have to swallow a bitter pill, namely, in the interests of a greater good, to encourage our young people to leave school instead of staying on into a third year sixth.

In the light of the research evidence it appears that there is nothing to lose by limiting sixth form to two years, and selection might even be improved by the removal of that often forgotten intervening variable—the time taken to satisfy matriculation requirements. As a preparation for university studies there seems little, if anything, to be gained by consolidating specialist subjects, particularly those which are not going to be followed up in university or college.

Two alternatives to the sixth form as a prelude to university and college selection are being currently discussed. One alternative is to admit to first-year university studies students with a wider range of ability, and select for further university studies only those who survive the first year. Because of its supposed harshness this has been called the 'slaughter-house method'. It is argued that students who fail in first year will suffer some trauma, and that, once they have been selected, students should be helped to attain their degrees. But, however laudable this latter proposition, this reasoning ignores the 'slaughter' that already occurs when growing numbers of applicants are turned down for admission, many of whom, though perhaps with lesser school examination results, are yet more highly motivated to university work than many of those accepted, and who would have made better students than some of those admitted.

Schonell, (85) when commenting on the Murray Report on Australian Universities, has written in the following terms of the limitations of selection procedures:

A first solution is to accept them all, or almost all. . . . This is obviously what Sir Keith Murray and his English colleague Sir Charles Morris, together with the three Australian members of the Committee, felt when they said, "the demand for graduates is so great, that rather than seek to make a selection of students, the universities should be put in a position to accept all those qualified and who wish to enter, and to give them the teaching and the facilities which will ensure each of them a reasonable opportunity to pass from first to second year and on to graduation".

Lady Venables, (86) expressing a similar idea about selection for technical colleges in England, said, "The best advice . . . is to let everyone try so that all the good candidates have a real chance." She found that second- and third-year examination results were unrelated to initial test scores; the only correlation being with the first-year examination results; the better these were the more likely was success in the final year. Once over the first hurdle motivation rather than ability is the operative factor. These findings are similar to those of Lord Penney discussed earlier in this chapter.

What is being suggested here is that in the first year in higher education, when students are wrestling with new methods of study, their motivation for higher studies is also being tested. Those who achieve best in that year would seem less likely to drop out and more likely to produce superior degree work. They would have proved by the end of first year that they are self-directed towards studies, in a way that no examination of their school work could. There is a marked contrast between the concentrated work in a small sixth form directed towards high A-level marks and the self-motivated work in a large student community, where personal attention might be minimal and the range of study far more extensive than in sixth form.

These propositions are backed by research findings. Sanders' (87) finding, that students in Australia who fail in their first-year examinations and are then permitted to repeat their studies are not good graduation prospects, applied *irrespective of their I.Q. or entrance qualifications.* Only about 33 per cent of these students succeed in graduating, and some of them only after further failure. Clearly this method of selection, using a high intake with a relatively high proportion of drop-outs, would be more efficient than raising entrance requirements, and fairer also, because it would give a larger number of students an initial opportunity to test their academic ability, and would sort out the most dedicated from the lesser. In short, there would be a greater chance of places and grants going to the most suitable students.

On this point Dale (88) considered that "Even with good selection a certain number of work-shy students will appear. If the selection line is drawn high . . . many worthy students will be excluded. If it is drawn low injustice to worthy applicants will occur seldom." He also points out that many unworthy students would also be admitted, but we might well ask to what extent this would matter if they were to be excluded at the end of the first year, and finally the best potential students were selected. Admission of virtually all students to the first year is not the only possibility, but it clearly has great merit, provided resources of staff and accommodation are maintained to achieve a reasonable staff-student ratio. Frederick (89) considered that the failure of students at the end of first year seldom constitutes a complete waste of time, and argued that it seems reasonable to assume that even if they have breathed the air of a university for no more than a year they will have had some stimulation from lectures, the reading, and the conversation and argument of the university community. If they leave without having received a degree or diploma they do not necessarily leave without having received benefit. Frederick raised the question whether the benefit is great enough to offset any frustration and humiliation of failure. It can be argued that if it is good to encourage more students to attempt sixth-form studies, logically it is good for more to have a taste of university. If it is bad to exclude students from university because they might be humiliated by failure, then it must be bad to encourage pupils to stay on at school in case they should suffer a similar humiliation.

A change in selection procedures on the lines suggested by this argument would necessitate, and might effectively bring about, a change in attitudes to students who do not continue their courses. As Brannan (90) has suggested, no one should ever be branded a 'failure' for trying to achieve something. This is consistent with the idea of the university as a place of learning, not a degree factory, and Lauwerys (91) takes us a step farther in this reasoning. Far from regarding first-year students who do not pass their examinations as total failures, Lauwerys favours the award of intermediate qualifications stating what courses students have satisfactorily completed, and the use of these in selecting alternative [and probably more suitable] courses for these students.

The Robbins Report (92) (Appendix 5) noted that in Holland and France the first year is used as a period of selection in conjunction with a liberal admissions policy, and this practice is much more usual in the United States, Sweden, and Australia than in English universities. It is perhaps not so elegant a method of selection as one might wish for. Initially it might demand more resources of accommodation and staff, and satisfactory staff-student levels should always be maintained—as in Sweden. It has merits that do not obtain where A levels are the main criteria, and those selected have had little chance to demonstrate their capabilities in a university or college atmosphere.

It is argued then that first-year university results provide a better criterion for the selection of undergraduates than school results because (i) only the most motivated students, of all abilities, would stay on; (ii) slower starters would be given a chance to prove their mettle in the independent work which is required in universities, and these might well include many who did not produce the best matriculation results in school subjects; (iii) broad-based entry would probably ensure a richer variety of character and social-class groupings among students; (iv) the mere crammers who have often been pushed and cajoled into university and college by well-meaning parents and teachers would be selected out with those who are too dilettante for undergraduate life—for example, those who should do well, yet succeed only in first-, second-, and third-year billiards, cricket, or rowing. It is conceivable that such a scheme is fairer than selection of students direct from school, and more efficient in selecting the best scholars, and ultimately the best graduates.

With a rapidly increasing percentage of young people seeking places in higher education, selection of school-leavers may become even more arbitrary than it has been. Husén (93) has been quoted as saying that in Sweden by 1980 possibly 75 per cent of school-leavers might qualify for university. If this happens it will be even more desirable than now to allow as many candidates as possible to test their capability for higher study by giving them a year in university or college, and selecting those who prove the best in the higher-education milieu, rather than using the less valid criterion of school achievement.

In concluding this section we may say that a selection procedure based on first-year performance, which seems from the literature to recommend itself, might be a salutary treatment for at least one form of malaise among some groups of students. Iliffe (94) at Keele cites Professor Mansfield Cooper, from his address to the Congress of the Universities of the Commonwealth 1963, as saying, "Students come up with little sense of obligation and a sharp sense of rights", and continues that students' comments bear this out, the common complaint being that a "lecture has not been interesting . . . the student expects as of right, to be interested". This seems a reasonable expectation, but Iliffe continues:

There is a widely shared failure to appreciate that an education programme involves long spells of hard application, unrewarding except in terms of the ultimate goal. . . . This is the result in all probability of a long period of schoolwork which has been largely devoid of intellectual stimulation combined with a somewhat romanticized picture of work at the university.

One is tempted to think that this malaise would to some extent evaporate if students were chosen from a wider range of ability and their motivations put to the test in first year, in the knowledge that it would be a trial period, to test their interests, ability, and academic motivation, there being no disgrace should they opt out or fail in that year. The trial period could also be used as a time to enable students to make more suitable choices of academic careers.

The cost of providing a far greater number of first-year places would present an immediate problem, though ultimately it might be more economic than present procedures. Keele already has a first-year general course, not used as a selection device. Dainton (95) envisages an uncommitted first year at university with a consequent four-year course at university to mitigate early specialization at Advanced and Ordinary level in the schools, and to encourage students to postpone their choice of academic discipline to a later and more mature period in their lives than is now the practice. The principle that students should be able to delay vocational choice [and presumably commitment to subjects which will decide career choices] is endorsed by Lauwerys. (96) If it is held to be economic to have a foundation year it would seem even more economic to use such a first year for selection. Vernon (97) too has expressed the opinion that first-year results would probably be a better predictor than matriculation results.

A second alternative, or additional method of selection, is the sixth-form college. Elvin (98) sees here the possibility of rationalizing those "vital resources in short supply" to which Dancy referred, sixth-form teachers, and writes of "too many small and ineffective sixth forms, far from the level of the remarkable best". Elvin also favours sixth-form colleges because "at this level the argument for separate teaching and learning gathers weight". Elvin notes the need for specialized teaching in the sixth form and that to have a good range of subjects requires considerable staff, which is neither practical nor economic in schools with small sixth forms. Concentration of sixth-form resources in sixth-form or junior colleges as Elvin suggests is therefore an excellent proposal from the viewpoint of rationalization alone.

Sixth-form colleges could serve an important purpose in the selection of students in a way that sixth forms at present do not.

This would be possible particularly if they were, as Elvin has suggested they should be, nearer to university than school in intellectual temper and methods of study. Students could attend them for a dual purpose, to complete their secondary education and to prepare for tertiary education. 'Failure' would thus carry no more stigma than failure in sixth form does now, and success in studies under these quasi-university conditions would indicate which students were most likely to do well in tertiary studies. There is much in common between the idea of a sixth-form college and a foundation first year of general education at the university such as that in operation at the University of Keele. Whether one or the other should be used as a selection or screening device is probably one of emphasis on practical economics and organization. The sixth-form or junior college would probably be by far the most economical and probably effective enough.

Locke's (99) study at Keele University supports the argument for the essential proposal. Although her research was based on small numbers it is interesting that a student who failed in the foundation-year examination and passed at the second attempt had a chance of graduating only slightly above 50 per cent. On the other hand students who passed foundation year without being referred showed a failure rate of only 2 per cent. At the University of Keele the function of the foundation year is to introduce the student to some of the methods and information necessary to an estimate of the inheritance, the problem, and the achievements of modern Western man. At the end of the year all students sit a common examination, which they are required to pass before proceeding to their degree work.

The sixth-form or junior college could be very useful for the dual purpose of completing secondary education and selection for higher education. Another outstanding advantage of the sixth-form or junior college is that the assemblage of sixth-form teachers into one such institution rather than their dispersal around in a large number of small sixth forms enables a huge range of course offerings, far more than an orthodox grammar school or even a large comprehensive school could arrange. Individual timetables could be arranged for students, in contrast to forcing a restricted choice of subjects upon pupils where sixth-form staff are small in number. Mumford (100) and Dancy have demonstrated the advantages of assigning sixth-form work to

129

separate colleges. However, Cochrane (101) has come down firmly in favour of a first university year to prevent expensive and uneconomic duplication of staff and plant in several institutions. Cochrane doubted if the right sort of staff would be attracted to junior or community or other quasi-university colleges, giving as his reason that people capable of performing the academic tasks which should be required in such institutions would prefer to be in universities. Cochrane also drew attention to the danger of allowing top-class students to mark time in such non-university institutions when they would be almost certain to attain their degrees without delay if they went direct to university. Nevertheless if the work in such institutions were confined to the equivalent of sixth-form or matriculation studies that argument would not apply.

To summarize: the overall proposition suggested by the research is therefore that a normal year of education could be used for the purposes described, whether in sixth-form college or junior college, or first or foundation year in college or university. This procedure would be likely to facilitate considerable improvement in selecting those students who are capable, by ability and temperament, of independent self-motivated study. It would also aid in selecting out, sooner rather than later, those who have little intrinsic interest in learning, but who may have gained high results in matriculation examinations merely because they have been closely supervised and coached for several years in a way that bears little relation to the kind of study which should be demanded in institutions of higher education, particularly universities. The evidence, English, Scottish, and Australian, suggests that second-, third-, and fourth-year sixth forms are of very limited use in finding the best university students.

Arguments expounded by Cochrane are strongly against the idea of junior colleges offering university subjects as a kind of half-way house between sixth form and university. His arguments apply with less force to sixth-form colleges because they would not be meant to serve a higher-education function. Sixth-form colleges come out unscathed through most arguments.

To attract students of the widest possible range of ability it would be necessary to make it clearly understood that the functions of sixth-form colleges were for three alternative, though not mutually exclusive, purposes: (i) completion of secondary education, (ii) preparation for higher education, (iii) selection for higher education. Students would be saved from any possible stigma of failure which might eventuate from using first year at university or college for selection. If the teaching in these sixth-form colleges were similar to that in universities, with an essential emphasis on student initiative and inner motivation to learn, rather than on closely supervized coaching, their use as an efficient screening and selection device does seem assured.

Cochrane deplored the waste of potential talent which lies in the lower rankings of matriculation results, talent which is in danger of being denied a university education if even mild quotas are applied. Having pointed out the serious limitations of matriculation marks as a predictor of undergraduate performance, he went so far as to state, "Unless some test is devised which provides a correlation at least three times as strong as matriculation marks, there seems no alternative but to expand university accommodation at a sufficiently rapid rate to permit all students who have matriculated to enrol." This proposal would almost inevitably lead to exclusion of some students at the end of first year. Although Cochrane was referring to Australian universities the same arguments surely apply in any other country which seeks to give the fullest opportunity to all of its gifted young people.

It has been suggested in this section that sixth-form or junior colleges, using university-type teaching methods to a larger extent than sixth forms generally do, would allow better prediction than we now have. Research clearly supports this. Perhaps ultimately the best answer to the problem of selection will lie in combined use of sixth-form colleges and the first year in higher education. Exclusion of the best students would thus be minimal, all would be given the fairest possible chance, and universities and colleges would be far less likely to be saddled with 'promising' students who fail to live up to that promise.

Selecting Postgraduate Research Students

This chapter on selection would not be complete without some reference to the selection of postgraduate research students. In Britain, to qualify for a grant for postgraduate studies, the candidate is generally required to possess a good honours degree—that is, a first or upper second. Students having lower-second, or third, or fourth honours in their initial degrees are thus seldom able to work for a research degree or to engage in other higher study.

The purpose of this section is to examine the appropriateness of such criteria in selecting and excluding candidates for higher degrees. As we have seen, the research literature indicates many shortcomings of school achievement as a predictor of under-graduate success. In the same way the literature indicates that prediction from undergraduate achievement to research achievement can be seriously questioned.

In contrast to the great amount of research on selection of undergraduates, there is a serious lack of research regarding the selection and success and failure of research scholars. Boyer and Michael (102) wrote as recently as 1965 that study of the performance of postgraduate students remains largely unexplored. Existing methods of selection rely heavily upon the assumption (which, in the absence of research, can be little more than an informed guess) that if the candidate has a 'first' or 'upper second' he will be a good researcher. There are some indications that this is a limited view. This question is a serious one because holders of higher degrees are generally strong candidates for academic appointments in teaching and research. It may well be that university and college graduates who have a 'good honours' degree plus a research degree are ideal people for teaching posts in higher education; but if we are trying to select the best potential *researchers* the standing of the first degree is possibly not so relevant as it has been held to be, as a criterion for allocation of research grants and places.

While research in this field is slight there is enough to warrant some thought and examination of the existing practice. Wright (103) traced the progress of 176 graduate students in the United States for eleven years. Of 115 candidates enrolling in 1950 for the Master's degree 46 had received no degree by 1961, compared with 58 who had, and 11 others who had attained doctorates. Of 61 Ph.D. candidates only 20 had received their doctorates eleven years later, and 8 had attained Master's degrees. The remaining 33, more than 50 per cent of the original candidates, had failed to gain a graduate degree of any kind. Wright found that intellectual endowment, including high grades as an under-graduate, was not significantly related to the acquiring of a Master's degree, and the age of the candidates was inversely related. Social adjustment was directly related to the performance of Ph.D. candidates. It seems highly likely that circumstances surrounding older students, such as greater family and other responsibility, could be acting as intervening variables so far as age is concerned and might militate against their research interests. It is also likely that social maladjustment could directly interfere with their research. It is further possible that graduate work, especially for older students, is socially disorganizing. Older students might be expected to have greater social responsibilities than younger students, and probably there are more aspects in their social lives that are vulnerable to maladjustment during the long sustained intensive work required of postgraduate students. This would be particularly true regarding financial pressures and claims made upon the student's time by his wife and family.

Interview assessments of candidates' favourable or negative attitudes to postgraduate studies failed in Wright's study to distinguish significantly between those who succeeded and those who did not. This suggests that selection interviews achieve little. Gough and Hall (104) have reported that in studies of scientists, architects, writers, and mathematicians at the University of California Institute of Personality Assessment and Research it has been repeatedly found that the highest levels of creative work are not closely associated with intellectual ability as ordinarily measured. Hudson (105) in England has questioned whether the criterion of 'class of first degree' is valid for selecting candidates for grants for postgraduate science students, and this question might apply with equal force to the selection of social-science and arts candidates. Hudson (106) studied a group of eminent British scientists, all Fellows of the Royal Society holding the doctorate in science, who had graduated from Oxford and Cambridge between 1930 and 1939. They were compared with other groups matched by class of degree, sex, year of graduation, university, and subject. They were not found to have better degree classes than their controls. More significantly, although Cambridge F.R.S.'s were roughly three times more numerous than those from Oxford they were far less likely to have first-class degrees. A large number of eminent scientists studied by Hudson had gained seconds, some lower seconds, and a few had thirds or even fourths. We might well ask, then, what relationship can there be between being awarded a first-class degree and achieving eminence in scientific research? Hudson calls for a distinction between the educational and the selective functions of university examinations. He suggests trial periods for research candidates which would enable tutors to assess their research ability. Whitehand (107) has also posed the same question. It has been the practice for many years in the Department of Geography at the University of Newcastle upon Tyne for students to carry out small research projects and to produce a minor thesis as an integral part of their undergraduate course. In a sample of 85 Whitehand found no correlation between students' subject markings and gradings on their undergraduate research thesis. Of those students with the highest thesis marks considerably less than half attained a subject examination marking equivalent to an upper second or better, which is the minimum mark of acceptability for a Government research grant. If research ability at undergraduate level is a reliable indicator of research ability at postgraduate level as Whitehand's research suggests, then the existing method of selecting grant-holders should be refined by the addition of some research assessment at undergraduate level.

It is true that the students who obtained the best subject markings generally produced competent theses. To that extent a high marking does seem a safe criterion, but the significant point this piece of research indicates is that the majority of these students who produced outstanding research projects did not receive comparable subject markings and would have had no chance to proceed to a research degree. In other words, present methods of selecting postgraduate students apparently ensures selection of safe, competent researchers, but only at the enormous cost of excluding more than half of the outstanding researchers. Bentley (108) considers that, since most of the evaluation in education consists in testing memory and cognitive or convergent ability and achievement, students with creative talents are unduly penalized. In a study of 75 advanced education students he drew that conclusion and advocated that tests should be constructed which would sample not only the candidates' ability to remember or recognize factual information but ability to seek new solutions and evaluate what has been learned. This proposition implies that a distinction be made between ability as usually measured and achievement in formal educational tasks on the one hand, and, on the other, the power to originate fruitful ideas, to search out data, and to synthesize. Gibson and Light (109) discovered that, of 148 science dons of Cambridge University, some scored as low as 110–114 on the Wechsler Adult

Intelligence Scale, the mean for the group being 126.5, with a standard deviation of 6.3. The significant finding was that most of them scored below 130. The mean and standard deviation are almost identical with the average student intakes described in some studies of undergraduates reviewed in an earlier chapter suggesting what has been posited already that academic ability and formal attainment are not adequate predictors of research ability.

Apart from demonstrated ability in small research assignments at undergraduate level in the rare instances where this is normal practice, and class of first degree, the usual method, what indications are there of other possible criteria for the selection of postgraduate students? Research in this field is extremely rare in Britain and the United States. Creativity is the variable that has so far attracted most attention, but it is doubtful if creativity, whose definition is in some doubt, can on its own predict research ability, except in so far as it coexists with other qualities. Chaney (110) studied two groups of scientists working in laboratories in America and Britain and compared them. Senior staff in the laboratories were asked to rate the individual scientists on their 'creativeness' in research. Chaney computed correlations between their ratings and a number of factors represented by 225 items used in previous studies, including life history, motivation, job behaviour, and working-environment variables. The results showed a significant relationship between the scientists' educational level and assessment of their creativity by senior staff. Educational level also correlated with the number of publications the researchers had produced, the scientists' own favourable self-assessments, and their expectations of future salary increments or other extrinsic rewards. Chaney's findings appear to have something in common with Bloom's (111) observation that science students who become deeply involved with research in their undergraduate studies tend to become the more productive researchers. Whitehand's study in England, to which reference has already been made, supports Bloom's observation. In view of the predictive value and generality of the kind of motivation items used in Chaney's and other studies, Chaney considered that an attempt should be made to develop more comprehensive scales to measure motivation of science researchers.

Morrison, Owens, Glennon, and Albright (112) conducted a factor analytic study of research achievements of some 200 petroleum-research scientists, using as criteria of research achievement, supervisor's ratings on creativity and overall performance, and the scientists' patent disclosures. The members of the sample were not candidates for research grants, but fully fledged science researchers, yet even for this select group 23 per cent of the variance on the criteria of research ability, based on supervisor's ratings, could be accounted for by five factors. There was a less clear relationship between the factors and patent disclosures. The factors which accounted for most of the variance (6.3 per cent) were suggestive of the subject's favourable self-perceptions of their ability and desire to work autonomously, their sense of responsibility and preparedness to take risks. The other 16.7 per cent of variance was accounted for by factors which suggested most strongly professional orientation, completion of the Ph.D., membership of a professional organization, ambition for sons beyond graduate level; also a desire for extrinsic rewards from business and society and preparedness to have several projects going at one time.

However useful these factors might be in petroleum science research, it does not follow that they would be useful for predicting research success in arts, education, or the social or biological sciences, though possibly there would be some common predictors. Anne Roe (113) has shown that clearly defined personality and ability differences existed between eminent scientists in different fields. Level of intellectual function was high for all groups, but there were pattern differences. For example, social scientists and theoretical physicists tended to have relatively higher verbal than non-verbal abilities. Experimental physicists tended to have relatively lower verbal than non-verbal abilities. Anthropologists tended to have relatively low mathematical ability. Roe considered it possible that these abilities were a factor in choice, not only of science, but of a particular science, though not necessarily a decisive factor, because there were exceptions. If we are thinking of prediction, however, the trends should be noted.

Roe found it possible to make further generalizations about personalities of scientists. For example, biologists appeared to have an orientation which strongly emphasized reliance on rational controls. Physicists and social scientists were less critical and less insistent on rational controls. Physicists showed less interest in people and were not so good at relating to them, social scientists were deeply concerned about human relations and were troubled about them in a way quite different from physicists and biologists, while physicists and biologists tended to prefer to maintain social distance. Against these generalizations there are exceptions, but Roe considered nevertheless that they gave some hint of the different needs of scientists in various fields. If needs of scientists differ their motivations are likely to differ also. If we wish to develop scales to help in predicting the research potential of candidates for grants it would be well to find out first if there are marked differences between *successful* candidates for the Ph.D. and other research degrees in different fields.

Glennerster (114) has discussed briefly the need for effective procedures in selecting the best research candidates. He has suggested that the first-degree papers of borderline candidates be assessed, and advocated the use of interviews. However, the usefulness of both of these criteria has been shown earlier in this chapter to be in grave doubt, and there is little point in extending their use. Glennerster's third suggestion is that aptitude tests be developed. This idea is better supported in the literature.

After discussing the limitations of formal examinations and degree classes as devices for selecting postgraduate research students, we may usefully consider the findings of Clements, (115) who studied the examination methods of the social-science departments of twenty-five British universities. He found that in deciding what class of degree to award graduates, while most weight was given to assessments of written answers to unseen examination papers, in no place were they relied upon exclusively. The dissertation or extended essay was given varying weight, but usually only the weighting of one or two written examination papers out of several. If such dissertations were to form a larger part of examination requirements to the extent that a good deal of research would be required to produce them, the markings from these dissertations could serve as useful criteria for selecting research students. This section of the overall examinations for undergraduates would require considerable development beyond its present form if it is to be as valid and reliable as it should be.

A Preliminary Outline for Research into Criteria for selecting Postgraduate Research Students
    In the work of Morrison *et al.,* Bloom, Roe, Pelz *et al.,* and

Wright, which were discussed earlier, and others reported in Taylor and Barron, (116) we have indications of the directions which such a search for useful criteria should take; hence the following outline. This is not a developed research project, but is offered tentatively to suggest the kind of start which it should be possible to make in this difficult but interesting and rewarding field.

The study would probably be based on:

(i) an experimental group of the most successful Ph.D.'s in arts, education, social science, physical science, biological science, as selected by their supervisors and/or on their output of publications. Other criteria are not excluded. All groups would be studied simultaneously to discover common factors between them. It would be necessary to analyse the data for each group separately, to allow for the differences between them which previous research evidence has shown to exist;

(ii) a second experimental group of postgraduate students who had not finished their studies, or who were taking an inordinately long time to finish, would be matched as far as possible for class of first degree, discipline studied, university attended, sex, and age;

(iii) a control group of graduates, matched in the same way, who had not applied for a research place would be necessary. It is possible that the greater contrast in research motivation would exist between this group and the experimental group.

The literature in this area has concentrated largely on measures of creativity. Other variables are probably of equal importance, and may correlate highly with, or be aspects of, creativity, and the results from such a study should give some indication of whether or not this is so. Variables for investigation might include curiosity, intrinsic interest in learning, persistence, determination, originality, tolerance of ambiguity, tolerance of complexity, flexibility, readiness to suspend judgment until fullest possible data are available, willingness to search out data and to sift them, independent work orientation, and selectivity in singling out and differentiating essentials. There are already tests for measuring some of these variables.* Developing tests for the others would form a very extensive operation, but, at any rate, a start should be made. The main hypothesis would be that there is a distinction between the extent to which these qualities are needed in research and in undergraduate work. Since there is serious doubt about how far undergraduate results serve as an adequate guide for selecting research students, there is a need for exploration to identify which of the above, and other, qualities correlate with success in research.

The work of Morrison *et al.* provides a useful methodological model, and suggests that a factor analytic approach would be the most fruitful in imparting some structure to the mixture of variables that we would need to consider as possible criteria.† Research in this field should proceed concurrently with experiments in predicting research ability from elementary research projects at the undergraduate level—say, in final year. This embryonic suggestion is offered as a starting-point for research in what is rapidly becoming a more serious problem—how to select the best research candidates from a steadily enlarging field. It is clear there will be more research candidates than places available. Therefore some form of selection is inevitable. We can go some way towards ensuring that the most appropriate criteria are used. A careful comprehensive study of the variables suggested should lead to some advance in finding a way to select those candidates who want the available opportunities the most and who would use them to the best advantage. This would be preferable to continuing to rely entirely on criteria the validity of which, research findings have thrown into doubt.

A study of selection of postgraduate research students would, however, be an incomplete operation. To enhance the effectiveness of such a study it would be necessary to consider aspects of the relationships between research students and their supervisors, the students' goals and how these fitted in with the research

---

* For example, the Omnibus Personality Inventory as used in studies at the Center for Research and Development in Higher Education, Berkeley, California.

† For a brief discussion of the uses of factor analytic techniques in educational research see G. V. Glass and P. A. Taylor, "Factor Analytic Methodology", *Review of Educational Research,* **36,** 5, 1966. For a demonstration of the use of factor analysis see R. F. Morrison *et al., op. cit.* For a clear, concise treatment of the rationale of factor analysis see H. J. Eysenck, "The Logical Basis of Factor Analysis", *The American Psychologist,* **8,** 1953.

interest of their supervisors, students' satisfaction with the research-topic choice, their ratings on the effectiveness of seminars, the exchange with other students which took place in and out of seminars, and the stimulus provided by the institution and its ethos.*

Summary

The selection of students, whether undergraduate or post-graduate, must be recognized as being only one of many factors related to the problem of success, failure, and wastage. The research literature makes this clear. Therefore it is necessary to look beyond selection—and, indeed, beyond research into selection—in order to find possible ways of developing students' potential after they have been selected. In the next chapter a large number of institutional characteristics are examined, since the literature on selection has made one thing clear above all else—that there is little point in trying to improve selection unless corresponding adjustments are made to other parts of an educational institution. The diminishing returns involved in imposing selection devices on a progressively higher level of student intake imply an increasing proportion of able students who become barred from entering higher education as more rigorous criteria are applied. Above a fairly modest level of ability, for every mediocre or unpromising student who is selected out, several others who would have done well if admitted are excluded also. This is because, although school results are the best single predictor of success at the tertiary level of education, they are grossly inadequate for this purpose and subject to very considerable error. To reduce wastage, then, selection must be kept in its place in the wider context of other factors affecting wastage. These are the subject of the following chapters.

---

* See Ann M. Heiss, "Berkeley Doctoral Students appraise their Academic Programs", *Educational Record,* winter 1967, for an example. See also the Royal Society studies of graduate research facilities in science departments of British universities.

REFERENCES

1. Maureen Woodhall and Mark Blaug, "Productivity Trends in British University Education 1938–1962", *Minerva*, 3, 4, 1965.
2. W. D. Furneaux, *The Chosen Few* (London, Oxford University Press, 1962).
3. Martha Maxwell, "An Analysis of the California Psychological Inventory and the American Council on Education Psychological Test as Predictors of Success in Different College Curricula", paper read at American Psychological Association Meetings (Mimeo), College Park, Maryland (University of Maryland, 1960).
4. Report of Commission of Inquiry (the Franks Report), (London, Oxford University Press, 1966).
5. E. A. Locke, "The Development of Criteria of Student Achievement", *Educational and Psychological Measurement, 23,* 1963.
6. J. L. Holland and J. M. Richards, "Academic and Non-Academic Accomplishment: Correlated or Uncorrelated?", *Journal of Educational Psychology, 56,* 1965; See also: J. L. Holland, "Creative and Academic Performance among Talented Adolescents", *Journal of Educational Psychology, 52,* 1961. D. P. Hoyt, *The Relationship between College Grades and Adult Achievement: A Review of the Literature,* American College Testing Programme (Iowa City, Iowa, 1965).
7. Report of Commission of Inquiry, *op. cit.*
8. Sir James Mountford, "Success and Failure at the University", *Universities Quarterly,* 11, 1957.
9. F. J. Llewellyn, "University and State", *The Times Educational Supplement,* October 6th, 1967.
10. W. D. Furneaux, 1962, *op. cit.*
11. J. G. Darley, *Promise and Performance,* Center for the Study of Higher Education (Berkeley, University of California, 1962).
12. A. B. Hood and R. F. Berdie, "The Relationship of Ability to College Attendance", *College and University,* 39, 1964.
13. W. D. Furneaux, "The Psychologist and the University", *Universities Quarterly,* 17, 1962.

14. K. Austwick, "G.C.E. to B.A.", *Universities Quarterly*, **15**, 1961; Hans H. Hohne, "The Prediction of Academic Success" (Faculty of Arts, University of Melbourne, (Mimeo), 1951); Robbins Report, para. 580; C. Sanders, "Report on Academic Wastage and Failure among University Students in Australia and other Countries: A Review of Research and Opinion" (Faculty of Education, University of Western Australia (Mimeo), 1958); Ethel Venables, *The Young Worker at College* (London, Faber, 1967); Philip E. Vernon, "The Pool of Ability", in P. Halmos (ed.), *Sociological Review Monograph No. 7* (University of Keele, 1963); Ruth Weintraub and Ruth Salley, "Graduation Prospects of an Entering Freshman", *Journal of Educational Research*, **39**, 1945.

15. A. W. Anderson, "A Note on High Intelligence and Low Academic Performance", *The Educand*, **4**, 1, 1960; D. S. Anderson, "Problems and Performance of University Students", Education Research Office (University of Melbourne (Mimeo), 1964); Hilde Himmelweit, "Student Selection: Implications derived from Two Student Selection Enquiries", in P. Halmos (ed.), *op. cit.*; G. W. Parkyn, *Success and Failure at the University, 1. Academic Success and Entrance Standard* (Wellington, N.Z.C.E.R., 1959).

16. G. W. Parkyn, *op. cit.*

17. D. Harris, "Factors affecting College Grades", *Psychology Bulletin*, **37**, 1940.

18. Hilde Himmelweit (1963), *op. cit.*

19. E. M. Williams, "An Investigation into the Value of High School Certificate Results in predicting Performance in First Year University Examinations", *British Journal of Educational Psychology*, **20**, Part II, 1950.

20. C. Katz, F. M. Katz, and W. B. Olphert, "What happens to Students" (Mimeo), (University of New England, 1965).

21. Hilde Himmelweit, "Student Selection—An Experimental Investigation: I", *British Journal of Sociology*, 1, **4**, 1950.

22. A. W. Anderson, 1960, *op. cit.*

23. C. Sanders, "Australian Universities and their Educational Problems", *The Australian University*, **1**, 2, 1963.

24. D. S. Anderson, 1964, *op. cit.*

25. Sir Fred J. Schonell, Ernest Roe, and Ivor C. Meddleton, *Promise and Performance* (University of Queensland and University of London Press, 1962).

26. D. S. Anderson and R. R. Priestley, "Notes on the Study of Failure in Australian Universities" (University of

Melbourne (Mimeo), 1960); G. A. Gray and L. N. Short, "Student Progress in the University" (University of New South Wales (Mimeo), 1961); P. W. Hughes, "Academic Achievement in the University" (University of Tasmania (Mimeo), 1960); N. B. Malleson, "Student Performance at University College, London, 1948–51", *Universities Quarterly*, **12**, 1958; John D. Nisbet and Jennifer Welsh, "Predicting Student Performance", *Universities Quarterly*, **20**, 4, 1966; F. J. Olsen, "Failure in First Year University Examinations", *Australian Journal of Education*, **1**, 3, 1957; G. W. Parkyn, *Success and Failure at the University*, vol. 2, N.Z.C.E.R, 1967; *The Times Educational Supplement*, "Gifted Failures", February 17th, 1967; Ethel Venables, "Why Do They Fail?", *Technology*, **5**, 38, 1961.

27. Hilde Himmelweit, "Folie d'Examen and University Entrance", Report in *The Times Educational Supplement*, September 10th, 1965.
28. C. Sanders, 1958, *op. cit.*
29. John D. Nisbet *et al.*, 1966, *op. cit.*
30. See reference to Brian Jackson's study in H. Himmelweit, 1965, *op. cit.*
31. H. Himmelweit, 1965, *op. cit.*; R. A. C. Oliver, "The Selection of University Students: A Scholastic Aptitude Test?" *Universities Quarterly*, **16**, 3, 1962; R. A. C. Oliver, "University Entrance Requirements: Whence and Whither", *Universities Quarterly*, **20**, 3, 1966.
32. Committee on Higher Education. *Higher Education*, Report of Committee appointed by Prime Minister under the Chairmanship of Lord Robbins, 1963. Cmnd. 2154. (London, H.M.S.O.).
33. "Selection System should be improved", Report in *The Times Educational Supplement*, March 31st, 1967.
34. G. A. Gray and L. N. Short, 1961, *op. cit.* C. Sanders, 1963, *op. cit.*
35. C. Sanders, 1963, *op. cit.*
36. C. W. Taylor and F. E. Williams (eds.), *Instructional Media and Creativity*, Proceedings of the Sixth Utah Creativity Research Conference, Torrey Pines Inn, La Jolla, California, 1966.
37. J. W. Getzells and P. W. Jackson, *Creativity and Intelligence* (London and New York, Wiley, 1962).
38. J. P. Guilford, "Creativity", *The American Psychologist*, **5**, 1950.

39. For example, H. E. Gruber (ed.); *Contemporary Approaches to Creative Thinking,* (New York, Atherton, 1962); Liam Hudson; *Contrary Imaginations,* (London, Methuen, 1966). See also Bibliographies in C. W. Taylor and F. E. Williams, *op. cit.*

40. Ruth Weintraub and Ruth Salley, *op. cit.*

41. J. A. Fishman, "Some Social Psychological Theory for selecting and guiding College Students", in N. Sanford (ed.), *The American College* (New York, Wiley, 1962).

42. Hilde Himmelweit and A. Summerfield, "Student Selection—An Experimental Investigation: II", *British Journal of Sociology,* **2**, 1, 1951.

43. A. W. Astin, "Personal and Environmental Factors associated with College Dropouts among High Aptitude Students", *Journal of Educational Psychology,* **55**, 4, 1964.

44. D. J. Prediger, "Application of Moderated Scoring Keys to Prediction of Academic Success", *American Educational Research Journal,* **3**, 2, 1966.

45. D. Hogben, "The Prediction of Academic Success in Relation to Student Selection in Medicine at the University of Western Australia", *Australian Journal of Higher Education,* **2**, 2, 1965.

46. W. D. Furneaux, "Background Factors and University Performance", *Sociological Review,* **11**, 3, 1963.

47. R. Lynn, "Two Personality Characteristics related to Academic Achievement", *British Journal of Educational Psychology,* **29**, 1959.

48. F. Di Vesta, Asahel D. Woodruff, and J. P. Hertel, "Motivation as a Predictor of College Success", *Education and Psychological Measurement,* **9**, 1949; L. D. Goodstein and A. B. Heilbrunn, "Prediction of College Achievement from the Edwards Personal Preference Schedule", *Journal of Applied Psychology,* **46**, 1962; Ethel Venables, *The Young Worker at College* (London, Faber, 1967).

49. Martha Maxwell, 1960, *op. cit.*

50. Hilde Himmelweit, 1951, *op. cit.*

51. C. Sanders, "Australian Universities and their Educational Problems", *The Australian University,* **1**, 2, 1963.

52. A. W. Astin, *op. cit.*

53. Derbyshire Education Committee, Report on Award to Students, (Mimeo), 1966.

54. D. Harris, *op. cit.*

55. P. W. Hughes, *op. cit.*

56. David C. McClelland *et al.*, *The Achievement Motive* (New York, Appleton-Century-Crofts, 1953).
57. "Murray's Personology", Chapter 5, in Calvin S. Hall and Gardner Lindzey (eds.), *Theories of Personality* (New York, Wiley, 1957).
58. David E. Lavin, *The Prediction of Academic Performance* (Russell Sage Foundation, and New York, Wiley, 1967).
59. John Summerskill, "Dropouts from College" in N. Sanford (ed.), *The American College* (New York, Wiley, 1962).
60. C. J. Craven, "Why We Withdrew", Ph.D. thesis, Syracuse University, 1951. Cited in J. Summerskill, *op. cit.*
61. Margaret Mercer, "A Study of Student Mortality in a Home Economics College", *Journal of Educational Research*, 34, 1941; and "Personal Factors in College Adjustment", *Journal of Educational Research*, 36, 1943.
62. C. Sanders, 1963, *op. cit.*
63. John Summerskill, *op. cit.*
64. R. R. Dale, "Psychological Tests in University Selection", *Educational Review*, 4, 1951.
65. Report of Commission of Inquiry, Vol. 2 (the Franks Report), *op. cit.*
66. Lord Butler, reported in *The Times Educational Supplement*, March 31st, 1967.
67. J. A. Lauwerys, in *Access to Higher Education*, vol. 2 (U.N.E.S.C.O., 1965).
68. R. R. Dale, *op. cit.*; W. H. Frederick, "Components of Failure", in E. L. French (ed.), *Melbourne Studies in Education*, 1957–58 (Melbourne University Press); G. A. Gray and L. N. Short, "Student Progress in the University" (Mimeo), (University of New South Wales, 1961); J. A. Lauwerys, in *Access to Higher Education, The International Study of University Admissions*, vol. 2, Section 11 (U.N.E.S.C.O. and the International Association of Universities, 1965); A. J. Morten and J. Wilkinson, "Staying for a Third Year in the Sixth", *Where*, Supplement Seven, "From School to University", February 1967; M. J. Theobald, "A Study of Some First Year Students of the University of Melbourne" (Mimeo), (N.U.A.U.S., 1961).
69. Ministry of Education, *Fifteen to Eighteen*, Report of Central Advisory Council for Education (England), (London, H.M.S.O., 1959).
70. Crowther Report, *op. cit.*
71. D. Hogben, *op. cit.*
72. M. J. Theobald, *op. cit.*

145

73. Sir Fred J. Schonell, *et al.,* op. cit.

74. G. A. Gray and L. N. Short, *op. cit.*

75. C. Sanders, 1963, *op. cit.*

76. D. S. Anderson, "Recent Developments in Studies of University Academic Performance in Australia", paper read at New Zealand A.U.T. Seminar on Tertiary Education (Mimeo), (University of Melbourne, 1968).

77. R. R. Dale, *From School to University* (London, Routledge and Kegan Paul, 1954).

78. J. D. Nisbet *et al.,* op. cit.

79. J. A. Lauwerys, *op. cit.*

80. Report of a Sub-Committee on University Entrance Requirements in England and Wales. Committee of Vice-Chancellors. Cited in J. A. Lauwerys, *op. cit.*

81. Hilde Himmelweit, 1951, *op. cit.* Hans H. Hohne, 1951, *op. cit.* C. Sanders, 1958, *op. cit.*

82. C. Sanders, "University Selection: Theory, History and Psychology", *The Australian Journal of Education,* **1,** 3, 1957; G. W. Parkyn, *Success and Failure at the University* (N.Z.C.E.R., 1967).

83. G. W. Parkyn, 1967, *op. cit.*

84. J. C. Dancy, *Sixth Form Studies in the Robbins Era,* National Union of Teachers, 1964.

85. Sir Fred. J. Schonell *et al.,* op. cit.

86. Ethel Venables, 1967, *op. cit.*

87. C. Sanders, 1963, *op. cit.*

88. R. R. Dale, 1954, *op. cit.*

89. W. H. Frederick, *op. cit.*

90. Paul Brannan, "A Comprehensive University", *Bulletin* of University of London Institute of Education, New Series 11, Spring Term 1967.

91. J. A. Lauwerys (Personal Communication), March 1967.

92. Committee on Higher Education (the Robbins Report), *op. cit.*

93. T. Husén, reported in *The Times Educational Supplement,* April 14th, 1967.

94. A. H. Iliffe, "The Foundation Year in the University of Keele", (Mimeo) (University of Keele, 1964).

95. F. S. Dainton, quoted in *The Times Educational Supplement,* January 6th, 1967.

96. J. A. Lauwerys, 1967, *op. cit.*

97. Philip E. Vernon, "The Pool of Ability", in P. Halmos (ed.), *op. cit.*
98. H. L. Elvin, *Education and Contemporary Society* (London, Watts, 1965).
99. Celia D. Locke, "A Record of Student Performance at Keele, 1950–58", *Universities Quarterly*, **15**, 1960.
100. D. E. Mumford, "The Case for Junior Colleges", *Where*, **29**, January 1967.
101. D. Cochrane, "Matriculation and First Year University Examination Results—Some Implications for University Policy" (Mimeo), (Monash University, Melbourne, 1962).
102. E. L. Boyer and W. B. Michael, "Outcomes of College", *Review of Educational Research*, **25**, 4, 1965.
103. Charles R. Wright, "Success or Failure in earning Graduate Degrees", *Sociology of Education*, **38**, 1964.
104. H. G. Gough and W. B. Hall, "Admission Procedures as Forecasters of Performance in Medical Training", *Journal of Medical Education*, **38**, 1963.
105. Liam Hudson, "Degree Class and Attainment in Scientific Research", *British Journal of Psychology*, **51**, 1, 1960.
106. Liam Hudson, "Several Systems for Admission", reported in *The Times Educational Supplement*, September 10th, 1965.
107. J. W. R. Whitehand, "The Selection of Research Students", *Universities Quarterly*, **21**, 1, 1966.
108. J. C. Bentley, "Creativity and Academic Achievement", *Journal of Educational Research*, **59**, 1966.
109. John Gibson and Phyllis Light, "Intelligence among University Scientists", *Nature*, **213**, 5075, 1967.
110. F. B. Chaney, "A Cross-Cultural Study of Industrial Research Performance", *Journal of Applied Psychology*, **50**, 3, 1966.
111. B. S. Bloom, "Report on Creativity Research by the Examiner's Office of the University of Chicago", in C. W. Taylor and F. Barron (eds.), *Scientific Creativity: Its Recognitions and Development* (New York, Wiley, 1963).
112. Robert F. Morrison, William A. Owens, J. R. Glennon, and Lewis A. Albright, "Factored Life History Antecedents of Industrial Research Performance", *Journal of Applied Psychology*, **46**, 4, 1962.
113. Anne Roe, *The Making of a Scientist* (New York, Dodd, Mead, 1952).

114. Howard Glennerster, *Graduate School: A Study of Graduate Work at London School of Economics* (Edinburgh, Oliver and Boyd, 1967).
115. R. V. Clements, "Degree Class Assessment for Arts and Social Science", *The Times Educational Supplement,* November 3rd, 1967.
116. C. W. Taylor and F. Barron (eds.), 1963, *op. cit.*

CHAPTER 4

OTHER INSTITUTIONAL FACTORS

In the previous chapters the argument and discussion of the research literature have been confined mostly to those areas in which the search is usually made for means to improve student performance and to decrease wastage—student factors and selection. Although there may be some advantage still in focusing research on student factors and selection, it is quite clear that any attempt to attack the problem of wastage which ignores institutional factors must be severely limited. For that reason the present chapter is devoted to a review of the less voluminous research literature on those characteristics of institutions which impede or advance student performance and their output of graduates.

Flexibility and rigidity of course requirements, teaching, counselling of students, staff-student relations, student residence, examinations, and interim qualifications are the main possibilities explored. Exploration of these areas may yield possibilities for lessening wastage and hence improvement in productivity of institutions, greater satisfaction of students, and more variety of graduates and other qualified people. Considerable increase in diversification of courses and in numbers of highly educated persons is desirable from the point of view of the individual and of society.

Evidence given to the Robbins Committee showed that of the 14 per cent overall wastage among undergraduate students in British universities, apart from medical students, about 80 per cent fail one or other examination during or at the end of the course, the remainder withdrawing for unspecified personal reasons. As the Robbins Report (1) points out, this information gives no indication of the weight that can be attached to lack of ability, application, or other student variables on the one hand and defective teaching on the other, but "one thing stands out from the statistics: the striking differences in wastage rates between different universities and different faculties of the same university". The 1968 report of the University Grants Committee showed that little change had occurred over the recent decade. (See Tables 1 and 2)*

In 1957 Sir James Mountford (2) asked whether student wastage rate of 10 per cent reflected upon the teaching students had received. Certainly both he and the Robbins Committee must have reacted unfavourably to the wastage rates of 20 per cent and higher which were included in the University Grants Committee tables.

Darley (3) studied the relationship between institutions and students' achievement, in four states. Concerning some of these institutions, he wrote:

> There is a significant relationship between the types of institutions entered and outcomes for the students [who were superior high-school graduates]. . . . The data warrant some concern about higher education's way of treating high-potential students. . . . There are only three chances out of five that they will graduate at all . . . [yet] this group might be expected to succeed without excessive effort if properly stimulated, advised and taught.

A large number of studies relating to characteristics of institutions are published or referred to in Sanford's *The American College*. There is no attempt here to duplicate the mass of material in that volume, since it is assumed the reader will be well acquainted with it. The object of this chapter is to complement Sanford's and other material and to lay particular stress upon those institutional characteristics which are most closely associated with academic performance.

There will be discussion in this section of the relation between students' achievement and different methods of teaching, teachers' ability and attitudes in teaching, personality characteristics of teachers, staff-student relations, institutional ethos, and several other institutional factors.

Teaching

In higher education it is almost universally true that teachers have no preparation in teaching methods, having been selected on account of their scholarship. While scholarship is of prime importance, there seems every reason for advocating a pro-

---

* Latest statistics from the University Grants Committee show an overall wastage rate of 13.3 per cent, and are in much greater detail than hitherto.

gramme of preparation to initiate new lecturers into such matters as defining their teaching objectives, student-lecturer rapport, styles of presentation, delivery, structuring of lectures, and new media. Although students' complaints about teaching are not the only criterion of the quality of teaching, the really good teacher is generally well recognized by students. The motivation of the student and the quality of the lecturer are interrelated, though each can be profitably examined separately.

It is possible to make a case for extending the effective use of the services of the best teachers by using closed-circuit television, open university courses on public television channels, or simply by having larger-sized normal classes within the campus. There is evidence which shows that these are academically viable propositions for certain kinds of studies, especially if supporting methods are used. Just a few researchers are cited here to indicate that student performance is not necessarily inferior where such methods are used.

Cassirer, (4) for example, cited evidence which showed that it is possible to teach large numbers of students in multiple classrooms by closed-circuit television in a variety of courses without an observable loss in quality of learning. Maclaine (5) has cited numerous studies of class size in American colleges. Classes ranged in size from 8 to 336 students, the typical upper limit of the small groups being 25 and the typical lower limit of the large groups 70. In thirteen American studies which Maclaine cites it was found that mere class size had very little influence on achievement in terms of the amount of factual information students were able to recall when tested, and that the quality of the lecturer is of prime importance, whether the class groups be large or small.

The use of larger classes appears from Macomber and Siegel's study (6) to be just as effective for other kinds of learning as for learning involving mere recall of information. These researchers compared the achievement of small groups of between 16 and 30 students with that of larger groups of up to 296. Subjects of study included chemistry, classics, economics, French, mathematics, and physics. Macomber and Siegel concluded that acquisition of subject-matter was not adversely affected by students being assigned to large classes. Students in large classes also compared well with those in small classes in their ability to think critically in the subject area and to solve problems.

Student motivation and interest in the subjects was not significantly less in large classes. The researchers confirmed that students' attitudes towards large classes appeared to be influenced not by size but by the content of the course and the ability of lecturers to handle large groups.

Connor (7) reviewed thirty studies of university teaching methods in a variety of subjects, including engineering, English, science, mathematics, psychology, political science, and chemistry. From these he too concluded that the size of the group did not affect student performance, except when a procedure inappropriate to the size of the group was adopted. Lecturing to large groups was appropriate for the systematic presentation of material, to introduce principles, to effect coverage of a topic, and to stimulate interest and enthusiasm for independent study. But discussions, tutorials, seminars, and other small-group methods were more effective for consolidating and integrating information and concepts and for applying those concepts and principles to practice. In small groups, as with large groups, the skill and preference of the teacher using any method were of more direct consequence than the actual method used. Moreover, preferences of the students themselves affected their performance under each method.

Macklin (8) said at the Home Universities' Conference in 1951, "It has always struck me as rather odd that universities, whose main function is, on one hand, teaching, and on the other hand, learning, should have done so very little about teaching the teacher to teach, or instructing the student in the art of learning." Cunningham (9) has argued that if teaching is not properly conducted success may be limited to exceptionally able and tenacious students, and Jenkinson (10) has suggested that we should aim at a situation where every recruit to teaching in colleges either goes through full-time training or during his first years in teaching takes in-service training, as a means of reducing wastage. Consultant services and research and experiment in university teaching methods are not very frequently undertaken or offered, though in the United Kingdom there are some recent moves to redress this.* The Hale Report is an authoritative and exhaustive

---

* For example, Dr Ruth M. Beard at the University of London Institute of Education University Teaching Methods Research Unit, supported by a Leverhulme Trust grant, is initiating exchange of ideas and stimulating studies of teaching among colleges of the University of London.

document on teaching in higher education in Britain.*

Student performance under any teaching method is also related to such variables as the sociability of the student. There are also sex differences. Smart, Owen, Hall, and Anderson studied the efficiency of a branching programme on electro-cardiography for fifth-year medical students. The programme was more effective than lectures for academically weaker students and for foreign students, and generally women learned better from lectures and men learned better from the programme. Inertia is a problem for some students, and they need some social stimulus to help them out of it. Unless the learning situation is also a social situation student performance may suffer. Hopson's (11) well-argued article supporting the uses of technological aids to teaching recognized this. In the enthusiasm for new techniques, however justified it may be, it would be folly to ignore the social ingredient of some learning situations. This is of critical importance to many students, though possibly negligible for others. The use of seminars for stimulating productive, critical discussion as a means of learning is an art which does not come naturally to all lecturers; indeed, for some it is an extremely difficult art to master. McKeachie's studies in the United States and Abercrombie's in Britain have explored this field, and a study of their work is recommended. (12)

Staff-student Relations and Institutional Ethos

Studies have shown that students favour tutorials in small groups. (13) The reason may lie in the social aspects involved. There is further evidence which suggests that different student groups vary in the manner and extent to which they need social reinforcement in the learning process. Hammond, (14) moreover, produced a general finding that participation in small informal discussions and attendance at small-group university seminars is specially associated with examination success. It may be that there are certain kinds of student relations which foster learning.

Malleson's (15) comments regarding the Oxford and Cambridge tradition of personal tutorials are probably relevant. He

* Report of the Committee on Teaching Methods, University Grants Committee (1964, H.M.S.O.).

For an excellent review of the literature on teaching the reader is referred to Dr Ruth M. Beard's monograph *Research into Teaching Methods in Higher Education,* published by the Society for Research into Higher Education, London, 1968.

asks why these universities can manage with such small wastage rates and others cannot. While recognizing there may be some truth in the rejoinder that they have first choice of students and can pick the best, he does not agree that this accounts for all the difference, since they accept some non-scholarship students. In the past, up to 1938, not only were students of high ability admitted to these universities, but also a percentage of students of lesser ability from privileged homes. Unless it be argued that Oxford and Cambridge selection tutors have insights and abilities denied selectors in other universities, he contends, they will still find themselves with a body of students covering a wide range of ability. Further, the staff-student ratios of those universities are not greatly different from many others, and many of the highest wastage rates elsewhere are found in departments where equipment and staffing are of the most lavish. Malleson thinks the difference in pass rates must lie in the handling of the problem, perhaps in a different attitude towards it. Great care is taken, for example, in assessing students' performance and in helping them to overcome their difficulties. Summary decisions to send students down, made by departments acting alone, are rare, if non-existent. There can be little doubt that the attitudes and practices of Oxford and Cambridge tutors in their extensive interaction with students are powerful influences promoting a high graduation rate. Abercrombie (16) has cited studies which refer to the accessibility of the teacher as an important ingredient in the learning situation, and the importance of feed-back in the acquisition of knowledge and development of concepts. Brookover (17) found that teachers who engaged in a great deal of person-to-person interaction with their students tended to be rated highly by them as instructors. All of these studies suggest that the nature of the teacher-student relationship may be critical.

The personalities of teachers and students and the nature of the interchange between them has been explained by Thistle-thwaite. (18) In a study of 2405 male undergraduates of high ability in 140 American colleges and universities he found their level of aspiration was associated with strong faculty press for enthusiasm, humanism, achievement, affiliation, independence, vocationalism, and supportiveness. Lamke (19) in a small study of 32 high-school teachers in their first year of teaching, using the 16 P. F. Inventory, found good teachers, more than poor teachers, to be gregarious, adventurous, frivolous, to have abundant emotional response and strong artistic and sentimental interests, more interested in the opposite sex, polished, fastidious, and cool. By contrast poor teachers were more likely than good teachers to be shy, cautious, conscientious, easily pleased, and more attentive to people. As with all findings, the reliability of the criterion is all-important. In this instance the teaching mark was used, together with a rating of the acceptability of the teacher to his principal. This may not be as reliable as one would wish, but the problem of accurate assessment of success is a fact of life in this kind of research. The possibility of having scientifically derived criteria is limited, and assessment must rest heavily upon some form of subjective evaluation.

Knapp and Goodrich (20) used a different criterion, though still a subjective one. They concentrated their research on specific disciplines rather than making findings that were meant to apply to all students. Biology and chemistry graduates were asked to assess their past teachers. On the basis of their assessments an index of the distinction of their teachers was derived. There were some slight differences, but a great number of similarities between biologists and chemists in the characteristics they regarded their most distinguished teachers as possessing. The qualities which most highly correlated with successful teaching were, in order of importance, participation in professional activities, enterprise and gaining of grants, dominance and demand for high standards, energy, research activity, physical vitality, pedagogic zest including accessibility to students, dedication to teaching rather than research, degrees held, warmth, command, presence, verbal and histrionic skills, and breadth of intellectual interests. Knapp and Goodrich considered that it is the quality of the teacher as a total human being more than his command of particular instrumental skills that determines success.

The most significant combination of characteristics emerging from the analysis of each group of scientists combined to form a factor which described a complex of energy, demandingness, masterfulness, and enterprise. As Knapp and Goodrich pointed out, these characteristics are those of the strong father figure and are peculiarly at variance with many of the attributes commonly ascribed to the 'democratic' teacher. In this study the eminent teacher, in biology and chemistry, has typically been a rather masterful figure possessed of considerable agressiveness and vitality, able to inspire his students, through their fear of his disapprobation and their desire to emulate his qualities and achievements. Knapp and Goodrich's general conclusion was that for teachers in biology and chemistry the traits yielding the highest correlations are those involving not particular pedagogic skills but general aspects of character, and suggested that for those who have conceived the process of education to be primarily the impersonal transmission of knowledge their findings represent a considerable challenge.

If Knapp and Goodrich's findings are true for chemists and biologists, what are the indications for other disciplines, particularly the humanities and social sciences? For students in these fields a distinctly different kind of teacher might be preferable. There is indirectly some suggestion that more democratic characteristics are requisite in faculties who teach social science and humanities. Social-science students were in the vanguard in the free-speech movement at Berkeley (21) in 1964, with humanities following closely, and no less than 75 per cent of the social-science students supported the movement. By contrast, students in vocational and professional courses were less critical of the *status quo* and more conformist. This may be in keeping with the scientists' teacher preferences found by Knapp and Goodrich. It seems highly likely, when considering these two reports, that social-science and humanities students would be less likely than scientists to need strong father figures as teachers. The free-speech movement was also more supported by students of high ability.

Several other recent studies (22) have shown that students in a number of countries follow a pattern. Liberals, radicals, and activists are most often humanities and social-science students, as found at Berkeley. Data from Buenos Aires, Mexico, Teheran, Pakistan, Puerto Rico, and the United States, cited by Spencer, confirm this. Students of engineering, business administration, education, and agriculture are generally more conformist and conservative. While conformists may accept authoritative attitudes in teachers, they are more likely to be questioned in free discussion and argument by radicals and liberals. From such studies it is reasonable to suppose that teaching style and staff-student relations should be appropriate to the different kinds of students who are attracted into the various disciplines. These studies all suggest that teachers' personalities have a decided influence upon students. It may well be that student performance itself is highly dependent upon staff-student relationship. In a study of 1500 National Merit Scholars and close contenders from 327 colleges and universities Thistlethwaite (23) found that colleges which considered students' views on course procedures were characterized by an absence of pressure for student compliance, and by student perception of an enthusiastic staff. Faculty enthusiasm was also important in the arts, humanities, and social sciences, and for these students faculty press for independence and achievement and humanism were of greater importance than for students of the natural and biological sciences. Many studies of student and institutional characteristics have been reviewed by McConnell. (24) He notes that institutions are differentially selective with respect to aptitudes, interests, values, social background, and intellectual disposition of students, and has suggested the possibility of fitting the student to the college so that optimum student development might be realized. It may be questioned, though, if students should be inducted into colleges which merely confirm their values, interests, and social outlook. It may be that superior student development occurs when institutional ethos does not so thoroughly coincide with the students' own interests and values. The small amount of evidence suggests that the optimal kind of relationship for academic achievement may not be the same for all students, but is different between disciplines and between ability groupings. This field requires much more research and replication in different countries, but hypotheses are already indicated.

Knapp and Goodrich and Knapp and Greenbaum (25) also studied the characteristics of institutions in relation to their production of scientists. Apart from a very small number of famous colleges—for example, California Institute of Technology and Massachusetts Institute of Technology—output tended to be inversely related to size of college. The most productive class of institutions were small liberal-arts colleges with a strong commitment to general education, whereas universities were seen to be less productive of scientists. Of the fifty most productive institutions 80 per cent were small liberal-arts colleges of limited reputation, mostly in the Middle and Far West. Only three of these institutions were universities of eminent reputation. The characteristics which appeared to promote the success of institutions in producing scientists were intense dedication to intellectual objectives and a corresponding lack of preoccupation with social life and intercollegiate athletics; a spirit of vanguardism or missionary zeal, a general quality of autonomy pervading administrative and disciplinary affairs, unique curricular features designed to emphasize individual initiative and consideration of the individual and an inclination towards broad achievement in social science and humanistic studies as well as science.

Factors showing no significant correlation with achievement of institutions in training scientists were: student-faculty ratio (though a trend existed), percentage of Ph.D.'s in science faculty, and proportion of total faculty teaching science. Privately controlled institutions were, on average, more than four times as productive as publicly controlled institutions. It is not clear whether these differences in productivity were related to administrative aspects or the prevailing social class of student intake, or whether the selection or teaching methods of private institutions differed significantly from public institutions. What is abundantly clear is that some institutional factors have a deep influence on production of graduates and on undergraduates' achievement.

Knapp and Goodrich noted that the higher productivity of small liberal-arts colleges, though it applied to scientists, did not apply to students in all disciplines. This they regarded as especially significant. Production of lawyers, physicians, and graduates in general is higher in larger institutions. The authors attempted to explain these contrary findings in terms of the vocational inclinations of students attracted to small institutions and the opportunity provided them for the development of creative student-teacher relationships. Astin (26) found that aspirations of talented students to seek the Ph.D. were negatively correlated with conventional college orientation and the existence of rigid hierarchies between faculty and students. According to students, faculty members in these institutions showing evidence of pronounced hierarchies had fewer contacts with students, were poorer teachers, and resented criticism.

There are important factors at work here. If the productivity of institutions is to be maximized, comparative studies of institutional characteristics and their differential influence on students' achievement and aspirations in various disciplines would be useful. American studies in this field are far in advance of those of other countries.*

---

* For some of these see N. Sanford (ed.), *The American College* (New York, Wiley, 1962).

Counselling, Health, and Psychiatric Services

There is a real need for counselling and health services, as the studies to which reference is to be made will show. The extent of the effectiveness of such services is difficult to demonstrate with accuracy, as is the case with clinical, advisory, consultant services of other kinds. It is dangerously easy to doubt their usefulness and to question if services should be created or extended because of the difficulty of assembling scientific evidence regarding their effectiveness, but Campbell (27) has demonstrated that counselled students at the University of Minnesota had a graduation rate 25 per cent higher than a control group of uncounselled students.

Although their effectiveness cannot easily be assessed, the need for them is clearly demonstrated. The Hale Report (28) refers to memoranda from the National Union of Students and the Scottish Union of Students. The former memorandum referred to the "deep gulf" between school and university teaching methods as a factor leading to psychological disturbances and failure, and emphasized the special need at this stage for guidance, while the latter said there was no serious attempt to bridge this gap or to help the student to adapt himself to university methods. Students were asked if they needed advice and if they in fact obtained the kind they needed. Two-thirds of students said they needed it, and, of these, 28 per cent had not been able to get satisfactory advice.

Lipset and Altbach (29) have reported a study which showed that for young people of student age seeking psychiatric help educational stresses were the main presenting problem in 74 per cent of cases in 1960–61. Reasons for referral to one counselling service in a New York college have been given by Watson. (30) The most frequent presenting problems, 25 per cent, were associated with maturational stresses. Next, 16 per cent were problems in the family situation, the students indicating that their parents were rejecting, punishing, or over-protective. Most students at this college were living at home or in lodgings. At one time or another 10 per cent of men and 18 per cent of women were depressed. The problems of young adults have been well described in general terms by Srole, (31) who said:

The jolting impact of role discontinuity on vulnerable personalities . . . may be viewed in part as a cultural failure to provide a bridge of training for the individual. . . . Role transitions occur in especially rapid sequence during adolescence and early adulthood, for example, entering college, dating and courtship, launching a career. At these transfer points in particular, signs of potential psychiatric morbidity may show themselves in relatively clear but transient forms.

After analysing students' reasons for withdrawal Howell (32) concluded, in evidence to the Robbins Committee, that lack of adequate guidance or interest on the part of teaching staff, with students left to sink or swim, played an important part in the withdrawal of students. Some lecturers did not appear to welcome questions, and some students were too diffident in asking them. If lecturers have too heavy a load a separate student counselling service would be necessary for students who need this help and are not at present able to secure it.

Parnell (33) and Malleson (34) have each pointed out that the students having serious breakdowns are merely the hard core in a problem which affects a much larger proportion of students having serious problems which may not entail absence, but which can nevertheless diminish their effectiveness in study. Malleson (35) has referred to social isolation, study difficulties, and remoteness of teaching staff as factors in wastage. Psychiatric disturbances affected 20 per cent of a student intake in one of his studies, though less than 2 per cent were major disturbances. Other researchers have referred to the variety of student problems which can affect academic performance. Lucas, Kelvin, and Ojha (36) considered that although emotional disturbance was common among 'wasted' and delayed groups, it was only one of many factors in wastage. From their study it was impossible to gauge how far emotional disturbance was an outcome of academic difficulty itself.

Macklin (37) discussed emotional disturbance among Aberdeen students, where it appeared to be related to unsatisfactory methods of study and living conditions. In an analysis of 132 cases of psychoneurosis among students, stress factors were associated with the university in 65 per cent of cases, and only 35 per cent were associated with factors outside the university. After a careful study of the literature it seems that the evidence produced by Priestley, (38) from research conducted in his student-counselling office in Melbourne, gives a fair picture of the distribution of problems students might have in almost any university.

Table 12 shows the distribution according to type of problem briefly referred to in Chapter 2.

TABLE 12

Distribution of Students' Problems in a Large Australian University

Type and severity of student problem	As Percentage	
1. Personal disturbances involving serious disruption of a student's life: psychosis, severe depression, severe family conflicts, sexual problems	6	⎫
2. Personal disturbances involving severe handicap, but not severe disruption of life: anxiety states, social isolation, less serious disturbance of the kind mentioned in 1	10	⎬ 16 ⎭
3. Doubts and worries about future vocation	27	⎫
4. Educational difficulties: difficulties in settling to study, reading and learning difficulties	21	⎬ 48 ⎭
5. Minor difficulties requiring brief information and advice	22	⎫
6. Financial difficulties	9	⎬ 36
7. Other problems	5	⎭
	100	

Source: R. R. Priestley, "The Mental Health of University Students", in E. L. French (ed.), *Melbourne Studies in Education*, p. 13 (University of Melbourne, 1957).

Psychological difficulties requiring referral to psychiatric services were present in at least 6 per cent of cases seeking help, and probably most of the 10 per cent in category 2 would benefit from psychiatric referral. In discussing categories 3 and 4 Priestley considered that a large number of the students would be passing through a disturbance normal in adolescence or early adulthood. Such crises can be severe and incapacitating while they last. Priestley recognizes that although some students may recover spontaneously, there are good reasons for providing assistance. In the first place, the student can be helped by sensitive counselling to get back to effective work with a minimum loss of time: secondly, and more important, he can sometimes be helped to adjust effectively or at a higher maturational level. Priestley considers that treatment of such cases is relatively brief and simple. Its lack of provision may result in failure in examinations and in some cases in the development of serious and persistent difficulties.

161

Malleson (39) supports this and takes the point farther. He discusses how students' anxiety can generate from basic study difficulties.

Secondary anxiety increases the student's distress and further decreases his efficiency, presenting a vicious circle which can take many weeks or even months to resolve spontaneously. . . . Helping the student make the best use of the university is not simply a matter of giving good advice. . . . Personal problems necessarily inhibit the student from making full use of the university. . . . Counselling him about his personal problems and helping him over his periods of distress, is therefore, as germane to the whole process of university education as taking seminars or writing essays.

In the previous chapter on student selection many studies were discussed which showed that more rigorous selection does not lead to a marked lessening of wastage. It has been suggested by Priestley and by Cunningham (40) that in any attempt to reduce wastage the university should be prepared not only to examine its selection procedures, but also to consider what it should do to help those students whom it selects. When universities have wastage rates of up to 33 per cent among students of superior ability, as is common in Australian universities with student intakes averaging 125 plus I.Q., (41) and just as great in some departments of British universities, it seems reasonable to suppose that improved counselling services as well as health services would help in reducing wastage, even if it is difficult to measure their present effectiveness.

WHEN IS COUNSELLING NEEDED?

There is evidence that students need guidance before entering university and college, beyond what is usually available in schools. Gray and Short (42) found that students' occupational interests were frequently incompatible with the courses upon which they had embarked. Priestley (43) found that 27 per cent of students who needed counselling were primarily worried about their future vocations, and Venables (44) found many students in colleges of technology lack clearly defined occupational goals, and are not aware of possibilities open to them at the time of taking up their studies. As a result they make unrealistic choices and become dissatisfied and uninterested, with a resulting loss in motivation. Thistlethwaite (45) found that even National Merit Scholars in the United States, a highly select group of students, were deterred from continuing their studies because closer acquaintance with the field of their choice, gained after starting studies, had caused them to lose interest. Had they been properly counselled better choices might have been made.

Jackson (46) found that students who were forced to abandon studies in English higher education had lacked information about courses which might have enabled them to make better initial choices, and Schonell (47) in Australia has also drawn attention to the same problem. Schools can help a great deal here, but it is not realistic to expect them to have all the information and facilities students need. Schonell suggests that new students and their parents should be interviewed by university counsellors to help in fitting students to the most suitable courses, partly because parents sometimes push students into inappropriate studies to satisfy vicariously their own ambitions.

Increasing numbers of students come from homes where parents have no previous experience of higher education. Kelsall found that 31 per cent of men and 19 per cent of women admitted to universities other than Oxford and Cambridge had fathers in manual occupations. (48) Counsellors could conceivably help students whose parents are hostile to higher education or who fail to understand students' needs, by arranging meetings and discussions with individual parents and encouraging their co-operation, especially when students live at home. Schonell (49) cited a study of pre-medical students by Anderson (50) showing the superior performance of students from professional and higher-status white-collar groups, and asked what universities should do about helping students from less favourable homes to make more effective adjustment to university demands. Should student counsellors try to help by making approaches to parents? In Schonell's own experience this was a practical possibility, even though a delicate matter. If university and college studies are to be properly open to all who are qualified, then some attempt in the solution of this problem appears to be necessary. Further, there is a clear need for better counselling of students before they enter a university or college. The present situation in Britain certainly falls far short of the ideal, yet the decisions made when entering any institution are often irrevocable. Once the student is committed to a course, generally speaking, it must be completed in three years, and there is little flexibility to allow changes to other courses. The British system of grants tied to a three-year period for most courses makes pre-college counselling of critical importance to an extent that does not apply in more open and flexible systems. Even the choice of institution is either faulty or inappropriate for a large proportion of students. In Marris's study less than a third of students found what they expected in their place of higher education. At Leeds 50 per cent of students were disappointed academically, socially, or both. Even at Cambridge, with a larger intake from public schools than most universities, after allowing for the closer links between them than exists between most schools and universities, for 38 per cent of students their expectations were not matched by what they found there.

Most student problems seem to occur in first year and decrease considerably in subsequent years. In Schonell's 1962 study the predominant worries were about studies and career choices. When most of the wastage occurs in the first year, students can be helped a great deal with their reading and study skills, their use of the library and references, and in understanding examination requirements. University requirements and methods can be very different from those of school, and, as Sanders (51) notes, orientation weeks and similar programmes do only a little to help individuals.

KINDS OF SERVICES NEEDED

Even in 1940 Harris (52) was able to cite studies showing that student performance could be improved by counselling in proper study methods. More recently Summerskill (53) reviewed a large body of literature showing that good and poor students can be differentiated by their patterns of work and study with fair accuracy; the time spent in study and in class, library usage, methods of study, ability to keep up with work, reading speed, and comprehension. Gray and Short, (54) and Pond, (55) came to similar conclusions, particularly for first-year students, and suggested the kinds of counselling services needed. In one study counselling by senior students led to better results than counselling by instructors. Gray and Short suggested that a study-skills centre could be provided to help new students with techniques of report-writing, reading, and note-taking from references. In their study 30 per cent of new students felt themselves to be lacking in these skills. While recognizing that schools have a responsibility to foster these skills we must concede that not all sixth forms are successful in imparting them. If universities and colleges and local education authorities who provide the grants are interested in making the best of their investment in the education of students, a sink-or-swim attitude towards those who require further tuition and assistance is unjustifiable and inappropriate.

Malleson (56) observed that it is rare in university practice to make any attempt to teach the student how to study and to make use of available facilities, and that, indeed, we have paid little attention to the techniques of learning at the higher educational levels. Hunter and Schwartzman's study (57) of medical students is one of many which have shown that this kind of help is needed. Unless something is done here is a potential source of avoidable wastage. Clearly we cannot assume that all students come to the university or college with a proper understanding of the kinds of study techniques which are required in higher education.

As Schonell (58) points out, universities unfortunately do not discover students' degree of understanding of what they have learnt or their attitudes to learning until after they have begun their courses. He suggests that for such students, particularly in departments dealing with such subjects as mathematics, physics, chemistry, and languages, diagnostic tests should be given early in the first term to discover those students with the worst deficiencies. There should then be small tutorial group discussions in places where these are not already available to impress on students the need for thorough understanding as well as mere memorization of subjects. Where these skills are lacking in students the schools they have left must bear some of the responsibility: this will be discussed later. But, having accepted students, the college or university has the responsibility, which is probably best shared by the departments themselves and the counselling office, as a team, in both diagnosis and treatment.

Knoell's (59) and Lawrence's (60) papers, while not necessarily representative, provide good illustrations of American ideas regarding student-counselling.* The functions of counselling services are seen to include helping students to decide on fields of study and to choose alternatives where these are necessary and feasible, encouraging students with motivational and study

---

* For a good up-to-date introduction to American thinking on student-counselling services see the *Harvard Educational Review, 32.*

problems, developing communications between the administration, faculty, and students, and conducting housing studies, especially to discover the kinds of housing which will help students to make their best adjustment to campus life, especially those who are away from home for the first time, and actively helping students to become integrated into university life, thus minimizing the sense of isolation and bewilderment felt by many in mid-adolescence upon entering a large institution. Although first- and second-year students are generally found to have most problems, older students are equally eligible for help.

It may well be asked if it is not going too far to attempt to supply all these services. Where a student health service is well developed and a good tutorial system is in operation the need may not be as great, but the indications are that they still are necessary, and this raises the question of the background and qualifications of student counsellors.

WHO SHOULD COUNSEL STUDENTS?

Research reviewed by Winfrey and Feder (61) suggested that the ideal counsellor should be characterized by the 'need for nurturance and intraception (need to understand people), by dominance and achievement to some degree, and least of all by autonomy and exhibitionism'. If this is a valid finding—and it would seem at least to have face validity—it suggests some possible shortcomings in a tutorial system in which tutors are merely good scholars who have been appointed to teaching posts. Conversations with graduates from institutions having individual tutorial systems disclose instances where the tutor has given advice rather than counsel. The difficulty here is that advice, however good, is not likely to be accepted or acted upon unless the recipient sees sufficient reason for so doing, and is ready for it and capable of using it. Counselling is quite different from advising. The counsellor takes up the problem from the counselled person's position and leads him, at his own pace, towards a viable solution, having considered the possible alternatives. This is vastly different from imposing a solution, however logical it may seem from the adviser's viewpoint. This kind of advice can be, and often is, useless.

Tutors are usually appointed on the basis of their outstanding academic careers, and may have little appreciation of the problems of less able students since they probably had few difficulties themselves which threatened their academic performance. They are specialists in their subjects and unlikely to have had professional preparation for counselling. It must be a matter of chance whether they have the requisite human qualities that will fit them adequately for this important role. Horle and Gazda (62) in the United States have found that much so-called counselling is done by untrained individuals without relevant educational background and experience. It is questionable how effective such 'counselling' can be in reducing academic wastage. Farnsworth (63) has stated that in American colleges the number of psychiatric and therapeutic interviews is determined not by need, but by the number of hours of psychiatric time available. Young (64) in England considered that even in Cambridge University, with its strong tutorial system, one student in six requires some sort of psychological help at some time before graduation, and of these one-third are severe or moderately severe cases. Young proposed a larger service, to include clinical psychologists and social workers, in addition to psychiatrists. This suggestion is sound because it recognizes that not all student problems are psychological or health problems, but are often social in origin. Hunter and Schwartzman (65) stressed that it is also desirable to build up a dynamic understanding of the psychology of educational processes rather than to make 'Procrustean efforts to fit the observed phenomena into traditional psychiatric nosologies'. To do this it is necessary to take into account the interaction between social, psychological, and educational processes. It is doubtful if students can be adequately helped when only one or two of these groups of variables are taken into account.

If, as Farnsworth says, the help available to students is limited by the amount of psychiatric time available, there is added reason for using the services of psychologists and social workers. Probably the most cogent reason why student counselling should not be restricted to doctors and psychiatrists is that students in difficulty do not often view their problem as medical or psychiatric, and, indeed, it seems that only a minority of student problems do in fact fall within either of these categories, though if the problem were allowed to develop the students affected might come to require medical or psychiatric treatment.

Still (66) has found that some students do not seek help until acute anxiety is precipitated by impending examinations. He refers to cases where reactions suddenly appear, and at the time of the breakdown treatment is sometimes hampered by a lack of knowledge of the circumstances which have led up to it. He suggests that calming of the students can best be done by one who has had earlier contact with them, perhaps a warden or tutor, who may be aware of the exact circumstances which have led to the students' difficulties. Discussing the increasing numbers of students, and the greater number of those who may be expected to experience difficulties because of lack of knowledge, poor organization of work, and the growing burden on tutors and supervisors who attempt to be aware of student problems, Still asks what can be done to improve student guidance. There can be little doubt that many students in trouble hesitate to see a staff member or a doctor in the student health service.

Summerskill (67) reviewed eighteen American studies of drop-outs in which the percentage of students citing medical reasons for dropping out was only 8 per cent; in Priestley's Australian study it was seen that, over a period of three years, only 16 per cent of students' problems warranted medical or psychiatric treatment. Had the remaining 84 per cent, whose problems were non-medical, not had a well-manned student counselling office to attend, it is extremely doubtful if they would have seen any need to consult a student health-service doctor until they had reached a state of acute anxiety. And had they no other person to consult about their problems they might simply have dropped out of studies. Malleson (68) has suggested that, apart from psychotic and urgent admission cases, there may be a number of students who suffer from profound neurotic disorders that will need prolonged treatment and who could be treated by non-medical psychotherapists. These are students whose psychological problems, though not minor, are of a circumscribed kind, but can have direct repercussions on the student's working capacity.

If, as American and Australian studies suggest, student problems are almost 90 per cent non-medical it is reasonable to ask why students should be required to consult a doctor. It is not appropriate to assume that a doctor is automatically qualified to be a student counsellor, nor is it prudent to expect a tutor to be able to recognize if a student requires medical or psychiatric treatment. Further, a student may have very sound reasons for not consulting his tutor or a doctor when he is in difficulty. In so far as this is so it indicates that what is needed is a non-medical counselling office, manned by professionals with the appropriate psychological background, interested in the social and study problems of students, whom students can consult with assurance of confidentiality, and even anonymity if they so wish. In the absence of a service of this kind student problems can develop seriously and unnecessarily.

Malleson, in arguing the need for assistance peculiar to the student, asks:

> Why does the distressed student need to find help? Young people in other walks of life, we must presume, are also subject to distress, yet get by without special help. The difference is in the nature of their work. The distressed apprentice or farmer's boy can, perhaps, carry on his manual duties without significant deterioration. The distressed student cannot so easily.

Although some students are able to perform well while under stress, Malleson asserts that in nearly every case distress impairs study effectiveness and renders the student unable to achieve as well as he might. The student inevitably gets progressively worried and anxious as he drops behind. This process is the spiralling interaction between failure and anxiety to which Priestley (69) referred.

It would not be right to assume that student problems and the services required are identical in all countries, but the literature suggests marked similarities. Serious thought should be given to relating findings in one country to the situation in another and to considering how far they are appropriate for any particular institution. Much that is useful may be applied locally.

Counselling services, as distinct from medical, psychiatric, and tutorial services, can do much to alleviate students' difficulties by preventing their development to critical proportions, especially in first year. Although it is virtually impossible to estimate their effectiveness, there should be no doubt that correct guidance given early on demand can prevent students from making persistent errors which would lead to ineffective habits of study and maladjustment in the learning situation. Where staff-student relations are tenuous the support which a good student counsellor is able to provide can do a great deal for morale. The main question would seem to be what functions a student-counselling service can serve which would minimize wastage and failure.

In *Success and Failure at the University* Parkyn (70) claimed that in the majority of cases failure does not seem to be caused by too low a standard of entrance or by lax and variable standards of accrediting. This was also clear from many other studies reviewed in Chapter 3. Parkyn suggested that the most promising approach to failure would appear to lie in an attempt to discover the nature of those factors which prevent so many students from achieving what it seems reasonable to expect of them. Some of these factors are institutional—for example, examination procedures and pass rates, but there are other more personal factors. It is clearly not the role of the student-counselling office to change policies of departments, though it is conceivable that findings from research and practice might make a useful contribution to departments' understanding of students who find themselves in difficulty and thus help to reduce wastage.

One American scheme of Student Personnel services, of a kind more often found in that country than in the United Kingdom, has been described by Lawrence. (71) Group and individual counselling methods are used to acquaint students with college services, traditions, regulations, course prerequisites, and to help in planning study schedules. Students are helped to clarify their educational and vocational interests and career goals. Free availability of counselling staff and faculty is central to the scheme. Student problems generally are not regarded as the domain of the medical profession, but college medical services are arranged through the Health Services Office of the Departments of Health and Physical Education. It is customary for all freshmen to produce a medical statement from their private doctors for the college health service. This gives the health service the opportunity to alert counsellors to special problems of physical or emotional disturbance.

A similar arrangement is planned for a new Canadian university* where the Division of Student Affairs will establish a comprehensive counselling service to work in conjunction with the Student Health Service. This plan is built into the overall university plan, and will draw upon research and practice in other American and Canadian universities extending over many years, and which has clearly confirmed the need for such services.

---

*Information from the Director of Student Affairs, Memorial University of Newfoundland, St John's, Newfoundland.

Reading clinics, consultations with parents of marginal students, and early treatment of students' social, emotional, and study problems to relieve the normal anxieties common among adolescents in new learning situations, can help. There are also at least two other important functions which counselling offices are well placed to perform and which should help in reducing wastage. The first of these is to accept for consultation those students who have not referred themselves but who have been recognized early by the academic departments as being at risk. Nisbet and Welsh (72) conducted a study of first-year science students at Aberdeen, the aim of which was to develop an early-warning system, students who were in the bottom third in two or more subjects in the December examinations being referred to regents. Before the scheme was begun the failure rate had been rising sharply, but in the two years following its introduction it was checked. The authors recognized that many factors affect performance, and do not claim that mere referral to regents has in itself caused the drop in the failure rate, but it is interesting that after referral some improvement followed. The action taken by the regents was not clearly defined, but it did not extend beyond an interview and perhaps some further general interest taken in the student. The Minnesota study by Campbell cited earlier has provided strong evidence that a well-manned counselling service can be very effective. In a study of architecture students at University College, London, Abercrombie and associates (73) found that half of the students requiring more than minimum time to complete their courses had been experiencing personal problems. The incidence of personal problems should not be a factor in the failure of students if this is in any way avoidable. Clearly the utmost help should be available to minimize their toll on academic performance.

Another way in which positive action could be taken to reduce wastage is in considering student records at conferences of faculty and counsellors where students are discussed before being sent down for poor scholarship. The decisions arrived at are fundamentally faculty decisions, but before 'wasting' a student it might be more productive to base assessment of the student's motivations and promise upon data to which probably only a good counselling office can have access. This procedure has been well developed for a very long time in some colleges in the United States. (74) In Britain, at Oxford and Cambridge and some other universities, the practice has developed of reviewing every aspect of a student's case before sending him down for poor scholarship. This has depended upon reports and opinions of tutors, and it is the practice to postpone irreversible decisions to as late a time as possible, generally the third year.

At a time of increasing pressure for places at all universities, and other institutions of higher education, and bearing in mind the practice of failing students at the end of first year, which seems more frequent than in the past, it seems fair to allow students the opportunity of having their extenuating circumstances, if they exist, made known to reviewing committees. Where students have felt it necessary to consult counsellors the counsellors' advice can contribute to a realistic assessment and may be crucial to a student's career. In at least one other English university, the University of Sussex, a Student Progress Board, composed of all Deans and the head of the Student Health Service, reviews the position of students who are not doing well, and devises plans to help. These practices should be instrumental in reducing wastage. It seems likely that the greater range of problems students would present at a counselling office would provide valuable material for the consideration of student progress boards in addition to that which health services can provide.

The counselling office is well placed to conduct and assist with research into academic wastage in so far as this is related directly to factors within the student himself. In some universities it is the practice to collect data about students at the time of intake, and the advice of experienced counsellors is useful in deciding the range of data needed to provide an adequate background for research into student problems and wastage, and by limiting it to sensible proportions, may prevent the collection of useless data. If agreement between large numbers of universities and colleges could be achieved about the kinds of data to be collected this could constitute the beginnings of a national data bank on the lines suggested by Astin and Panos. (75) A national data bank containing equivalent information from many universities and colleges, relating to students' abilities, motivations, and background, courses undertaken, reasons for withdrawal, and postgraduate intentions, would yield useful samples for follow-up studies and secondary analysis and for comparative cross-national studies.

At the local level, counselling offices can study when and why students begin to fail, and can compare drop-outs with persisters. They can study the special problems of drop-outs and explore alternatives to dropping out which may be open to the student. Frequently in Britain there is no alternative. Where failure is related to institutional factors, research based on counselling data could be useful for those departments and faculty who are receptive and sufficiently flexible to consider the possibility of modifying policies. Individual differences among students are not always adequately considered. Greater flexibility in administration and course requirements may help in limiting student wastage. This is discussed more fully in a later section.

Student Residence

It is doubtful if student residence is ever provided with the simple aim of fostering high academic performance. Higher education aims at something more than grades, and residential halls are generally considered important in promoting wider goals of education. Research into the relationship between type of student residence, whether in hall, lodgings, or at home, and the student's academic performance is the essential theme of this section. However, relationships which have been found bristle with intervening variables. Findings are inconsistent and inconclusive. Harris (76) in 1940 reported conflicting findings, and to the present time the situation seems hardly to have changed. Harris thought that the relationship depended on the local tradition and situation, and this is probably still true, though some forward steps in the study of student residence have been made.

In Britain, Hopkins, Malleson, and Sarnoff (77) reported finding no significant differences between residence of graduates and of those students who left university without a degree. Marris (78) found that students who had lived in halls at two British universities achieved only about one-third of the above-average results in their examinations, and in one university residents achieved average or below average 30 per cent more often than non-residents. It cannot be assumed that being in hall was responsible for the inferior performance of residents. Perhaps they were unadventurous, dependent, or weaker academically in the first instance than those who lived in lodgings, flats, or at home. The study was not controlled for these factors, and the total number of students in the study was only 178. Nevertheless, this is a very striking finding, when it is so often taken for granted that halls help, not hinder, academic success. Albrow (79) compared 32 first-year students residing in halls with 32 in lodgings, and found that hall residents tended to perform better academically, but the trend was statistically insignificant. Students in halls studied slightly more hours per week, but the difference was very small.

However, other research has shown residence to be more favourably associated with student performance. Anderson and Priestley (80) found that students in halls do perform better academically than those living at home, and students in lodgings do least well. Though there was some evidence in their study that selection of residence students was based partly on scholarship, they instanced one hall in which this was not so, and in which students were selected on need. In this hall students from rural high schools, who are often found to be weaker than other students in university performance, constitute a large group. Yet their performance had, at the time of the study, been surpassing that of students in other halls. The researchers found that the physical comfort and facilities provided in halls were not greatly superior to those in most lodgings, and considered that the superior performance of hall students could be explained by the greater degree of social integration that they enjoyed. Also emancipation from parental overprotection might be a further explanation. This was an Australian study. It is commoner there than in most other countries for young people to stay in the parental home until marriage, and it is likely that parents' influence remains strong throughout the student years for most students living at home. The researchers thought that, for the increasing body of students living in homes with no previous experience of higher education, their rapid acquisition of new ideas and free expression often created tension and conflict in the home, and this often led to discouragement of academic effort and withdrawal of the student from studies.

Schonell (81) found in another Australian university that women residents' performance was markedly inferior to that of women living at home or in lodgings, and for men a similar, though non-significant trend in the same direction was found. For men and women this applied across all academic disciplines. Some women residents performed better than non-residents, and Schonell attributed this to continuous residence in halls which provided adequate tutorial assistance. He considered it may well be that, without adequate tutorial assistance, conditions for study in halls are inferior to those of home or good lodgings, particularly in regard to freedom from distractions.

There are differences between types of halls which confound efforts to generalize. Suddarth, (82) for example, found that students in halls had by far the greatest drop-out rates and the lowest graduation. The second poorest group in academic achievement were those living at home with parents. Next came students living in private homes or apartments. By far the greatest proportion of graduates and least proportion of drop-outs were among students in sororities and fraternities. But several factors combine to produce these clear-cut differences. The most important of these is probably that students are not invited to join fraternities and sororities until late in the first year. As we have seen in other studies, the first year is the critical one for undergraduates : students who survive first year have far higher probability of graduating than the freshman group as a whole, and in many universities the first year serves as a selection device. Therefore, students invited to join sororities and fraternities late in first year are a selected group on that account alone. Secondly, there is a social class bias favouring students of middle-class origins ; and, thirdly, because of the practice of inviting members to join, there is a built-in likelihood that the membership will be homogeneous and mutually supportive. (83) For these reasons it cannot be concluded that the students achieve the best simply because they live in a certain kind of student residence.

Matson (84) found that fraternities of low prestige had a negative effect on student performance, but the drop-out rate was higher for the off-campus group and the residence-hall group than for any of the fraternities. And another point should be considered. It is interesting to speculate, for example, whether students in off-campus groups with the higher drop-out rates were as financially well supported as those in fraternities, and whether lower financial status of off-campus students compelled their withdrawal. Also it is likely that since fraternity and sorority members are generally survivors from first year this ensures that they are academically strong.

Some decrease in the popularity of fraternities and sororities occurred in American universities between 1950 and 1960. Bacig and Sgan (85) offered some hypotheses that might explain the decline and which might well be relevant to thinking about student residence in other places; for example, racial and religious discrimination and other factors which operate in selection for some halls can alienate the students from the rest of the campus culture.

Two other factors are of importance in assessing the influence of students' place of residence upon their performance. These are year of study and student satisfaction with residence, both of which have been already hinted. Whatever kind of residence is open to students, there will be varying degrees of satisfaction, depending upon the individual's personality and his social, academic, and practical needs. A study by Holbraad (86) of 3174 students in most of the British universities showed overall differences in performance between those who were satisfied with their place of living and those who were not. Students were asked if their accommodation was on the whole satisfactory with regard to food, warmth, privacy and quiet, light, bathing facilities, place to study. Forty per cent of satisfied, but only 30 per cent of those who were dissatisfied, received good degrees. Thus students in satisfactory accommodation had 30 per cent higher chance of getting a good degree. The difference was greatest for women. Thirty-seven per cent of those satisfied with their accommodation received good degrees, compared with only 26 per cent in unsatisfactory accommodation. All told, failures were more than twice as high among students in unsatisfactory accommodation. The distance of students' accommodation from the campus made no difference to performance.

Types of accommodation, whether hall, lodgings, or home, produced less marked overall differences in performance than the subjective satisfaction of the student with his living space, but within each university group there were more marked differences. Holbraad considered that generalizations about the relative effects of home, lodgings, and hall residence were not valid except in the context of particular universities. For example, in Oxford and Cambridge those in residence gained a higher proportion of first- and second-class honours than those in lodgings. In London and other English universities there was practically no difference between the degree levels of those living in hall, lodgings, or home. The proportions of best degrees and poor degrees were similarly distributed between all kinds of accommodation. However, delays in taking degrees were related to type of accommodation. Howell (87) found that when students of all universities *who were satisfied with their accommodation* were taken together as one broad group, home-based students least often sat finals, and students in hall contained the highest proportion of those who sat finals on time, in universities other than Oxford, Cambridge, and London. In those three universities students had the same delay rates, whether in home, lodgings, or hall. In Wales students in lodgings received a higher proportion of good degrees than those living in hall; and in most universities other than Oxford, Cambridge, and London students living at home did slightly better than other students.

Howell considered briefly the arguments favouring halls of residence. For example, it is often argued that students living at home, and especially those from working-class homes, are subject to greater tensions and conflicts and are less integrated into university life than students in colleges and halls. Home residence is therefore often thought to be one cause of poor academic performance. Residence in lodgings, on the other hand, is believed to bring a different set of problems, such as low standards of comfort, loneliness, and insecurity, all of which are said to affect performance. It is a common assumption that halls of residence avoid these disadvantages to the student and are more desirable than other types of accommodation because students enjoy a relatively higher standard of comfort and have better opportunities to participate in the corporate life of the student community. On the whole, Howell found that hall residents obtain slightly fewer good results than those in lodgings or at home. On the other hand, they meet with failure slightly less often. The outstanding finding made by Howell and Holbraad was the striking similarity in the performance of students living in different types of accommodation, not the differences. This is summarized in Table 13 overleaf.

It is important to keep in mind that these findings apply only to students who were satisfied with their accommodation. Individual working-class students in noisy homes with no encouragement to study would clearly be at some disadvantage. Similarly, students in poorly run halls unsatisfactory for a variety of reasons, overcrowded, over-disciplined, and with fellow-students not oriented to study would also be disadvantaged. Satisfaction with residence, home, or lodgings seems more important than type of residence, and any study of residence related to performance should include some consideration of students'

TABLE 13

Percentage Distribution of Final Examination Results by Social Class and Third-year Accommodation

Finals Results	Non-manual (as percentage)				Manual (as percentage)			
	Home	Lodgings	Hall	Total	Home	Lodgings	Hall	Total
Good	41	41	38	40	42	40	34	38
Mediocre	54	55	60	57	55	57	63	59
Fail	5	4	2	3	3	3	2	3
(100%) n=	756	2,580	2,160	5,496	290	990	590	1,870

satisfaction with accommodation. Working-class students' performance in Howell's study was less affected by dissatisfaction with accommodation than middle-class students' performance. This could mean that the latter are less adaptable, or that working-class students who manage to get to university are more able. The fact that they are in a smaller minority of their reference group entering higher education suggests the latter may be true. The possibility of further intervening variables cannot be ignored. As Howell pointed out, it is possible that personality differences affect students' choices in where to live. He cited studies which showed that students in lodgings valued the independence made possible by lodgings, and reasoned that those attracted to halls may be more dependent and less mature. This is only speculation, but if it were found that students who sought places in halls were in fact lacking in independence or ability, or any other factor that might affect performance, the fact that these students do no worse in examinations than those in lodgings might mean that residence in hall has a favourable effect on performance. Several recent American studies of freshmen groups have revealed no significant differences in freshmen grades among students in different forms of residences (88). However, Langley (89) found differences between the performance of students according to whether they spent first, second, or final year in residence. In her study students living in college or hall in the first year of studies performed better than those who lived at home or in lodgings, but in second and third year students living at home performed better than hall residents. Those living in lodgings did less well in first year than the hall

178

and home-based students. In the third year the situation was reversed, and students in lodgings performed better academically than either the home-based or the hall students. These findings suggest that students in first year benefit academically by being in residence, because they require some cushioning of the shock of having independence while still young. Going into lodgings is perhaps too large a step for young people of freshman age, and it may be that where conflict between ethos of the home and that of the university exists, this can be ameliorated by the student taking up residence. The advantages of first-year residence are probably greatest for students from rural centres and foreign countries, but all students are likely to benefit from the opportunity to become oriented to the university or college situation at this early stage.

By third year students are more mature and independent. They have had time to streamline their study methods and have learnt to organize their social life and living needs, and will have learnt from others how to find suitable flats or lodgings better than they could have done at 17 or 18 years of age. They should have learnt by then how to cope with and to make use of independence, and it is reasonable that, given the experience of a year or two in residence, they would be ready to seek opportunities to be independent. By comparison, students still seeking places in halls may well be lacking in independence and enterprise. In so far as these are correlates of academic performance, which they may well be, it is not surprising that third-year students in lodgings perform better than those still in halls or at home. This hypothesis requires confirmation by empirical investigation.

In the literature little mention is made of the staffing of halls of residence. Horle and Gazda's study, noted in the previous section, showed that in some American colleges staffing in student residences left a great deal to be desired. The Niblett Report (90) emphasized that the quality of the staff was crucial if halls of residence were to fulfil their educative function, and called for wiser selection and higher status to be given to staff members who are prepared to live and work in halls. If it is agreed that halls can or should be regarded as instruments in the educative process, either in the academic or in the more general or liberal sense, then staff should be most carefully selected and greater encouragement given to suitable people.

Whatever the uses of student residence, it seems certain that there will be increasing demand for residential accommodation in one form or another in almost every country. The Robbins Committee's estimates of future demand for higher education in Britain were much higher than anything envisaged in the past, and appeared exaggerated to a great number of informed and experienced educationists, yet the demand already is even greater than the Robbins projections forecast. Similar dramatic increases in demand are occurring everywhere in the world. It is imperative to consider, therefore, what *kinds* of student accommodation are likely to encourage the best academic performance. This consideration is at least as important as the practical considerations of having somewhere where students can reside and the more fundamental purpose of fostering the general education of students.

Discussing investment in college housing in America, Riker (91) has reported that college and university enrolment has doubled in ten years.

> Numbers and expansion have often shifted student housing into a warehousing operation. . . . Plans for new construction have boiled down to the question of how many students can be bedded down. . . . Other than his desk and a few text books in students' rooms nothing about the typical residence hall will suggest that the building is an educational facility and part of an educational plan.

There is a great deal of discussion but very little research about how to plan halls of residence as educational units.

Riker continues:

> Nothing about some hall climates serves to stimulate students to investigate some features of the academic life. . . . The bright recreation room says "You are here to play". The expensive lounge says "You are here to relax". The long corridors and congested lobbies say "You are really not very important here". The disciplinary system and staff procedures state flatly, "You are juvenile." Typically but with exceptions, this is the climate that surrounds [many students in halls].

Riker claims that many halls are designed merely as comfortable shelters, the planners not having conceived of the housing unit as an educational building, and that administrators frequently see control and discipline of the student as the chief educational function of halls. Riker sees halls of residence as having an intellectually stimulating role and, ideally, as being designed in such a way that anti-intellectualism cannot grow.

Boyer's study (92) of student peer groups in residence suggests that student needs for affiliation and environmental press of the school for achievement frequently conflict. In a peer group where play is emphasized more than study it can be difficult for a student high on need for affiliation to do satisfactory work. But if the same student is in a group where study rather than play is emphasized, and acceptance and mutual respect are high, performance tends to be enhanced. Studies of the formation of small groups may lead to some suggestions about how students can be allocated to minimize excessive anti-intellectual orientation. In Boyer's study it seemed that persisting patterns of behaviour developed very early in the semester, probably in the first six weeks. It is conceivable that studies of the kind Boyer suggests could identify some of the more wasteful errors in planning and organization of residence. It may be that flats, bed-sitting-rooms, study towers shared between residents and non-residents, student houses on the campus for study, and other activities for home and lodgings-based students, or traditional houses arranged in small, flexible suites, serve academic purposes better than halls planned in the traditional manner. It may also be that students achieve better in those halls in which they have the responsibility for self-discipline rather than in those where discipline is imposed on them. This hypothesis may be related to age, sex, and academic discipline.

Student preferences change, and it would perhaps be prudent to allow for flexibility in physical planning of student accommodation. Schonell (93) reports that there has been a change in students with regard to residential requirements in recent years, increasing numbers perferring to live in flats. In Britain the same trend is noticeable, and planning for student requirements is allowing for these changes.

The few researches studied suggest that the greatest attention should be given to the special needs of vulnerable groups, the potential drop-outs, students from families indifferent or hostile to higher education, rural students who find it hard to integrate, and first-year students in particular. It should be ensured as far as possible that students will be satisfied with their accommodation with respect to privacy and quiet (not always to be taken for granted in halls), light, heating, bathing facilities, food, and place of study. In private homes, lodgings, and flats these are the aspects in which shortcomings are most often found.

Instruments such as those developed by Pace and Stern (94) to measure college environments, the College Characteristics Index, need to be used in research likely to reveal which type of student residence will facilitate academic achievement. After reviewing a large body of literature Yonge (95) concluded that the systematic study of interaction between students and their environment, and the dynamic analysis which this made possible may be considered a major break-through in the study of students in higher education. Our knowledge of the residence correlates of academic performance is limited, but we may discover much more as dynamic interactional studies of students in their institutional context become more common.

Schools and Preparation of Students for Higher Education

In so far as the main body of research into academic performance has centred upon student and institutional variables, the relationship between performance and antecedent variables has been comparatively disregarded. Antecedents can be critical, and those which are capable of being observed at the school stage merit greater attention from researchers. It is curious that, though preparation of candidates for higher education is done in schools and the results of examinations in school subjects constitute a major part of selection criteria, so little thought has been given to the study of schools and the ways in which they prepare young people for higher studies.

From the limited number of studies it is possible to review in this section, some patterns emerge which suggest that modes of teaching in schools may have a strong influence on students' later performance in higher education. Types of academic orientation also appear to play a role, differences having been noted between types of school in the way they stress rigorous concentrated and convergent study attitudes on one hand, and evolution of general academic interest on the other. There appears to be an overall difference in these respects between public schools (meaning broadly those financed by local authorities in England and state governments in the United States and Australia) and private schools.

In the United States, Britain, and Australia there is more than suggestive evidence that students from 'state schools' or their equivalents and those from direct-grant schools achieve the best academic results. Though the differences are not enormous they are consistent between the three countries and between several studies in Britain. So far as men are concerned, Tables 157 and 158 from the Franks Report (96) are representative of findings.

TABLE 14

Degree Performance by Type of School—1006 *Men Graduates and* 162 *Women Graduates who entered the University of Oxford* 1958–59

Type of School	Sex	1st Class	2nd Class	3rd Class	4th Class	Other
Independent	Men	7.8	47.9	37.3	3.8	3.3
Boarding	Women	10.0	60.0	26.7	3.3	—
Independent	Men	11.5	57.5	27.6	2.3	1.1
Day	Women	5.6	55.6	27.8	5.6	5.6
Direct Grant	Men	12.1	53.9	29.8	3.5	0.7
	Women	7.0	62.8	18.6	7.0	4.7
Maintained	Men	9.8	61.8	24.6	3.5	0.3
	Women	—	55.4	43.1	1.5	—

Source: Tables 157 and 158 from *Report of Commission of Inquiry*, vol. 2 (Oxford University Press, 1966).

The table shows that male students from independent boarding-schools were awarded the least proportion of firsts and seconds and easily the greatest proportion of third- and fourth-class degrees. Students from independent and direct-grant schools led the field in firsts, and students from maintained schools, while not achieving the greatest proportion of firsts, achieved the greatest percentage of firsts and seconds taken together and the least proportion of thirds and lower. It is important, however, to note that women's results were generally the reverse of men's, with best performance from women who had attended independent boarding-schools: those from maintained schools received the least proportion of first- and second-class degrees, but also the least proportion of fourth and other degrees.

Howell's national study (97) of 13,471 students resulted in similar conclusions regarding men students; his most outstanding finding was the poor performance of the boarding-school men. His finding was the more remarkable because these included a large number of college scholars who can be expected to do well. Howell cited other studies by Evans, Worswick, and Malleson

(98) which supported his own. Malleson found striking differences also in the proportions of students at University College, London, from different kinds of schools, who failed to graduate. The highest failure rate was among students from independent schools: 27.8 per cent failed to graduate, compared with only 12 per cent from grammar and direct-grant schools (difference significant at the .01 level). Malleson thought this might be explained by the possibility that the best students from independent schools go to Oxford, but since the Franks Report on the University of Oxford came to similar conclusions for Oxford to those of Malleson at University College, that explanation is not sustained. At the opposite extreme Malleson (99) also found that, as well as having a smaller failure rate, 11 per cent of students from State-sponsored grammar schools obtained first-class honours, compared with 3 per cent from independent boarding-schools and 9 per cent from direct-grant schools. The grammar-school group also had a much higher proportion accepted for postgraduate studies. In two separate studies Marris (100) and Himmelweit (101) made similar findings at other English universities.

Two other variables may be affecting the British findings, social class and ability. Malleson thought that pressures to achieve exerted on middle-class boys might be excessive and harmful. There is an alternative to that possibility: students from grammar schools are more highly selected for ability than those from independent schools, and they are thus more likely to achieve the better results. These interpretations should be treated with caution, however, because, as we have seen in the earlier section on ability, there seems to be a threshold effect, and ability is not all-important above a certain level. Himmelweit thought that the inferior performance of independent-school boys might be accounted for by their lesser motivation.

Whatever additional variables may be influencing the British findings, we must still take account of findings in America and Australia. MacArthur (102) in the United States has found repeatedly that students from public ('state-supported') schools achieve better results than those from private schools, and Hogben (103) found the same to be true of a group of Australian medical students. MacArthur went so far as to claim that the public-private dichotomy excels all psychological variables, and cited other studies showing that the performance of public (state) school graduates was superior to that of private-school graduates when I.Q. was held constant, and that these differences remain even when scholastic aptitude and grades are comparable for the two groups. He suggested that I.Q. profiles were different for each group, that private-school boys were more socially and aesthetically oriented than state-school boys, and that state-school boys were more science- and success-oriented. He also links his findings with social class. He suggested, in Florence Kluckhohn's terminology, that higher-middle-class boys are more 'being-oriented' and lower-middle-class boys are more 'doing-oriented'. While the latter measure themselves by achievement, the former measure themselves by personality and social criteria. Values associated with 'being' and 'doing' involve different aspects of education. Thus, more doing-oriented boys enter college with a clear choice of major study, often in technology, and get an 'A'; the being-oriented come up with a vague choice, usually in the humanities, and settle for a gentleman's 'C'.

Differences undoubtedly exist between schools in different countries, but the question whether they are publicly or privately organized, though of sociological and educational interest, is of secondary importance compared with differences in the kinds of academic interest they foster. 'Being-orientation' and 'doing-orientation' are probably useful concepts because they represent very different educational objectives, each valid in its own way. There are, however, other aspects of schools which in the present context are more relevant. The aspect which has attracted most attention is what schools might do to prepare students for learning from internal motivation, curiosity, and initiative in the demanding, though relatively unstructured situation of university or college.

In an extensive review of the literature Summerskill (104) considered that we need to know a great deal more about candidates' preparation for the job of scholarship, an area scarcely touched by research.

He cited a study by Mercer (105) which showed that ratings on students' intellectual and working characteristics predicted college success better than other personality characteristics or assessments by secondary-school principals. The question raised by this research is what schools do to help students develop these characteristics. It is not reasonable to suppose that students who have been closely supervised and crammed in school will suddenly become self-propelled when they enter college or university.

The Hale Report (106) on teaching methods made this point clearly in 1964. It stated:

> The magnitude of the leap forward depends . . . partly on the extent to which his school has launched him on the process of thinking for himself . . . even at the best students coming to a university straight from school find themselves suddenly saddled with more responsibility for ordering their lives than they have had to take before; and in their approach to their subjects many, perhaps most, students on entry to university have hardly got beyond the stage of taking their opinions from authority and expecting to find the 'right' answers to all questions in a textbook. [Para. 94.]

Other writers have regretted the fact that students come to university with an unsuitable approach to learning. Forster (107), for example, thought that among the many factors which may account for failure to fulfil high academic promise could be included the fact that students have not learned the art of independent study.

> Ideally, universities ought to be able to take for granted that all their students, by the time of admission, are able to plan and pursue studies without close supervision and direction; to exercise a measure of independent and critical judgement when faced with new material and ideas, to make full use of the library. . . . In practice, many students arrive at the university without this basic equipment, and even a promising school leaving examination may sometimes reflect an exceptional aptitude for cramming and rote memory rather than a developed capacity for thought and judgement.

There can be no doubt that students in some schools experience kinds of teaching and atmosphere which encourage dependence upon the teacher rather than self-motivation, initiative, and independence. This is no preparation for university studies. The Derbyshire study (108) named inability to study at a higher level (in spite of good school results) as a source of wastage. There would be much point in study of the kinds of school teaching which the best and poorest higher-education students received while at school. Australian writers (109) have also referred to the problem of the abruptness of the change from the school regime to the university, and the fact that some students appear to have been crammed, over-coached, and over-protected in schools, and are ill-prepared in their attitude towards study and immature in their ability to seek out knowledge for themselves. Olsen stressed the need for a year at school before entering university in which teachers who also had the knowledge and skills, and were willing, would have time to conduct discussion groups and to stimulate students to discover information for themselves through small research projects and giving papers. Pond (110) found that students who had acquired this sort of initiative and knowledge were generally the high achievers in the crucial first year. By contrast, low achievers were more primitive and random in their study methods.

Dale (111) considered that a professional pride in his pupils' examination results leads the mediocre teacher to use spoon-feeding methods which so condition the pupil that he is ill-adapted to the individual study methods of the university. Relying on A levels and interviews for selecting candidates, universities do not discover whether students have any real understanding of what is learnt and what is their capacity for independent learning until after they have begun their university studies. Schonell (112) believes that the major solution lies in teaching and encouraging students to think for themselves. "If schools adopt cramming methods . . . and if teaching methods do not involve something of the Socratic approach with periods for discussion, undue emphasis will often be placed on memorizing." At worst such methods can amount to the exclusion of active learning, thinking, and reasoning. Schonell cited evidence that where teachers are better trained and their teaching is more permissive and less authoritarian, placing more responsibility upon students to develop their own study methods, and where discipline is based on co-operative working with less punishment for errors in work, the scholars from such schools tend to do better in surmounting the first-year hurdle of university. By contrast, students from regimented schools tend to take longer to adjust to university, and the probability that they will not survive the first year is greater. Dale suggested that student failure may be due to reaction to the strain of gaining requisite A-level results and the sudden change to the self-discipline of university studies. There is also the possibility that in school the students have been pushed along to high-level school performance and specialization by external pressure from their teachers and parents rather than by internal motivation and curiosity. Carr-Saunders (113) made the point that whereas success at the university depends upon exploring interest, wide-ranging curiosity, and initiative, the examinations on which selection to university is based tend to over-emphasize capacity for absorption. Laslett (114) found at Cambridge that an appreciable proportion of open-entrance scholars, though they obtained good results in first year, did less well thereafter, whereas many students who did not gain entrance awards did gradually better as they progressed through university. These studies suggest that cramming, though it may achieve its purpose in getting the candidate a place, is ultimately inferior to the less rigid preparation of students, which, though not so effective in gaining places for candidates, has the merit of keeping their minds open and flexible, enabling them to overtake the others through the university years.

These ideas are, to some extent tentative. Research findings are not plentiful in this area, but they are certainly more than suggestive. Apart from the recognition that more research is necessary, we can draw some other conclusions. We can recognize that students fail for social, psychological, personal, economic, and environmental reasons. However, as Olsen (115) wrote, success in university is dependent upon skills and knowledge acquired in schools. Schools which give opportunity and encouragement to students to develop independent learning habits and do not impose straitjacketed thinking, nor confine their preparation for university to a search for the 'right' answers, seem to produce better undergraduates.

There is a conspicuous dearth of research into sixth-form teaching as preparation for higher education. Close supervision of sixth-formers may be necessary to prevent any possible deterioration in morale extending downwards to lower forms. If these fears are justified this would support the case for separate sixth-form or junior colleges which has been debated over many years in Britain. Apart from required academic standards, an entry would be largely self-selected in the sense that students would be making a declaration of intent to finish their secondary education or to prepare for university or college. Once accepted into sixth-form colleges, students would be taught under quasi-university conditions, not crammed or over-supervised, but encouraged to think and reason as well as to remember. The students who dropped out or failed because they could not achieve under these conditions would likely be the same ones who would have failed in university or have had to be led by the hand throughout. By contrast it is likely that the survivors of such a year would be the most stable and persistent students and would use their university places to greater effect. The essence of the sixth-form college as the present writer conceives it would be in its mode of teaching through seminars and individual and group assignments. Another important aspect would be respect for the independence which older youths rightly demand as part of the process of assuming adult responsibilities, which would be encouraged by the absence of uniforms and the sometimes foot-ling rules and regimentation. Many young people consider these childish enough to affect adversely the decisions of young people to stay on at school. They can scarcely be held up as important factors in preparation for university. Ian McMullen, (116) director of the Resources for Learning project at the Nuffield Foundation, reporting on his studies of secondary education in several countries, maintains that secondary-school children can be left alone in small groups to work independently. He suggests, for example, that half the pupils' time could be spent in class groups, a quarter in seminar groups, and a quarter in indepen-dent study, the last-named being used for following up assign-ments arising out of class or group work, to be completed within a limited period and requiring reference to books, slides, tapes, and the teachers. Two possible advantages of these methods over a more didactic approach are that the children become more internally motivated or inner-directed, and that increasingly rare resources of good sixth-form teachers can be distributed more efficiently, which is reassuring at a time when sixth forms are proliferating. The National Extension College has shown that even by correspondence children are capable of independent study in some subjects. Studies reviewed in earlier sections suggest that school teaching which brings out these qualities in pupils can have an important influence upon students' aptitude for higher education.

The onus to improve student quality cannot be placed only upon schools. Universities and teachers' colleges can clearly make a contribution. The criticisms of teaching in secondary schools in the Hale Report and those of Dale and researchers in Australia provide material for serious thought about what can or should be done to correct the situation. The consensus of several studies is that, at the secondary level, pupils are 'taught', even crammed, but not nearly often enough 'taught how to learn'. Colleges of education in Britain have for many years impressed upon student teachers the need of the child to learn through discovering rather than to be 'taught'; they have been so emphatic about this as to risk and sometimes to attract ill-informed criticism for 'airy-fairiness'. Since only a minority of teachers from colleges of education enter secondary education it is not surprising that the benefits have been felt principally in primary schools.

It is commonplace to assume that a degree qualifies a person to teach at secondary level. Apart from those graduate teachers who have completed a postgraduate certificate in education or the equivalent, there are many who must be forced to rely heavily upon their own school experience to enlighten them in their approach to the art of teaching. The assumption that because the graduate has studied his subject in depth he can impart that knowledge appears rash; moreover, it ignores the question of whether the teacher in a secondary school should do more than teach his 'subject'. Education of pupils towards open-minded curiosity, thirst for knowledge, and free critical thought in the search for understanding may be left to chance in some instances. To the extent that this is so, perhaps it helps us to understand why 'promising' students with high A levels come to university or college and fail to fulfil their promise—unfit for independent learning in a setting less structured than school.

Children in primary schools are encouraged to learn through discovery, and university students are certainly expected to do the same at a higher level. It is odd, then, to assume that intellectual initiative and curiosity at the secondary level can suddenly flower in the sixth form and the first year in the university if they have not been nurtured in the earlier years. If the memoranda given to the Hale Committee by the National Union of Students and the Scottish Union of Students are accepted (and the Hale Report gave some weight to them), it seems that too much spoon-feeding occurs even in sixth forms. Olsen's study (117) led to his belief that universities can help to reduce wastage by co-operating more with schools in their task of preparing students for higher education, and Schonell (118) has taken this up. It is not enough for universities to complain about the inability of new students to study independently when they enter the university. As Schonell put it, any system of higher education depends upon an incoming student population that has been well taught at school. Yet universities are too stuffy still about teacher-training, though the quality of their students depends on effective teacher-training.

The responsibilities of universities and schools of education in the education of graduates for teaching careers is also discussed by Tibble. (119) The absence of education from the undergraduate curriculum to which he refers is deplorable. Nice arguments about whether education is a discipline, and, if it is not, that it must necessarily be excluded from university undergraduate studies, appear irrelevant. Exclusion must strike at the foundation of education. In Britain the inauguration of degrees in education is welcomed as a sign that universities are beginning to view their responsibilities *vis-à-vis* education at least as seriously as they view preparation for the professions of science, law, medicine, and engineering. The extent to which they do so, and the extent to which they accept that the quality of incoming students in general depends upon the effective education of teachers, must be reflected in the quality of students entering universities in future years.

Lord James of Rusholme, Vice-Chancellor of the University of York, summed it up very succinctly: "The absolute error of the universities over the past twenty years has been the failure to realize that to get good people from school good people are needed in the schools to teach them originally."*

Examinations

Over the years there has been critical inquiry about the reliability of examinations and their efficiency in fulfilling their supposed purposes. There have been suggestions for experimentation and possible improvements or alternatives, and much questioning about the criteria which are applied in judging this usefulness. The Hartog and Rhodes studies (120) of the 1930's are still quoted in discussion of the limitations of essay-type examinations in schools. Differences in estimates of examiners give rise to inaccuracy, and although studies of examinations are not very common, there is enough material to suggest that continued awareness of examiners regarding the limitations of examinations and further study of the problems of examining could lead to greater improvement in examinations and perhaps reduction in wastage.

---

* Cited in *The Times Educational Supplement*, November 3rd, 1967.

This question of the relationship between examinations and wastage is closely associated with the problem of 'policies' on pass rates and productivity in higher education, because examination results are the main criteria upon which decisions are made about the proportions of students to retain and the proportions to be sent down, and hence whether they should be admitted to their intended professions. Cox's review of the literature (121) has provoked a great deal of informed and frank thought in British institutions of higher education, and an issue of the *Universities Quarterly* (vol. 21, June 3rd, 1967) was devoted to the problem of examining in universities. Typical criticisms of examinations are: (i) much examining is inconsistent and arbitrary, (ii) they measure merely the examination-passing ability of the candidate, placing too high a premium on speed and fluency and the short-term memory, (iii) they do an injustice to the slow but more thoughtful worker, and (iv) we do not know exactly what the purposes of examinations are, what they are meant to measure, whether they measure what we think they measure, their relation to what lies in the student's future, and if, indeed, they should be regarded as relevant to it.

Universities are meant to have objectives other than training students to pass academic examinations. Knowledge for its own sake is important, but discipline of the mind, enjoyment of intellectual and cultural activity regardless of examinations, tolerance of complexity, curiosity and liberal-mindedness, and a distaste for dogmatism, are a few of the intellectual, social, and moral qualities which many still think universities are intended to foster. Unless examinations sample at least some of these qualities it is possible even for students who have profited in other than purely academic ways to be failed in their finals, thus barring them from working in fields for which they might be eminently suited. At the same time it is possible that those who have profited the least from the social, moral, and cultural objectives of higher education will be among those successful in their examinations and welcomed into their chosen fields. Success and failure in the student role should bear some relation to performance of adult roles. As Lavin (122) has put it, "An important feature of the student role is its transitional character. . . . If career success, critical-mindedness and creativity [and the values mentioned above] are valuable for a variety of personal and societal goals, what is the meaning of grades? . . . There is a question as to why and for what grades are important." Any assumption that students who obtain high grades are more intellectually curious or possessors of any of the above-mentioned other qualities has yet to be proven. If higher education is concerned with producing these qualities educationists may have to pay attention to criteria other than grades in examinations as they are now generally conceived. Lavin puts another question : are the more eminent people in science or commerce necessarily those whose college performance was exemplary, as indexed by examination results? Evidence by MacKinnon (123) in America and Hudson (124) in Britain shows that the two do not necessarily coincide, and Holland (125) also found that factors which predict high examination performance tend to be negatively associated with creativity. Examinations are sometimes a blunt instrument for predicting graduates' potential in their professions. If we believe that one of the important aspects of education at the university and elsewhere is the development of social and moral values, we may well wonder if these should receive more attention from examiners. It is highly questionable if dons should attempt to assess social and moral development, and even dangerous, yet ethical standards are demanded of graduates in medicine and law, and a case could be made for some equivalent requirements in other professions.

Lavin (126) summed up this important aspect of the problem of examinations :

If grades will not predict future eminence and if the early identification of outstanding talent is a task worth pursuing, there is a need to develop additional criteria of good student performance. . . . As soon as education is considered in the context of certain societal values and needs, it is evident that in addition to grades, other dimensions of student behaviour need to be considered. . . . Grades are not unimportant . . . but within the context of some personal and societal goals [and some supposed objectives of higher education] reliance upon grades as the *only* criterion of student performance is unwarranted.

Bearing these arguments in mind, so long as grades are the sole criterion for assigning students to wastage, objection to preoccupation with grades must be even stronger. Piaget (127) wrote :

The two essential defects in examining are that it does not

as a rule produce objective results and that it inevitably becomes an end in itself. . . . It implies an element of chance and . . . lays more stress on memory than on constructive capacities. . . . Anyone can verify how little the classification based on examination results corresponds to the contribution made by individuals in later life.

What of the more mechanical aspects of examining, even assuming that examination criteria are perfect for their purpose? One of the more outstanding aspects which have a very direct bearing upon wastage is rigidity of examination procedures. In some courses students are required to pass all their examinations each year before proceeding to the next year. There are probably administrative reasons for this which are sound in the immediate sense, but which are more difficult to justify in the wider sense, in terms of students and productivity. *Rigid* adherence to a pass mark, especially where this is in one subject only of a particular course, can be wasteful of places. Such rigidity must have the effect of depriving candidates in the succeeding year of places which would otherwise have been open. The cost to the university of having to provide marginal candidates with places for an additional year unnecessarily, to the individual students and their families in having to support themselves for an extra year, and to society in being deprived of badly needed professionals for a further year must be considerable. Some of these students may have been obliged to drop out permanently, producing a permanent deprivation of society and of the economy of professional people, and wasting the financial investment which had been made in them in providing them with places up to the time of failure. More reasonable procedures could be developed to supersede this rather savage one of failing students for a whole year because of poor showing in one subject.

In addition to rigidity is a near relation which is probably farther-reaching in its contribution to wastage and more dangerously persistent because it is, for the most part, unconsciously applied. Pass rates and wastage rates are often extraordinarily stable over long periods within departments. Vernon (128) has referred to this as a well-known phenomenon in universities and technical colleges, and further, that one department may differ quite arbitrarily from another in the same institution. The phenomenon has also been noted by several researchers in Australian universities. (129) In one institution it was found that failure rates in different departments varied between 5 per cent and 70 per cent, and courses with high failure rates tended to have similar high failure rates in successive years. As selection standards rise, which they inevitably do as pressure for places increases, it should be possible, other things being equal, to fail fewer students and to raise the pass rate. However, Hohne (130) found that failure rates did not improve concomitantly with student quality. University examiners passed and failed almost identical proportions of students year after year instead of ascertaining the true calibre of their students and adjusting failure rates accordingly. Hohne thought there must be fixed departmental pass policies to account for this otherwise puzzling failure of demonstrably better prepared students. Vernon too noted that if the pass rate is raised it usually soon regresses to its traditional value. Vernon sees this as an inevitable characteristic of the subjectivity inherent in our marking of examination papers. Hughes (131) in Australia and Forster (132) in Britain are others who have discussed the responsibility of the universities themselves for unnecessary wastage, particularly this problem of stable pass rates and ways of making objective assessments of examination candidates in times when student quality is manifestly improving.

Dale (133) considers that the principal reason for the wide variation between facilities in degree standards lies in the subject-matter, and that in subjects with a high mathematical content there is a greater spread of marks than in subjects like English and history, where the essay type of answer is more common. In between these come classical and foreign languages, so that unless there is conscious correction on the part of university examiners it is likely there will be more firsts in mathematical and science subjects, while in subjects examined by the less objective essay-type methods there will be a greater band of mediocrity in terms of given marks. In fairness to students, Dale made a plea that universities examine the possibility of finding a rough approximation to equity between faculties and departments.

Returning to the more central problem of gross wastage rather than gradations of academic success, there is the question of constantly raising the standards expected in examinations. A very real argument can always be made for raising standards in any enterprise, but this must affect wastage levels in higher education. Venables (134) has noted instances in which, despite the entry of better-prepared students, examiners graded candidates according to their own concept of the normal curve and an agreed cut-off. The 'good' teacher produces students with above-average attainment in his particular subject, but it is possible that he will deprive them of this advantage by setting papers of above-average difficulty or marking them according to the 'normal' curve.

It is, of course, nonsense to grade candidates according to some notion of the normal curve because the candidates are already highly selected by virtue of their achieving a place in an institution of higher education, and the normal curve is not appropriate for such a group except in the fancy of the examiner. If all the students in a year were excellent, and this must be the case sometimes, it would be foolishly unfair to the candidate, and wasteful in terms of scarce university resources and public money, to assign any student to wastage. Cunningham (135) made a further point on the question of standards: "Those who defend high failure rates are almost sure to say 'it is unfortunate, but those who failed were simply not up to standard'. . . . Whose standard? . . . How was it arrived at?" He argued that the fixing of some level of difficulty between so easy a course that all pass, and so difficult a course that all fail, is an arbitrary matter, and that the only criterion for setting standards is what the actual body of students is found to be able to achieve under efficient teaching. He suggested that the standard for a selected group such as university students should be low enough to secure a pass for practically all students who work well and who work under satisfactory conditions. If the question of growth of knowledge arises, or increased content in the syllabus, it can be dealt with equitably by lengthening courses or by better teaching or by dropping outmoded sections of the course. The Robbins Committee recommended the review of first degree courses periodically to prevent overloading (Robbins Report, Recommendation 13). Limiting the number of passes to a few exceptional students who can stand the pace, as happens in some colleges and departments, must contribute unnecessarily to wastage of students themselves, and wastage of resources in providing places under unsatisfactory conditions.

The problem of pass ratios is essentially the same whether the proportion passed is large or small. The question is on what basis are the pass ratios decided? It is probably true that if no student fails in any course for several years academic standards may fall, but there can be little justification for failing good students just in case some relax their effort. 'Raising standards' can sometimes be a euphemism for failing more students, just as 'keeping up standards' can be a euphemism for a policy of failing a certain percentage each year. Apart from student discipline, there seems little justification, if any, for an established ratio of pass rates, because it ensures that some good students may be failed, and, in the absence of accurate objective tests, it rests upon the supposed ability of examiners, as Dale has put it, "to carry in their heads unchanged from year to year, and from one examination paper to another, an exact conception of a 40 per cent pass mark."

There is no ready solution to the problems of examining. It is easy to criticize examinations, but more difficult to improve them or suggest alternatives. The purpose of this discussion is to focus attention upon the implications of unnecessarily failing students and to point out possible sources of avoidable wastage. The Robbins Report (136) (paras. 580–581) summarized the aspect of examinations discussed here and policies on pass rates in the following terms:

> Differences in wastage rates are not explicable solely in terms of the quality of students admitted or in terms of the way they are taught. It is difficult to avoid the presumption that an important factor affecting wastage is that in some faculties there is an approximate percentage of students whom it has been customary to fail. This supposition is borne out by the fact that wastage rates have remained nearly constant in faculties whose entrance standards are known to have risen. In so far as there are grounds for this presumption they should be removed. It is essential that a student should feel confident that his success or failure depends only upon his ability and attainments.

Cunningham's statement is relevant in this context: "the only criterion . . . in determining pass and fail rates, and hence wastage, is what the typical student, who is usually in the top 12 per cent of ability, can compass in view of the total work load the university allows, or requires, him to carry." It should be an essential part of the responsibility of any university department towards its students to investigate this problem carefully, as the Robbins Report suggests.

Returning to the question of the purposes of examinations and leaving aside the more general objectives of higher education, let us consider what academic purposes they should serve and ask if they can be modified in acceptable ways to make them more valid. Bloom's (137) taxonomy of educational objectives falls, so far as the cognitive area is concerned, into the following major classes: knowledge, recall of material directly taught; comprehension of the material and its application in a new situation; analysis and breakdown into essential components; synthesis or the assembly of previously learned material into something new; and evaluation involving judgments. In so far as an examination does not sample whichever of these are appropriate for a given subject, failure of students and hence wastage is ill-based. Examinations are seldom as well designed in these terms as they might be. Fensham (138) has described an experiment in examining first-year chemistry students by traditional methods and a method using Bloom's criteria. Although there was no great difference in the pass-fail ratio, there were differences in the number of honours grades. In subjects less formal than chemistry, there might well be differences in the pass-fail ratio. If we could establish further criteria for validity of examinations we might revise our ideas about how they could be modified to reduce wastage. If, for example, we think they should be purely tests of the amount of ivory-tower knowledge students have acquired, then they should perhaps be left well alone, and there might be a strong case for that. But should they also be tests of the ability to synthesize and to be creative? Should they be tests of research ability? This is one of the uses to which they are put. Or should they assess professional promise in those fields for which the major study has made it most likely the student will enter?

Upon the answers to these questions will depend the kind of examinations that will be required, the rigour with which they are marked, and the degree of wastage through academic failure which will be permissible. If it is agreed that a student's professional promise should be a criterion of examination success, then it might be wrong to 'waste' him because he failed in a highly theoretical paper that has little to do with his probable future career. If the essential requirement of a profession were that the student should be able to synthesize and think clearly it would be foolish to 'waste' him because of failure in an examination testing his memory of factual material on a certain day.

However important memory may be, it cannot be regarded as a principal and universal criterion. If the capacity to work persistently and to seek out data is required for the kind of work he is most likely to do it might be incorrect to fail him because of failure in examinations requiring speed under stress. Because pursuit of knowledge is the main end of education these examples will be regarded as heresy by many, and perhaps rightly so, but there is a case for some common ground between the academic world and that outside because there are several kinds of knowledge. If it is known what sort of profession the student will enter, some occasional compromise to avoid wastage may be in order.

Cunningham (139) put this argument very cogently. Many university courses are taken by people having vocational objectives in mind, such as medicine, architecture, teaching, chemistry, law, music, engineering, business administration, and possibly, to a less definite degree, psychology, sociology, economics, public administration, and town planning. Since some of these fields and professions cannot be entered without the appropriate university qualification, the act of passing or failing students becomes, in effect, a decision that they can or cannot practise the profession in question. The act of failing a student on some of these courses, or in one of the subjects he must 'get' to complete the course, is tantamount to declaring that the student in question is not fitted to practise his profession in the community. The question might seriously be asked whether the university or college is in a position to make such a declaration with any confidence. It is possible that in some departments there is little interest in the more pedestrian students who nevertheless have the ability to become satisfactory professionals. Academic courses can sometimes become remote from the practical world, and it is conceivable that excellent practitioners are lost because we rely too heavily on the criterion of examination success or the examination ability of the student.

The arguments of the 'consumers' must also be considered. If corporations and government agencies are to be deprived of graduates because students are failed on strictly academic criteria, is this completely justifiable? Industrialists sometimes claim that students are assessed on purely academic criteria. For example, it was feasible for Sir David Pye (140) to entitle his Presidential Address to the Institution of Mechanical Engineers

(1952) "The Yawning Gap between the University Graduate and the Competent Engineer". In 1964 Bosworth (141) wrote that students are conditioned to reject the professional approach to such an extent that they are "often unwilling to concentrate on the job in hand. They are further conditioned to think that a job is only a stepping stone to something better, and therefore not worthy of whole-hearted effort. The industrial impression of the graduate as a passive bystander, not willing to work, is not entirely unfounded."

This criticism of graduates is not confined to engineers. Sir Paul Chambers, (142) the former Chairman of Imperial Chemical Industries, said in 1964:

Some top-rank public schools and university colleges produce men of brilliant academic achievement who have poor judgment, no power of decision and no capacity to delegate work or to control men . . . their deficiencies are not revealed in their academic record and are hard to detect at a selection interview. . . . On the other hand, the same schools and colleges can produce second-rate graduates who are first-rate men with all the characteristics I have listed. . . . All aspects of education are important—the acquisition of knowledge, the development of the power of thinking and reasoning, specialized vocational training, the inculcation of moral values and the development of all those elements of character which enable a man to work effectively and harmoniously with his fellow workers. . . . How often have I met men of high academic achievement . . . [being] sheltered from the harsh need to make important decisions which has left them timid and irresolute, or stubborn for fear of making a mistake. . . . In some men of high intellectual ability there is failure of another kind. Concentration and success in a narrow field . . . can lead to an arrogance which reveals itself in a contempt for the problems of other and broader fields. The pure scientist who is infected in this way will regard applied work as needing a lower standard of intelligence. He will also regard the problems of management, and of working harmoniously in a heterogeneous team, as non-existent or just simple matters to be dealt with *ad hoc* by anybody with average intelligence.

What have these opinions of distinguished industrialists to do with examinations? Surely, a great deal. It is doubtful if they will be shrugged off by any with the slightest realism who feel there should be even a remote connection between what goes on in a university and what goes on outside.

Ought university examiners to pass *only* graduates who are strong theoretically with little interest in applying that knowledge and who are perhaps unwilling to work in groups across disciplinary boundaries? The reluctance of graduates who are blinkered to their own learning and who are unwilling to come to terms with workers in disciplines other than their own, or unwilling to work with people whom they do not recognize even as having a 'discipline', is clearly to be seen in many interdisciplinary situations, and can amount to philistinism concerning others' academic interests: it could be called academic bigotry. John Gardner,* former United States Secretary of Health, Education and Welfare, once said, "The average department holds on like grim death to its piece of intellectual terrain. It teaches its neophytes a jealous devotion to the boundaries of its field. It assesses the significance of intellectual questions by the extent to which they can be answered without going outside the sacred territory." And Jencks and Riesman in their *The Academic Revolution* have referred to academic disciplines as administrative categories. (143) Ought examiners, then, to fail borderline candidates with a wide-ranging awareness and appreciation of other disciplines which their peers, whose virtues are more easily measured by examination results, may noticeably lack?

If all these considerations in assessing graduates are to be ignored in favour of the pure academic assessments which the literature shows to be unreliable (and therefore not so pure), wastage in the form of lower productivity of graduates to man the professions will be greater than it need be. In this discussion there is no intention to denigrate academic values. They are affirmed to be the essence of learning, but it is maintained that there is a strong case for broadening the criteria of pass-failure, at least in some instances. Lord Robbins (144) has said that there are mistaken conceptions of what at the present time is appropriate for universities to do:

> For instance, there still seems to be a considerable number of people who conceive the life of a modern university as of some community of scholar-students pursuing their work regardless of its bearing on their subsequent careers, and of staff having the sole duty of inculcating appropriate habits of

* Reported in *The Chronicle of Higher Education*, August 1968.

thought and advancing knowledge with no practical application—a conception rather on a par with the conception of the life of the middle ages often entertained by people who do not have any knowledge of economic history. Of course, if you have this kind of conception you will wish to keep the universities free of any contamination with every-day life and anything vocational . . . [but] a substantial number of students would not be at the university at all if it were not for vocational ambitions. . . . The importance of the universities as centres for the advancement of knowledge is fundamental—we must never lose sight of it or we are lost. But if we are to be realistic we must face the fact that this function has to be combined with the training for life in the outside world of many young men and women who will never advance knowledge and who are not going to be dons or school teachers. We have to organize so as to provide for the discharge of both functions.

There is no question of lowering the standards of graduates, and it is possible to infer that graduate standards might actually be raised by applying wider criteria to student assessment. In medieval times, as at the present, the ancient universities prepared students for the professions of law, medicine, and the Church, and there is no valid argument for thinking that universities should confine themselves only to less practical criteria. Practical professional criteria can coexist with the purely academic. If we agree to that, there is perhaps support for the idea that some students should be assessed in part on other than pure academic grounds; professional criteria should be given due weight.

Academic Flexibility

Reassessment is now in progress of some of the issues discussed under the heading of examinations, and some of these issues also bear upon academic flexibility.

The so-called swing away from science in Britain is thought to be partly due to shortage of good science teachers in the schools, a shortage itself caused by a loss of science graduates in the past, stemming from excessive wastage rates in science faculties and technical colleges, many of whom might have become adequate science teachers. In Gibson's view, two years' successful study of science at the university was sufficient to teach A-level science. He pointed out that at universities in Britain the failure rate in science has been increasing by just over 2 per cent annually and now stood at 30 per cent. It may follow that as the shortage of science graduates becomes worse there will be a further corresponding increase in the shortage of science teachers, followed by a still more serious lack of applicants for under-graduate science places, and so the vicious downward spiral will gather momentum of its own. At a conference on the problems of transition from school to university Professor Gibson* pre-dicted that because of the swing away from physical science, and an increase in the popularity of the arts, humanities, and social sciences, the stage was approaching when any English sixth-former with two A-level passes in science would be assured a place in a university. It might even come about that science departments will stop arguing for A-level passes at all.†

Lack of flexibility in course arrangements can take on many forms—for example, degree arrangements in which students are expected to study one subject only without the possibility of including others. In British universities it is rare for a student to be allowed to follow a joint science/humanities or a science/social-science programme. Even in the 'new universities', with all their flexibility, students generally are expected to confine themselves to science on the one hand or humanities and social sciences on the other, yet an individual may have quite sound reasons for wanting to pursue studies in both fields, as will be discussed later. Some of these students would be likely to lose interest in courses which do not cater for their breadth of interests.

Not only have subject options been limited, but possibilities of change-over between courses at school and at university are seriously lacking, and many students have been wasted because they did not fit into a set scheme of study.‡ Malleson (145) has referred to the enormous variability of individuals, particularly adolescents, and remarked on how extraordinary it was that we get so many to march in locked step through a three-year course. Some consideration of individual differences among students'

---

* A. F. Gibson, Dean of the School of Physical Sciences at Essex University, June 30th, 1967, at a conference on the problems of transition from school to university. Reported in *The Times Educational Supplement,* July 7th, 1967.
† Dr F. S. Dainton, F.R.S., Vice-Chancellor of the University of Nottingham, is highly critical of A levels as a preparation for university studies.
‡ Professor L. R. B. Elton, of the University of Surrey, is experimenting with a first-year course in physics for freshmen without A levels in science.

interests must surely be relevant to the problem of wastage. It is extraordinary to suppose that students who have already spent years in studying for A levels in certain subjects, and then go on to university often to pursue the same or closely related subjects, should progress through the same courses at a uniform speed. Such an assumption almost amounts to a prescription for wastage.

Katz at Stanford* concluded after a longitudinal study of student development, involving a sample of over 3000 students, that colleges should capitalize on the diversity of students' interests and talents by offering a wider range of educational alternatives and more freedom to choose, to enhance individual learning and institutional reform. Katz found that for most students college offerings do not adequately coincide with students' own personal motivations. The fault was mainly seen to be in universities' preoccupation with abstract knowledge at the expense of exposure to experience. Katz claims that educational planning must begin with the recognition that students differ greatly in their interests and abilities, purposes, learning styles, backgrounds, and personalities, and that colleges have not sufficiently linked these varied styles and approaches to their education.

Even so to a large extent, compared with Britain, this is a meaningless issue in the United States where course flexibility is taken for granted in the majority of institutions. Its absence in Britain is deplorable since it implies a severe denial of liberal education which traditionally we are supposed to favour, and the academic freedom of the student to pursue those branches of learning which he may wish to choose for himself. Some people will object that broader courses will have the effect of depriving us of the specialists we need, who have studied for three years 'in depth'. The obvious answer to this is that America does not appear to be very short of specialists. With diversity and flexibility it is possible to have specialists who have broad education. This must to some extent aid communication between disciplines.

The implications of this are being considered more carefully than previously by British academics. Gibson at Essex, for example, has suggested that if universities are forced to stop

---

* J. Katz (ed.), *Growth and Constraint in College Students*, cited in *The Chronicle of Higher Education*, 2, 3, October 12th, 1967.

asking for A levels in science it will at least mean that selection will be based largely on performance in first year at the university, thus diminishing the need for specialization in schools. That could be an advantage. More important, Gibson suggests that an alternative route to science degrees might be arranged for students who show less interest in pure academic rigour and are more practically oriented. Instead of these students being wasted and lost to science by being written off as failures they could successfully satisfy industry's and the school demands for the second- and even third-echelon scientists in their particular fields. Barnard* has also discussed the needs of industry, not only for top-ranking scientists, but for ordinary competent scientists who would go into the administration side of scientific establishments. The needs of individual students and the institutions they will work in are thus complementary, and both depend on criteria which are not entirely academic.

Flexibility in another sense is built into the new courses in the Honours School of Engineering Science and Economics at Oxford, (146) the aim of which is to train a technical élite for management and the Civil Service and to stimulate interaction between engineering and economics, which are seen as two disciplines with a mutual affinity. Students who have specialized at school in physics, pure or applied mathematics, chemistry, and any other subjects relevant to engineering often have a latent interest in economics but have not had a chance to study it at school. That they wish to broaden their interests is shown by the fact that a sizeable proportion opt for the combined course. A proportion of these students would probably not be satisfied by the more highly specialized engineering courses, and would drop out or be wasted because they lacked the interest to pursue them to the required academic level. A similar course is available at the University of Warwick, and the Council for National Academic Awards is sponsoring combined science-arts courses. Gibson suggests that equivalent combined courses in education could be arranged for students of science who did not wish to study science in the greatest possible depth and who had an interest in teaching. In the older British universities such combined courses are probably more the exception than the rule,

---

* Professor G. A. Barnard, Dean of the School of Mathematical Studies, University of Essex.

though at Cambridge there is the possibility of taking Parts 1 and 2 in different subjects. However, it may be that students who are not enabled to engage in such inter-disciplinary studies at undergraduate level are frequently among the wasted. This is the more serious when we remember the common criticism in industry of the stereotype 'pure' engineer who is often narrowly confined to his specialism and who cannot communicate with management; and the 'pure' arts man who is technically deficient. Industry and management must find it difficult to tolerate either, though it must be recognized that the United States appears to have no such difficulty. The comparative rarity of combined courses has not often been seen as a factor in wastage. Their growing popularity and the demand for the 'products' of combined courses suggest that more of them should be developed. How far are the difficulties students have in finding combined courses, or of changing courses after a mistaken original choice of study, or the impossibility of receiving credits for work done, related to wastage? This is certainly a viable research problem. It may be that this is a major source of wastage, and it has been little explored. Students tend to achieve best in directions which they find interesting or rewarding. Once this fact is recognized there is a strong case for the kind of flexibility in courses which allows for combinations, changes, and delays. Such a prospect might be anathema to purists in some disciplines who fear that standards will deteriorate, but there is nothing to suggest that by accommodating the broad-minded person of wide-ranging curiosity we shall see the last of those students who wish to study their discipline in as great a depth as possible.

New combined physics-philosophy and mathematics-philosophy courses at Oxford, and Keele's combined education/chemistry, mathematics, or physics courses, are examples of courses which will, it is hoped, be forerunners of others designed to include arts and science subjects. Even in the 'new universities' of Britain, although there is flexibility within social sciences and humanities, combined arts-and-science courses are still very rare.

Kendall (147) in Britain and Knoell (148) in America have found that some student wastage is better described as student mobility. In these British and American studies, drop-outs, and 'push-outs' as some may be better described, frequently found ways to conclude their studies in other institutions and to gain qualifications, in the same field, or in other fields more suitable for them than their original choice, in spite of the absence of formal arrangements which would have made it possible.

Because these students ultimately succeeded is no argument for doing nothing to facilitate flexibility in the belief that students will succeed in the end despite difficulties. Rather it is an argument for having built-in institutional arrangements to help students find more suitable courses and to allow credits where possible. For each one who eventually finds success there may be another who is permanently wasted. Knoell's paper points out that student mobility sometimes involves temporary dropping out and later return to the same college, with various kinds of intervening experience, or drop-out and transfer, with or without a time lag, to another college. Although in some instances the student is dismissed on account of poor scholarship, in other circumstances it is his own decision to withdraw. This might be because the course did not turn out to be as suitable as expected, since the data available at the time of choice were an inadequate basis for decision. In other instances, as a result of increasing maturity and experience, changes in students' objectives and motivations may have taken place. Sometimes the goals or objectives of the drop-out are incompatible with those of the college. In one study cited by Knoell 60 per cent of male freshmen dropped out instead of graduating, but only one-third of these were permanent drop-outs.

Students who transfer might be expected to proceed to inferior colleges which would have to accept them as second-hand or second-rate students, but the opposite is true. The most prevalent pattern of transfer was upward to the major state universities by students who 'dropped out' of colleges which could not offer the study programmes in which they were interested. Many institutions expressed favourable opinions concerning the performance of the transfers they admitted as compared with freshmen who entered from high school.

Some other significant findings emerged from Knoell's analysis of attrition. Apart from the large number of drop-outs who made unrealistic or otherwise unsuitable choices, financial factors appeared to affect the decision to drop out after transfer to more suitable courses; though about 50 per cent of drop-outs after transfer were dismissals, and about one-third of the voluntary withdrawals cited motivational problems. One of the values of higher education often cited is that it teaches students to value learning. If this is true there should be no objection if a student wants to drop out and return to studies after a period of other experience, perhaps in industry, commerce, teaching, travelling, or merely earning money to finance later study. Academic conservatives might object, and there might also be objections from administrators, yet if academic and administrative procedures could be made more flexible, wastage might be lessened in the long term. One of Knoell's main conclusions is that decisions concerning their college attendance, withdrawal, re-entry, and graduate work are made by people of all ages and in different stages of their lives and careers. "The only really permanent dropouts appear to be the deceased, since as new opportunities are afforded the public—new two and four year colleges, new programs in existing colleges, new financial aid programs— dropouts of all ages and varying interests leave the ranks of the attrition group and become college students once more." She suggests courses should be less rigid, and suggests it should be possible for a student, when a break seems desirable, to drop out of college, to have some worth-while experience outside college, and to re-enter with minimal disruption to his or her degree programme. In Douglas's research (149), cited earlier, he showed an appreciable proportion of students at the London School of Economics looked upon their undergraduate days as a moratorium, an interim period during which they sorted themselves out, as it were, and tried to decide what they wanted to become. There is nothing necessarily wrong with that because it is a necessary phase of adolescence, and university may be a good place to do that. But it means that although they see it as a moratorium, their choice is, in fact, becoming crystallized because the studies they are pursuing will largely decide their ultimate life situation. Nevertheless, in terms of student motivation and productivity it might be better if students could have this moratorium before coming to college or even half-way through. Expensive investment in university places, grants, and in academic staff is surely not warranted for this purpose, and they might be more usefully deployed for students who have had long and diversified enough experience to make up their minds to some extent concerning their future intentions. Adolescence is a time when developing adults have a psychological need to be individuals, yet rigid systems of academic organization must seriously limit this.

As Knoell puts it,

The challenge of colleges is to find ways to accommodate the thousands of students who differ from the efficient stereotype who attends college right after high school and persists until graduation. We need to incorporate these people into our long-range planning in a positive way, in order to make maximum use of our educational facilities and to offer maximum opportunities to worthy dropouts of all ages. Modifications will need to be made in our assumptions about progression through degree programs, and specialized services.

It is not so unusual as it perhaps was to hear academics in Britain speak in terms favouring greater academic breadth and flexibility. The Robbins Committee recommended that arrangements should whenever possible allow a student to postpone his choice of special subject until the end of the first year or to change his course of study then, if necessary with an extension of grant. They also recommended that students who do not live up to their early promise should be transferred, after their first or second year, to less exacting courses, and that a higher proportion of students should receive a broader education for their first degrees. The Swann Report (1968) advocated more general science degrees to enable graduates to be more flexible and adaptable in their careers, implying that there was a danger that holders of specialist degrees would be unsuited to continue long in careers requiring understanding of new knowledge in related sciences, and hence a tendency to fall out of date more quickly than those with a background of more general study. (150)

Venables* has proposed that greater diversity in the structure of degree courses in Britain could be achieved by having two-year courses for some who did not wish to be committed to a three-year honours course, a three-year honours degree course for some, and a four-year Master's course for others who wished to specialize beyond what the shorter courses would permit.

Not every drop-out from present courses is necessarily a failure. A student who leaves university after three years of a five-year course is not, or should not, simply be wasted. The knowledge

---

* Sir Peter Venables, cited in *The Times Educational Supplement,* October 13th, 1967.

S.F.W.H.E.—O

he has acquired is valuable, and it makes no sense to prevent him from using it. Students who have chosen courses which they later find are not satisfactory for their purposes, interests, and aptitudes should be able to change across, being credited with all the relevant studies in which they have previously passed. Lauwerys* considers that no initial selection, particularly for professional courses, should be final. There should be a second chance. Students should be encouraged to accept what they may consider a less desirable alternative. And for those who may wish to study for a degree in a university faculty but find it possible only to enter a course for a national diploma should, if performance is satisfactory, be enabled to move back from the diploma course to the degree course. Lauwerys suggests that intermediate qualifications should be awarded at, say, the end of two years of university studies, or later in some disciplines. In many professions—for example, medicine and engineering—for every one who has taken the full course there is a need for several persons with middle qualifications. It might be wise not to admit students to the full course without completing the short course. This would help to ensure the preparation of the large number of middle-level technicians and professional men which society needs. To diminish wastage, alternative courses should be offered which take into account knowledge already gained.

In America Harold Howe II, then United States Commissioner of Education,† attacked "routine rigidity in most fields". He advocated entrance of high-risk students to colleges and special support services for them when they have been admitted. There was no advocacy of lower standards, but rather the introduction of major adjustments in the institutions themselves to maximize flexibility, the purpose of which would be to identify unconventional talent and give it the chance to develop. These sentiments are the opposite of those which maintain rigidly defined academic courses and make little allowance for those students who may need or wish to deviate from the three-year degree system which is general in Britain.

Plans which would implement the ideas put forward by

---

* Private communication, March 1967, from Professor J. A. Lauwerys, Professor of Comparative Education, University of London Institute of Education.

† *The Chronicle of Higher Education,* 2, 4, October 26th, 1967.

Lauwerys, and those of Barnard and Gibson cited earlier, would require flexibility in administration as well as flexibility of mind among academics, but are far from impracticable. In Germany* students can change courses and place of study as they can in the United States, and systems of credits operate in a great many countries; for example, U.S., Dutch, and Australian universities. While recognizing objections that may be made about other countries' systems of higher education and the snares and pitfalls involved in transplanting ideas from one country to another, we may reasonably submit that an eclecticism which makes use of the best of other systems while discarding their unsuitable aspects can lead to profitable syntheses. The main obstacles are conservatism and lack of flexibility. In the course of time some such changes will probably occur in any event, but only after wasteful periods of delay which make their eventual implementation more difficult.

More obvious sources of flexibility which are not always fully exploited and which can contribute to a reduction in wastage relate to examination procedures; for example, supplementary examinations for borderline candidates and those who consider they could have done better if it were not for illness, nerves, or other human frailty, or accident on the day of the examination. Mountford (151) has pointed out that supplementary exams held in September are frequently given as an excuse for a June slaughter. Supplementaries are wasteful if this means that students have to work during the summer on subjects in which they should have been judged competent. On the positive side supplementaries give students a second chance and save repeating the whole year. Unnecessary repeating of years constitutes wastage not only of places but also wastage of qualified candidates who will have been prevented from entering university or college.

Annual examinations place a high premium upon students' examination ability, which is far from perfectly correlated with other attributes desirable in a graduate. Course assignments in conjunction with formal examinations can enable a better all-round assessment of the candidate to be made and allow the final degree mark to reflect more accurately his known ability. They can partially eliminate examination stress and its contribu-

---

* See Robbins Report on Higher Education, Appendix 5, H.M.S.O.

tion to failure. Some academics* suggest that equal weighting should be given to assignments and formal examinations. Greater number of examinations increases the chances of reliability and stimulates a steady effort, and discourages belated effort near examination time. Reliability is better also, because different kinds of student ability can be tested.

There is no reason why students in some departments, provided safeguards are adequate, should not be given time (perhaps a fortnight) in which to hand in examination answers, as is done in at least one department of the University of York. Open-book examinations assess students' ability to solve problems and synthesize, when given all the data available in books which are allowed to be taken into the examination room. This reduces the premium on mere memory, for which formal examinations are notorious, and gives students an opportunity to show how well they can *use* knowledge.

All of these suggested methods take into account individual differences among students and their different working styles, and the different working styles employed by any one student. Used together, they offer opportunity for more reliable assessment. When students are assessed in a number of different ways it is safer to assume that wastage is minimal. By contrast, when examination is confined to formal papers there is bound to be wastage of students low in examination ability. What is perhaps more serious, there is another kind of wastage in which students high in formal examination ability obtain the highest grades and go on to get the greater number of research grants and senior posts in the Civil Service, and industry, when others who are in fact more suitable might have made better use of these opportunities. This may be one source of the unexpectedly low correlation between class of first degree and later scientific

---

* For example, A. R. B. Etherton in *The Times Educational Supplement,* October 28th, 1966. This is, of course, done most extensively in subjects requiring the presentation of laboratory notebooks for examination purposes; but essays in other subjects, particularly in arts, are not always taken into account as far as they might be. See also R. V. Clements in *The Times Educational Supplement,* November 3rd, 1967, reporting his survey of departments in British universities, some of which require dissertations; these are given status equal to one or two formal written papers. One university stipulates that course work marks shall be at least $33\frac{1}{3}$ per cent, but not more than 50 per cent of the total. Most universities do not yet reach that maximum.

productivity among postgraduate degree-holders which was discussed in an earlier section.

Apart from the wastage problem, arguments for flexibility and diversity in course structure and openness of higher education to greater numbers can be expanded in terms of preparing people for roles other than élitist roles. McConnell says that in a democracy advanced education is necessary not only in science and technology, but equally in humanities and social sciences if ordinary citizens are to follow in civic affairs and society generally the leadership of men of intelligence, sensitivity, and idealism. These views were based on his belief that a democracy cannot exist and grow merely through the leadership of an intellectual élite, and that society must have a large body of citizens who possess a deep understanding of the problems of modern life. McConnell expressed the view that a highly educated few are unlikely to be recognized or accepted as leaders in a democracy if the great body of citizens have no basis of communication with them. (152)

Arguments about the division between history and geography and accusations of 'superficiality' whenever cross-disciplinary attempts are made are likely to be resurrected whatever the combinations of subjects which might be suggested. Paradoxically, effective study of a problem is in some ways hindered when knowledge is fragmented artificially into subject departments. This must certainly be so when, for example, an educational problem is seen in sociological terms, while the psychological aspects are ignored, or an economic or political problem is tackled in such a way as to ignore the psychological, sociological, and even historical aspects. Jencks and Riesman's reference to disciplines as mere academic categories is applicable here. There are arguments for broader courses in great variety— diversification as an insurance against sterility. Lord Robbins, in his Installation Address as Chancellor of the University of Stirling, was highly critical of too much academic specialization. While agreeing that the main outstanding contributions to culture and civilization in the arts, humanities, and sciences have come from men who were specialists, he pointed out the disadvantages in limiting mutual understanding, versatility, mobility, and adaptation. Furthermore, he recalled that even in the concentrated work of the graduate school he had found that graduate students with first degrees having a broad-based content compared favourably with first-class honours specialists. Their greater universality and flexibility of outlook were an advantage he had observed over several decades of supervising graduate students at the London School of Economics. (153)

As a source of considerable wastage, broadly defined, there can be little doubt that lack of academic flexibility is of serious importance. The examples discussed in this section are not exhaustive, but those included are representative of the types of rigidity that impose wastage and so lessen the productivity of institutions unnecessarily. The remedies which the literature suggests are not universally applicable, but a flexible and open-minded approach to this problem reveals a large number of ways in which suitable ideas might be adopted in institutions and departments where they were not previously considered practicable. Examples of flexibility which could reduce wastage and release more qualified people include: (i) combined courses for the non-purists; (ii) opportunities to change courses or transfer to other institutions, while being allowed all relevant passes as credits; (iii) provision for students to drop out and return to studies without penalty in time or grant; (iv) supplementary examinations, independent assignments counted more frequently as part of the overall examination, open-book examinations to test candidates' ability to use knowledge and not merely to reproduce material; and (v) all types of examination in combination where possible to enhance the reliability of examinations by sampling several attributes; and (vi) a conscious refusal of examiners to adhere blindly to fixed pass rates year after year. The increased opportunities for students, who might well be wasted in a rigid academic regime, to satisfy their academic aims and aspirations in the ways they choose would in itself represent no mean gain.

Summary

To what, then, can we attribute wastage? As we have seen, the research from several countries over a long period has shown that students' ability, personality, and motivation are important factors. But it is an oversimplification to suppose that because a student joins the 'wasted' group he must therefore have been lacking in one or more of these. The generalized claim that students fail because they are lazy may well be true for some students, but it is extremely unwise to disregard the possibility of defects in the policies and practices of institutions themselves. Whenever a student fails it is in a sense a reflection upon those who selected him. It could be argued that some error is due to pure chance factors. This can be conceded. The questions which remain are: how much wastage is tolerable? Can it be reduced further? And what are the most promising ways in dealing with it? Since 1938, according to Woodhall and Blaug, (154) productivity in British universities has declined. To put it another way, we might say wastage has increased, yet in that time the student intake has become progressively more selective. Prior to the Second World War student intakes were more comprehensive and included a wider range of ability than now. With the exception of a minority of outstanding scholars, entry into higher education was largely a function of financial ability. Mediocre students whose parents could afford it took up places—students who today would not so easily gain entry. Entry is now far more justly a function of scholastic ability. There are indications that standards for admission to most university departments are steadily being raised. Before the War the average I.Q. of university entrants in Australia was 120: since the War this has risen to 126, and each year stricter quotas exclude increasing numbers who would have gained entry in former years. In Britain the Robbins Committee (155) in 1963 forecast that enormously greater number of qualified applicants would seek entry into higher education. Even their forecast has proved to be conservative, and university departments and colleges in Britain, like those elsewhere, are demanding higher entrance qualifications as pressure for places mounts.

Clearly there is less wrong with students' ability each year, in so far as this can be judged by marks in school subjects. If productivity of universities is decreasing, as Woodhall and Blaug claim, or even if it remains fixed, one or more of the following must *increasingly* be at fault: (i) selection, and the limited criteria which are applied in the selection process, (ii) the way schools prepare students for higher education, (iii) teaching methods in higher education, (iv) inflexibility of course arrangements and structure, (v) examining, (vi) pass rates and examination procedures, and (vii) the manner in which institutions help or do not help the students they have selected towards their goal of graduation. There may be other institutional and student variables, but these are those which the research literature has shown to have the greatest bearing upon wastage. Student variables cannot be disregarded, but since student quality, as measured using the criteria of performance at school, is likely still to improve, the time seems ripe for institutions and departments to assess ways in which they might modify their assumptions, procedures, and structure. On this point Nevitt Sanford (156) has asked, how can we discuss attrition without recognition of the goals of the institution. In discussing research on drop-outs and on student performance and wastage Summerskill (157) pointed out that "institutional variables have been taken for granted or treated as constants". But clearly they are not constants. In the following chapter opportunities for research are discussed—research which would take into account some of the institutional variables which have been shown to contribute to wastage.

REFERENCES

1. Robbins Report (1963), *Report of the Committee on Higher Education*, Cmnd. 2154 (London, H.M.S.O.).
2. Sir James Mountford, "Success and Failure at University", *Universities Quarterly*, **11**, 1957.
3. John G. Darley, *Promise and Performance*, Berkeley Center for the Study of Higher Education (University of California, 1962).
4. H. R. Cassirer, *Television Teaching Today* (U.N.E.S.C.O., Paris, 1960).
5. A. G. Maclaine, "A Programme for improving Teaching and Learning at Australian Universities", *The Australian University*, **3**, 3, 1965.
6. F. C. Macomber and L. Siegel, *Experimental Study in Instructional Procedures* (Miami University, 1957).
7. D. V. Connor, "Effectiveness of Teaching Methods at the University Level", *Educational Research Unit Bulletin, No. 7* (University of New South Wales, 1957).
8. A. D. Macklin, *Proceedings of Home University Conference*, 1951.
9. K. S. Cunningham, "Success and Failure in Australian Universities", (Mimeo), (Australian Council for Educational Research, 1953).
10. A. J. Jenkinson, "Seven Ways with Wastage", *The Vocational Aspect*, **13**, Spring 1961.

11. Barrie Hopson, "Modernising University Teaching", *New Society*, December 1st, 1966.
12. For example, W. J. McKeachie, "Research in Teaching: The Gap between Theory and Practice", in *Improving College Teaching*, American Council on Education, 1966; M. L. J. Abercrombie, "Small Groups", in B. M. Foss (ed.), *New Horizons in Psychology* (Pelican 1966), and *The Anatomy of Judgment* (London, Hutchinson, 1965).
13. John McLeish, "Lecture, Tutorial, Seminar: The Students' View", paper given at Annual Conference of Society for Research into Higher Education, London, 1966; L. F. Thomas and Alison Webb, "University Staff and Students' Views of each other and of the Learning Situation" (Mimeo), (London, Brunel University, 1966).
14. S. B. Hammond, Draft Report of the First Year Student Survey, University of Melbourne (Confidential), 1957. Cited in W. H. Frederick: "Components of Failure", *Melbourne Studies in Education*, 1957–58.
15. Nicolas B. Malleson, "Must Students be Wasted?", *New Society*, May 2nd, 1963.
16. M. L. J. Abercrombie, "Educating for Change", *Universities Quarterly*, **21**, 1, 1966.
17. W. B. Brookover, "The Relation of Social Factors to Teaching Ability", *Journal of Experimental Education*, **13**, 1945.
18. D. L. Thistlethwaite, "Rival Hypotheses for Explaining the Effects of Different Learning Environments", and "Fields of Study and Development of Motivation to Seek Advanced Training", *Journal of Educational Psychology*, **53**, 1962.
19. T. A. Lamke, "Personality and Teaching Success", *Journal of Experimental Education*, **20**, 1951.
20. R. H. Knapp and H. B. Goodrich, *Origins of American Scientists* (University of Chicago Press, 1952).
21. *Education at Berkeley*: Report of Select Committee on Education (the Muscatine Report), (University of California, 1966).
22. S. M. Lipset, "University Students and Politics in Underdeveloped Countries", *Comparative Education Review*, **10**, 2, 1966; M. Spencer, "Professional, Scientific, and Intellectual Students in India", *Comparative Education Review*, **10**, 2, 1966; R. J. Still, "Aegrotat Degrees for Psychological Cases?" cited in *The Times Educational Supplement*, January 20th, 1957.

23. D. L. Thistlethwaite, "College Press and Changes in Study Plans of Talented Students", *Journal of Educational Psychology*, **51**, 4, 1959; D. L. Thistlethwaite, "Diversities in College Environments: Implications for Student Selection and Training", in K. M. Wilson (ed.), *Research Related to College Admissions* (Atlanta, Georgia, Southern Regional Education Board, 1963).

24. T. R. McConnell, "Problems of Distributing Students among Institutions with Varying Characteristics", *North Central Association Quarterly*, **35**, 1961.

25. R. H. Knapp and H. B. Goodrich, *op. cit.*; R. H. Knapp and J. J. Greenbaum, *The Younger American Scholar: His Collegiate Origins*, Chicago, Illinois (University of Chicago Press, 1953).

26. A. W. Astin, "Further Validation of the Environmental Assessment Technique", *Journal of Educational Psychology*, **54**, 4, 1963; A. W. Astin, "Differential College Effects on the Motivation of Talented Students to obtain the Ph.D.", *Journal of Educational Psychology*, **54**, 4, 1963.

27. D. P. Campbell, *Results of Counselling Twenty Five Years Later* (Philadelphia and London, Saunders, 1965).

28. Report of Committee on Teaching Methods (Hale Report), University Grants Committee (H.M.S.O., 1964).

29. S. M. Lipset and P. Altbach, "U.S. Campus Alienation", *New Society*, September 8th, 1966.

30. Gladys Watson, "Happy College Years": A Report on the Specialised Counselling Program (Mimeo), (Brooklyn College of the City University of New York, 1963).

31. L. Srole, "Sociologists' Sight Lines: Retrospective and Prospective", in L. Srole (ed.), *Mental Health in the Metropolis* (New York, McGraw Hill, 1962).

32. D. A. Howell, "A Study of the 1955 Entry into British Universities", Evidence to the Robbins Committee on Higher Education, 1962.

33. R. W. Parnell, "Mortality and Prolonged Illness among Oxford Undergraduates", *Lancet*, March 31st, 1951.

34. Nicolas B. Malleson, *A Handbook on British Student Health Services*, Pitman Medical, 1966.

35. Nocolas B. Malleson and John Hopkins, "University Student, 1953, I: Profile", *Universities Quarterly*, **13**, 3, 1959.

36. C. J. Lucas, R. P. Kelvin, and A. B. Ojha, "Mental Health and Student Wastage", *British Journal of Psychiatry*, **112** (484), 1966.

37. A. D. Macklin in *Proceedings of Home Universities Conference,* 1951.
38. R. R. Priestley, "The Mental Health of University Students", in E. L. French (ed.) *Melbourne Studies in Education,* 1957.
39. Nicolas B. Malleson, 1966, *op. cit.*
40. K. S. Cunningham, *op. cit.*
41. Sir Fred J. Schonell, et al., *Promise and Performance* (University of Queensland and University of London Press, 1962).
42. G. A. Gray and L. N. Short, "Student Progress in the University, 1958–60" (Mimeo), (University of New South Wales, 1961).
43. R. R. Priestley, *op. cit.*
44. Ethel Venables, "Placement Problems among Engineering Apprentices in Part-time Technical College Courses, Part 2", *British Journal of Educational Psychology,* 31, 1, 1961.
45. D. L. Thistlethwaite, 1959, *op. cit.*
46. Brian Jackson, "Students who Fail", *Where,* 20, spring 1965.
47. Sir Fred J. Schonell, *et al., op. cit.*
48. R. K. Kelsall, *Report on an Inquiry into Applications for Admission to Universities.* Committee of Vice-Chancellors and Principals of the Universities of the United Kingdom, 1957.
49. Sir Fred J. Schonell, "Student Adaptation and its Bearing on Academic Achievement", *The Australian University,* 1, 1, 1963.
50. D. S. Anderson, "Failure in the 1959 Preliminary Course in Medicine" (Mimeo), (University of Melbourne, 1960).
51. C. Sanders, "Report on Academic Wastage and Failure among University Students in Australia and Other Countries: A Review of Research and Opinion". Faculty of Education (Mimeo), (University of Western Australia, 1958).
52. D. Harris, Factors Affecting College Grades: A Review of the Literature 1930–37", *Psychological Bulletin,* 37, 1940.
53. John Summerskill, "Dropouts from College", in N. Sanford (ed.), *The American College* (New York, Wiley, 1962).
54. G. A. Gray and L. N. Short, *op. cit.*
55. L. Pond, "A Study of High Achieving and Low Achieving University Freshmen", *Australian Journal of Higher Education,* 2, 1, 1964.

56. Nicolas B. Malleson, "Student Performance at University College, London, 1948–51", *Universities Quarterly,* **12,** 1958.
57. R. C. A. Hunter and A. E. Schwartzman, "A Clinical View of Study Difficulties in a Group of Counselled Medical Students", *Journal of Medical Education,* **36,** 1961.
58. Sir Fred J. Schonell, 1963, *op. cit.*
59. Dorothy M. Knoell, "Undergraduate Attrition, Mortality or Mobility?", paper presented at Princeton University Conference on the College Dropout and the Utilization of Talent, October 1964.
60. Ray Margaret Lawrence, "Student Personnel Services at Brooklyn College" (Mimeo), (Brooklyn College of the City University of New York, 1965).
61. J. K. Winfrey and D. D. Feder, "Non-Instructional Services", *Review of Educational Research,* **25,** 4, 1965.
62. R. F. Horle and G. M. Gazda, "Qualifications, Training, and Duties of Directors and Staff of Men's Residence Halls", *Journal of Student Personnel,* **4,** 1963.
63. D. L. Farnsworth, "Social and Emotional Development of Students in Colleges and University", *Mental Hygiene,* **43** (358), 1959.
64. R. M. Young, "One in Six", *Cambridge Review,* May 28th, 1966.
65. R. C. A. Hunter and A. E. Schwartzman, *op. cit.*
66. R. J. Still, "Psychological Illness among Students in the Examination Period" (Mimeo), Department of Student Health, Leeds, 1963.
67. John Summerskill, *op. cit.*
68. Nicolas B. Malleson, 1966, *op. cit.*
69. R. R. Priestley, *op. cit.*
70. G. W. Parkyn, *Success and Failure at the University,* 1: *Academic Success and Entrance Standard* (Wellington, New Zealand Council for Educational Research, 1959).
71. Ray Margaret Lawrence, 1965, *op. cit.*
72. John Nisbet and Jennifer Welsh, "Predicting Student Performance", *Universities Quarterly,* **20,** 4, 1966.
73. M. L. J. Abercrombie, S. Hunt, and P. Stringer, *Selection and Academic Performance of Students in a University School of Architecture,* Society for Research into Higher Education Monographs, London, 1968.
74. Ruth Weintraub and Ruth Salley, "Graduation Prospects of an Entering Freshman"; *Journal of Educational Research,* **39,** 1945.

75. Alexander W. Astin and Robert J. Panos, "A National Research Data Bank for Higher Education", *Educational Record* (winter 1966).
76. D. Harris, *op. cit.*
77. J. Hopkins, N. B. Malleson, and I. Sarnoff, "Some Non-Intellectual Correlates of Success and Failure among University Students", *British Journal of Educational Psychology*, **28**, Part I, 1958.
78. P. Marris, *The Experience of Higher Education* (London, Routledge and Kegan Paul, 1964).
79. M. C. Albrow, "The Influence of Accommodation upon 64 Reading University Students", (Mimeo), 1965.
80. D. S. Anderson and R. R. Priestley, "Notes on the Study of Failure in Australian Universities" (Mimeo), (University of Melbourne, 1960).
81. Sir Fred J. Schonell *et al.*, 1962, *op. cit.*
82. Betty M. Suddarth, "Factors Influencing the Successful Graduation of Freshmen Who Enrol at Purdue University" (Mimeo), (Purdue University, 1957).
83. "Fraternities and Sororities", University of Purdue, Indiana, 1964–65, Bulletin.
84. R. E. Matson, "A Study of the Influence of Fraternity, Residence Hall and Off-Campus Living on Students of High Average and Low College Potential", *Journal of the National Association of Women Deans and Counsellors*, **26**, 1963.
85. T. D. Bacig and M. R. Sgan, "A Ten-Year Fraternity Membership Study", *Journal of College Student Personnel*, **4**, 1962.
86. Christina Holbraad, "The Accommodation of Third Year University Students and their Performance at Final Examinations" (Mimeo), (London School of Economics, 1962).
87. D. A. Howell, "A Study of the 1955 Entry to British Universities" (Evidence to Robbins Committee on Higher Education, H.M.S.O., 1964), (Mimeo), 1962.
88. R. E. Prusok and W. B. Walsh, "College Students' Residence and Academic Achievement", *Journal of College Student Personnel*, **5**, 1964; J. K. Winfrey and D. D. Feder, "Non-Instructional Services", *Review of Educational Research*, **25**, 4, 1965.
89. Doreen Langley, "Student Performance and Student Residence", *The Australian University*, **3**, 2, 1965.

90. University Grants Committee, Report of the Sub-Committee on Halls of Residence (London, H.M.S.O., 1957).
91. H. C. Riker, *College Housing as Learning Centers,* American College Personnel Association (Washington, D.C., 1965).
92. R. K. Boyer, "The Student Peer Group: Its Effect on College Performance" (Mimeo), (Case Intitute of Technology, 1966).
93. Sir Fred J. Schonell, 1963, *op. cit.*
94. C. R. Pace and G. C. Stern, "An Approach to the Measurement of Psychological Characteristics of College Environments", *Journal of Education Psychology,* **49**, 1958; G. C. Stern, "Environments for Learning", in Nevitt Sanford (ed.), *The American College* (New York, Wiley, 1962).
95. G. D. Yonge, "Students", *Review of Educational Research,* **25**, 4, 1965.
96. Report of Commission of Enquiry, vol. 2. (The Franks Report), (Oxford University Press, 1966).
97. D. A. Howell, *op. cit.*
98. Warren Evans, "Study of Academic Careers of 1955 Entry", Cambridge University Sociological Society (Mimeo), 1959; Nicolas B. Malleson and John Hopkins, *op. cit.,* 1959; G. D. N. Worswick, Report in *The Times Educational Supplement,* May 3rd, 1957.
99. Nicolas B. Malleson, "University Student, 1953, II: Schooling", *Universities Quarterly,* **14**, 1960.
100. Peter Marris, *op. cit.*
101. Hilde T. Himmelweit, "Student Selection—Implications derived from Two Student Selection Enquiries", in Paul Halmos (ed.), *The Sociological Review Monograph, No.* 7 (University of Keele).
102. C. MacArthur, "Personalities of Public and Private School Boys", *Harvard Educational Review,* **24**, 4, 1954; and "Sub-Culture and Personality during the College Years", *The Journal of Educational Sociology,* **33**, 1960.
103. D. Hogben, "School of Entry and First Year Performance of Medical Students in the University of Western Australia", *Australian Journal of Higher Education,* **2**, 1, 1964.
104. John Summerskill, *op. cit.*
105. Margaret Mercer, "Personal Factors in College Adjustment", *Journal of Educational Research,* **36**, 1943.

106. Report of Committee on Teaching Methods (the Hale Report), *op. cit.*
107. Michael Forster, "An Audit of Academic Performance" (Queens University, Belfast, 1953).
108. Derbyshire Education Committee, "Report on Awards to Students" (Mimeo), 1966.
109. K. S. Cunningham, 1953, *op. cit.*; C. Sanders, 1958, *op. cit.*; F. J. Olsen, "The Distribution of Academic Talent among the Larger Faculties of the University of Queensland, 1953", *University of Queensland Gazette,* **29**, 1954.
110. L. Pond, "A Study of High Achieving and Low Achieving University Freshmen", *Australian Journal of Higher Education,* **2**, 1, 1964.
111. R. R. Dale, *From School to University* (London, Routledge and Kegan Paul, 1954).
112. Sir Fred J. Schonell, 1963, *op. cit.*
113. Sir Alexander Carr-Saunders, in *Proceedings of Home Universities Conference,* 1952.
114. P. Laslett cited in A. T. Welford, "Stress and Achievement", *Australian Journal of Psychology,* **17**, 1, 1965.
115. F. J. Olsen, "Failure in First Year University Examinations", *Australian Journal of Education,* **1**, 3, 1957.
116. Ian McMullen, reported in *The Times Educational Supplement,* June 30th, 1967.
117. F. J. Olsen, 1957, *op. cit.*
118. Sir Fred J. Schonell, "Higher Education and National Progress" (Presidential Address to Australian and New Zealand Association for the Advancement of Science), *Australian Journal of Science,* **29**, 8, 1967.
119. J. W. Tibble, (ed.), *The Study of Education* (London, Routledge and Kegan Paul, 1966).
120. Sir P. Hartog and E. G. Rhodes, *The Marks of Examiners* (London, Macmillan, 1936).
121. Roy Cox, "What Use are Exams?", *New Society,* May 26th, 1966.
122. David E. Lavin, *The Prediction of Academic Performance* (Russell Sage Foundation, and New York, Wiley, 1967).
123. D. W. MacKinnon, "What do we Mean by Talent and How do we Test for It?" in *The Search for Talent,* College Entrance Examination Board, New York, 1960.
124. Liam Hudson, "Degree Class and Attainment in Scientific Research", *British Journal of Psychology,* **51**, 1960.

125. John L. Holland, "The Prediction of College Grades from Personality and Aptitude Variables", *Journal of Educational Psychology*, **51**, 1960.
126. David E. Lavin, 1967, *op. cit.*
127. P. Mansell Jones, "The Fallacies of the Examination System", in *Universities Quarterly*, **19**, 3, 1965.
128. Philip E. Vernon, "The Pool of Ability", in P. Halmos, *op. cit.*
129. D. S. Anderson and R. R. Priestley, *op cit.*; K. S. Cunningham, *op. cit.*; H. H. Hohne, *The Prediction of Academic Success*, Melbourne, A.C.E.R., 1951; C. Sanders, *op. cit.*
130. H. H. Hohne, 1951, *op. cit.*
131. P. W. Hughes, "Academic Achievement at the University" (Mimeo), (University of Tasmania, 1960).
132. Michael Forster, *op. cit.*
133. R. R. Dale, "University Standards", *University Quarterly*, **13**, 1959.
134. Ethel Venables, *The Young Worker at College* (London, Faber, 1967).
135. K. S. Cunningham, *op. cit.*
136. Robbins Report, *op. cit.*
137. B. S. Bloom, *Taxonomy of Educational Objectives* (London, Longmans, 1956).
138. P. J. Fensham, "An Experiment in Examining First Year Chemistry Students", *Vestes*, **4**, 4, and *Nature*, **194**, 4824, 1962.
139. K. S. Cunningham, *op. cit.*
140. Sir David Pye, "The Yawning Gap between University Graduate and Competent Engineer" (Presidential Address to the Institution of Mechanical Engineers), 1952.
141. G. S. Bosworth, "Towards Creative Activity in Engineering", *Universities Quarterly*, **17**, 286, 1963, and "The Education and Training of Engineers in the Light of the Feilder and Robbins Reports", *The Engineer*, September 1964.
142. Sir Paul Chambers, *Education and Industry*, Chuter Ede Memorial Lecture, National Union of Teachers, June 2nd, 1964.
143. C. Jencks and D. Riesman, *The Academic Revolution* (New York, Doubleday, 1968).
144. Lord Robbins, *Universities Quarterly*, **20**, 1, December 1965.

145. Nicolas B. Malleson, "Must Students be Wasted?", *New Society*, May 2nd, 1963.
146. N. G. McCrum and R. J. Van Noorden, "Technical Elite in Training and Management", *The Times Educational Supplement*, July 7th, 1967.
147. Michael Kendall, "Those Who Failed—1:The Further Education of Former Students", *Universities Quarterly*, **18**, 4, 1964.
148. Dorothy Knoell, *op. cit.*
149. Lawrence F. Douglas, "Types of Students and their Outlook on University Education", Ph.D. thesis, London, 1964.
150. *The Flow into Employment of Scientists, Engineers and Technologists*, Report of Working Group on Manpower for Scientific Growth. Cmnd. 3760 (H.M.S.O., 1968).
151. Sir James Mountford, "Success and Failure at the University", *Universities Quarterly*, **11**, 1957.
152. T. R. McConnell, *A General Pattern for American Public Higher Education* (McGraw Hill, 1962).
153. Lord Robbins, Installation Address as Chancellor of University of Stirling, 1968.
154. Maureen Woodhall and Mark Blaug, "Productivity Trends in British University Education, 1938–62", in *Minerva*, **3**, 4, Summer 1965.
155. Robbins Report, *op. cit.*
156. Nevitt Sanford, "Personality Development during the College Years", *Journal of Social Issues*, **12**, 1956.
157. John Summerskill, "Dropouts from College", in N. Sanford (ed.), *The American College* (New York, Wiley, 1962).

CHAPTER 5

FUTURE RESEARCH STRATEGY

THERE is no point at which it is possible to assume that more research is unnecessary. When frontiers of knowledge are pushed back newer and more exciting problems emerge in greater detail than had previously been envisaged. This applies to all fields of knowledge. Education is no exception, and a modest strategy is proposed. The research into higher education is not voluminous, certainly not in Britain and other European countries. Research into higher education has scarcely started to become proportionate to its importance. It will have been noticeable that much of the research reviewed in this volume did not originate in Britain. Comparative educationists and administrators rightly ask to what extent research findings in other countries can be applied to local educational policy. There is scope for enlightened eclecticism here. Application locally of research done in other countries is often more valid than hunch or tradition, though one of the conclusions from this study is that local research is necessary as a sound basis for policy. According to Halsey in 1963, (1) "There is more mythology than information available to new Vice-Chancellors and Principals who seek to create effective centres of learning". He was paraphrasing in a way what Sir Fred Clarke (2) had said twenty years earlier, that if medical and engineering services were conducted with the same lack of careful inquiry, analysis, and research as we find in education, "most patients would die, most bridges would fall down and most manufacturing concerns would go bankrupt".

It is true that in Britain educational research has gathered momentum since 1963, and the time is opportune, therefore, to think strategically in order to avoid unnecessary duplication, while at the same time attempting to ensure that studies are replicated where needed.

Research into wastage in higher education requires a two-pronged approach. At the local and national level the two main subjects of concern are (i) student variables and (ii) institutional and departmental variables; and to these are added at the national level statistical and economic studies.

The justification for local studies is that wastage is a complex problem, and the reasons for it are probably different for each department and for the types of students attracted to studies in different departments. Faculty attitudes probably vary between disciplines. The justification for national studies is that wastage is a national problem and must be tackled nationally.

Research into student variables should continue, but the literature has made us uncomfortably aware that campus and departmental values may be just as critical a factor in wastage as student variables. According to Sanders, (3) "There is no easy road to the production of more graduates of better quality. If teaching is improved, and if all failing students who can be rehabilitated psychologically, educationally and socially, are rehabilitated, the extent of student wastage will still depend on the educational philosophy from time to time of each faculty and university." Sanford (4) too has suggested that research into the environmental determinants of attrition might show that wastage had less to do with factors in the student than with certain conditions in the college itself, and that these conditions might assume greater practical importance than factors within the student, because they affect all students. The research of Pace and Stern provides models of the kinds of studies which could be done in individual institutions.

Universities and colleges do not often have much information about their students who fail or drop out, yet if progress is to be made in reducing wastage it is essential that these data be collected, if not by departments themselves, then by an education research unit in each institution which would conduct other research in addition to that into wastage. This kind of research merits local projects in individual institutions, because, as Summerskill (5) has lucidly pointed out, when a student fails on purely academic grounds he testifies to inadequate admissions procedures or inadequate instruction or other help. Local studies can provide the kind of findings which will best help individual departments to see how far they can reduce their wastage problem. The following discussion deals briefly with the main areas in which research is necessary at the local and national level, and for each of these areas a next step is suggested.

Student Variables

It can be said that students who have a history of democratic, equalitarian family interaction accompanied by encouragement to self-reliance and initiative are better equipped to achieve academically than those who have been dominated. When submissiveness to authoritarian ideas has accompanied domination the limitations of the student are multiplicatively increased. Deprivation of social, emotional, cultural, or intellectual nature also seriously affects the ability to profit from education. Social class is of lesser direct importance than these, though it correlates with some. Those which correlate with social class, and those which do not, need to be identified if we are to get beyond pondering the simple, well-known fact of association between social class and academic performance.

Lavin (6) listed the student variables most often reported in studies as being related to academic performance and categorized them. He produced the following classification of student variables: social maturity, emotional stability, achievement motivation, cognitive style (including curiosity, flexibility, originality, tolerance of ambiguity, liking for abstraction), achievement via conformance, achievement via independence. Some of these factors varied between students of different academic disciplines. Mori (7) studied the structure of motivation for deciding on teaching as a career and found five categories of motivation: economic, social, inter-personal, intellectual, ethical. Vernon (8) found that student teachers with the best academic results were less liable to depression and instability, though tense; and more dependable than weaker students. In a similar study of student teachers Warburton, Butcher, and Forrest (9) found that the more successful students were characterized by high conscientiousness, self-control, and level of culture, and were socially active and sensitive. Roe's work showed that scientists of different disciplines varied in social orientation and motivation.

If we could discover which personality and motivational variables *go together with success in specific disciplines,* selection might be improved. Separate studies should be done for each discipline. Engineers and social scientists, doctors and historians may have markedly different characteristics.

Factor analytic methods would help to show which kinds of traits and groups of characteristics are most closely associated with each discipline, and multiple correlations would indicate which of these taken together are the best predictors. It would not necessarily follow that we should wish all students in any one discipline to be characterized by the same personality traits. Nevertheless, assuming it were desirable to have a mixture of personalities in each discipline, students of 'inappropriate' personality who were falling behind could be diagnosed and their deviance within the group allowed for, rather than they should simply be assigned to wastage.

Selection of Undergraduates and Postgraduates

The research literature on selection almost unanimously declares that present methods of selection are seriously lacking in predictive validity. In Britain the Vice-Chancellors' Committee has commissioned research into the development of scholastic aptitude tests which might be used in place of, or to augment, A levels, interviews, heads' assessments, and other procedures. While it is true that A levels or matriculation examination results are probably the best single predictor of success in higher education in Britain, their effectiveness varies between subjects. The Scholastic Aptitude Test and its equivalents have distinct advantages over traditional selection methods. They are more reliable and can be designed for specific disciplines. Their use might well remove some of the tyranny of O and A levels of which Dainton (10) and many others have complained over the years, including the early specialization they evoke in schools at a time when children should be receiving a broader education. Oliver (11) for several years has drawn attention to the advantages of scholastic aptitude tests: for example, flexible patterns of sixth-form attainment, more freedom for schools, and enhanced capability of universities to discern promise. However, Oliver has also emphasized that a great deal of research is required before it will be possible to introduce them and to assess their effectiveness. Studies comparing selection by S.A.T. and equivalents and by traditional methods should be promoted on a scale large enough to demonstrate conclusively the extent to which selection can be improved by such means.

Research has shown that students who have satisfied matriculation requirements in one or two years tend to achieve better at university than those who have required longer, and further replicative studies should be made to test this finding. There are two other possible ways of selection: by performance in a sixth-form or junior college where studies are conducted under quasi-university conditions with independent study assignments and consultation with teachers rather than using class methods, and by the use of a foundation or first year at university for gauging an individual's possibilities of graduation. The value of academic performance under quasi-university conditions as a predictor should be carefully compared with the predictive power of academic performance under school conditions.

The economics of selecting students by each of these methods also require investigation. If second-, third-, and fourth-year sixth forms could be reduced, and if it were found that those who qualified in one year or survived sixth-form college or the first year at the university were the better students, considerable economies of sixth-form resources and more effective use of college and university places would be possible, provided other factors were held constant, particularly pass rates in universities and colleges. As well as economic studies, studies of comparative academic productivity should also be made of institutions who select students by each of the four principal methods, as a test of the effectiveness of those methods of selection. Several studies* have already shown that students who survive first year at university generally have a far better chance of attaining degrees than those who have merely satisfied the initial entrance requirements, but replication in other colleges and universities is desirable and would cost little to execute.

If we seriously intend to improve selection, all these methods will have to be compared dispassionately. Considerations of the trauma, if any, suffered by students rejected at the end of first or foundation year at the university or college, and that suffered by rejection at 18–19 plus on the criterion of A levels, scholastic aptitude tests, or performance in sixth-form college, would influence our application of the findings. Concern only about the reactions of students selected out at the end of first year need not stand in the way of objective research. The objection usually

---

* For example, at Keele University a Foundation Year in general studies is shared by all students. Degree work begins in second year. Celia Locke has shown that a student who takes two years to pass the Foundation Course has only about 50 per cent chance of getting his degree. On the other hand, students who pass Foundation Year first time show a failure rate of only 2 per cent. Australian studies produce substantially the same findings.

Since publication of the Keele Report it has been found that in later years the difference between successful and unsuccessful students in the Foundation Year has narrowed considerably. This possibly suggests some change in marking and departmental pass rates or other policies.

voiced against selection in first year of university or college is that 'failures' would feel rejected, but strangely it is rare to hear about the trauma experienced by sixth-formers who fail to gain a university place. The proper procedure would be to shelve these sentiments until the necessary research is finished, and then to apply the findings as humanely as seems appropriate.

Research of a very different kind into selection should be done to test whether students' first choice of course could be more realistic and suitable if it were based on fuller knowledge of the possibilities open to them. It is extremely doubtful if every school can have all the data available. Computer studies could be made of the possibility of matching interest, attitudes, vocational aims, and A levels of prospective students with courses in various institutions which make use of or assume the qualifications and attributes the prospective students possess. As Summerskill (12) has said, "It is inadequate to ask whether a student has sufficient and appropriate motivation for college. The more meaningful question is: does the student have sufficient and appropriate motivation for a specified college [or course] with specified characteristics and objectives?"

English and American researches have already shown that, because of ill-informed original choice, many students spend a year or more in courses not suitable for them before dropping out or failing. Of these a high proportion then go on to other, more suitable studies and gain a qualification. The random, trial-and-error enrolment of these individuals could be reduced. A more realistic choice based on consideration of all of the suitable alternatives rather than 'hit-or-miss' with respect to a narrow range of alternatives would help prevent later wastage of university and college places and frustration of students and faculty. Regional studies could be made at first, later extending to a national study and development of a more comprehensive scheme of guidance and selection.

Postgraduate Research Students

Selection of postgraduate students is a field in which only fragmentary research has been done. The small amount of research literature suggests that the criterion usually applied, class of first degree, is limited as a predictor. Anne Roe's studies of eminent scientists and other research by Liam Hudson have shown that the qualities required for outstanding undergraduate work are not necessarily the same as those which are required for original research. Yet in awarding grants and postgraduate places a good first degree—that is an upper second or a first—is almost automatically and often uncritically accepted as a measure of the candidate's potential research ability. Rudd and Hatch (13) in Britain also found only a weak relationship between class of first degree and success in postgraduate studies.

Courses requiring undergraduates to conduct original research studies offer an opportunity to study the relative merits of selecting research workers, using as criteria class of degree and the mark given for a thesis during the undergraduate course. Whitehand (14) in a small study confined to geography students found that by excluding from research opportunities all students with degrees below 'upper seconds' the majority of the outstanding thesis writers would not have had the opportunity to enter the research field. Whitehand's study is in line with the findings of other researchers and is of such interest that it should be replicated on a larger scale in other disciplines. Research is costly, and not to have selected postgraduate students by the use of appropriate criteria must mean that the best use of research funds—never in over-supply—is not achieved. The cutting edge of research into the frontiers of knowledge surely must be less sharp than it should be. Better criteria for selecting researchers than we now have should be sought, using follow-back studies of eminent researchers for interim, and follow-up studies for the more conclusive, findings.

Wastage among Research Students

In Britain and even in the United States research into graduate education is not common. Published research on attrition is mostly concerned with undergraduate students. Wright (15) has documented some of the American work, but overall it is meagre in volume.* Even simple statistics of the number of persons who drop out of graduate schools are often hard to obtain. One study cited by Wright revealed that faculty in a group of institutions believed that only about 20 per cent of doctoral candidates dropped out, yet the true proportion was about 40 per cent. In one university the rate of attrition was

* Professor M. J. Lighthill, F.R.S., has been conducting a study of graduate education of scientists at the Imperial College, London, under the auspices of the Royal Society.

65 per cent. Of no less than 63 student variables studied by Wright few had any association with success or failure in earning the M.A. or Ph.D.

There was little attempt in Wright's research, as reported, to explore personality and motivational factors. Crude motivational items asking, for example, whether or not the candidate would be prepared to rewrite his thesis if requested to do so by the examiner yielded little. It seems that, while the sociological variables should not now be ignored, there is need to go beyond these and to explore motivational variables more scientifically than has yet been done. Postgraduate students who are prepared to accept the isolation and loneliness which is often involved in the protracted task of formulating a viable research problem, acquiring, analysing, and sifting the data and writing it up, and who have the determination to see it through, probably comprise a unique group, with a motivation which differs in quality from that required for undergraduate studies. This hypothesis, if proven, would help in selection and might explain more fully why present criteria for selecting postgraduate students are inadequate. Basic research is necessary and feasible.

Wright's failure to find significant variables must also provoke thought about the possibility that departmental and institutional variables exert as great an influence on research performance as variables within the student himself. The Robbins Committee (Robbins Report, paras. 284–307) referred to the lack of formal training and seminars available to the postgraduate student, and was critical regarding supervision. There was no far-reaching criticism of the quality of those who finally achieve postgraduate degrees. Glennerster's (16) statistics for the London School of Economics showed *a drop-out rate of graduate students as high as 42 per cent for full-time students and 70 per cent for part-time.* It is true that overseas students, who form a significant group, may drop out because of inability to finance themselves beyond the minimum time and because of the social isolation common to visitors. But this is only an informed guess. Selection on the criterion of class of first degree as a predictor of research ability must come into serious doubt when such high drop-out rates are shown. Alternatively, is the standard of supervision so poor? Is the drop-out rate general or does it apply to only a few departments?

Reasons for higher-degree student wastage are probably as

complex as for wastage among undergraduates. The implied criticism of the Robbins Committee in its question, "Who supervises the supervisor?" demands investigation. Some departments have a strong orientation to producing holders of higher degrees, while others are more exclusive or rejecting in their attitudes to students, or are unable to provide adequate facilities, as the Robbins Committee appeared to suspect. Perhaps the burden of undergraduate teaching limits what they can do. Comparative studies of the facilities provided in different disciplines and the difficulties of supervisors in sponsoring students' research are desirable. It would also be useful to conduct follow-up studies of successful postgraduate students and drop-outs from graduate school, to compare the experiences of those in different fields of research, as suggested by the work of Berelson.*

Teaching

There is little real evidence in the literature which has been reviewed to show the ways in which teaching in colleges and universities should be developed in the future. There is obscurity about the place of the lecture, the seminar, the tutorial, and the optimal size of classes and the value of different kinds of audio-visual aids. Few lecturers have any training in methods of teaching; indeed, it is largely a speculative question what kinds of training should be given.

The multiplicity of disciplines and the different teaching methods appropriate for each complicate the problem of research into teaching. For example, experimental work in the laboratory which requires demonstration and notebooks for assessment of progress requires a different kind of teaching than introductory lectures in arts subjects. The physical requirements of the different teaching situations and the curricula often dictate the teaching method. The kind of material to be learned and the availability of aids such as closed-circuit television may dictate the numbers of students who can be taught at once. The widespread criticism of teaching students in large numbers is that the method is too impersonal, but this may not be a valid criticism if lectures are augmented by small-group seminars. Research into teaching methods should be specific to the individual departmental situa-

---

* B. Berelson, *Graduate Education in the United States* (New York, McGraw-Hill, 1960).

tion, because generalizations across disciplines are frequently invalid.

The problem of the 'best' kinds of teaching is complicated also by the differences between students in different disciplines. This is reason for advocating research into teaching at the departmental level. There is some evidence, for example, that students of engineering, medicine, and management are less radical in their political and social attitudes than students in the humanities and social sciences. This was seen in the free-speech movement at Berkeley in 1964. Management and engineering students were not to the forefront in that movement. This raises the question of staff-student relations in teaching. Knapp and Goodrich found that science graduates saw their best teachers as having been strong, masterful, authority figures. It would thus seem, at any rate from Knapp and Goodrich's study, that a strong, perhaps even autocratic method of teaching is appropriate for teaching scientific and management subjects. Quite different faculty-student relationships might be more appropriate for teaching in arts, social sciences, and humanities. The social and emotional concomitants of the learning situation have rarely been studied. Lavin, after reviewing much of the literature, concluded that grades are a function of the interaction between student and teacher. In their relationship with their teachers students have different needs. Some have high needs for affiliation, and others would prefer to learn without affiliating. The warm teacher is therefore not necessarily the effective one, and the effectiveness of a teacher must depend partly on the characteristics of his students.

Yonge (17) reported that two areas of research conspicuously absent in the period 1960–65 were studies of student satisfaction in relation to educational experiences and the study of faculty attitudes, values, and interest in relation to student characteristics. Research into university and college teaching could develop on two main lines—in connection with specific disciplines and students' social and emotional characteristics,* bearing in mind that there seems to be some relation between student characteristics and the disciplines they study.

---

* Research would be conducted at two levels, each complementary to the other. Individual departments would probably be best able to conduct detailed studies, but more often it will be essential for some guidance in methods of research to be given by research officers who have themselves been teachers. Such officers would also gather together findings for dissemination.

Examinations

The recent literature in Britain has focused attention upon the traditional limitations of examinations, their reliability and structure. Locke (18) has pointed out, as recently as 1963, that an important but frequently neglected problem in the evaluation of educational achievement is the meaningfulness of the criteria by which achievement is to be judged. What is it that examinations are meant to test? Is it capacity to work at speed under stress during a three-hour period without 'nerves'? There is little doubt that a student with this capacity has an advantage compared with a nervous student, even if the latter's performance would otherwise be superior. In so far as this is true the better student might sometimes be 'wasted' because he lacks examination ability, perhaps for temperamental reasons. In Locke's study a high-level group of science students could be distinguished by their self-initiated achievement and by their standard grade achievement. How far can the former be measured by examinations? Should examinations measure persistence in working at a problem and ability to work independently; or the ability to see the essentials and to formulate strategies in problem-solving? Should the criteria take into account the cognitive style required in the proposed profession of the candidate?

These are questions which might well have direct relevance for different disciplines. What formulation based on valid research procedures has been achieved in this field? Formulation of criteria for use in examinations is an essential step towards solving the problem of wastage, for if the wrong criteria are applied in assessing graduates it follows that wastage of some who should have passed will occur, and others will get through the net who perhaps should have been failed.

Simultaneously with research for better criteria, research into examination reliability should continue. Objective tests offer greater possibilities of reliability, but it is often argued that they only measure recall and do not test the ability to synthesize and solve problems or literary style. These objections must be recognized for the planning of research in this field.

These are real problems. While they are being studied research into the use of course assignments and supplementary examinations should also be pursued. It may be found that wastage and delay is less in departments which employ these methods than in those which do not. The Robbins Committee (Robbins Report,

Appendix IIA, Part 4, para 132) reported evidence from a study at Imperial College, London, which it cited as "one of the few pieces of direct evidence" regarding delay. In many cases the alternative to requiring students to leave is to require them to repeat a year of their course. Over a period of eight years wastage was reduced by almost half by this method alone. Sixteen per cent of students failed their first-year examination at the first attempt. Of these one-third were allowed to repeat their first year at the college, and 80 per cent passed at the second attempt. Of the other two-thirds of the original failures who left the college about a third resat the examinations a year or more later, and half passed. At the second attempt the first-year failure rate of about 16 per cent was thus reduced to some 9 per cent. The same practice in later years of the course reduced wastage in these years by about the same proportion. By offering a second chance to students in other disciplines there seems no reason why similar reductions in wastage should not be achieved. Further, in some cases, the use of supplementary examinations might reduce wastage just as successfully and without the delay involved in requiring students to repeat a whole year.

In arts, science, technology, and agriculture only 7 to 13 per cent were studying beyond the period normally required, at the time the Robbins Committee was collecting evidence. In medicine, dentistry, and veterinary science 30 per cent of students were permitted to study beyond the normal period. Individual departments might profitably conduct their own research into the extent to which the use of delays and supplementary examinations can reduce wastage, though this might preferably be the concern of universities as a whole rather than departments if they wish to attack the problem of wastage generally. The tendency for departments to have more or less fixed wastage rates has already been discussed. It seems eminently desirable for universities to compare the wastage rates of various departments and to inquire into the assumptions made by the examiners in each. This kind of study would need to take into account the quality of student entrants into each department, and their work loads, and should lead to the possibility of assessing the extent to which rationalization and reduction of failure rates was feasible. Inquisitions would be deplorable. This is a delicate problem, but, by developing constructive consultative relations, defensive and intransigent resistance among faculty could be made redundant.

Halls of Residence

Among the advantages of living in halls of residence it is often held that they offer a liberalizing and socializing education to the student, of the kind higher education is meant to foster. These apparent advantages do not necessarily correlate with academic success. It is debatable whether students are or should be assessed solely in academic terms; nevertheless the influence of halls of residence or other student accommodation on academic achievement is as valid a research question as their influence upon the less tangible qualities it is hoped that halls promote.

The small amount of research in this specific field is not conclusive, and more is needed. Policies of wardens in selecting students for residence are not dependent necessarily on the question of how to maximize academic achievements, yet it is possible that these policies are crucial to students' academic performance. For example, one study (19) has shown that first-year students in residence perform better than non-resident students, while for third year the opposite is true—non-resident third-year students perform better than residents. If this were a general finding we might well conclude that those wardens who insist on first-year students living out are contributing to wastage. Whatever criteria are held to be important in selection of residents in different years, it is rash for wardens to ignore the question of potential wastage, and how they might be influencing wastage in applying selection policies. This study would be simple to replicate, and the findings could be far-reaching. For more accurate findings such a study should preferably be controlled for sex, social class, criteria for admission, ability, age, subject of study, and kind of tutorial assistance given in the hall.

On the results of experimental findings will ultimately depend the kinds of student residence and other facilities which should be built. What, for example, should be the policy of a university or college which found that students who live out perform better than residents? This affects costing. Perhaps the ideal arrangement in terms of overall academic achievement will be to build student houses where students can live and work at all hours on the campus, but sleep at home or in other accommodation. Such an arrangement would be cheaper than residential places for all, which obviously cannot be afforded, and the benefits would be more evenly spread. Against any possible overall gains in academic performance would need to be considered the degree to which the traditional values of higher education are fostered by one kind of accommodation or another. In spite of the long tradition of residence, this is an almost unexplored field in research terms.*

Schools

The literature on wastage contains few reports on the role of schools in preparing students for higher education. By the time students enter college or university the influence of their school experience is largely irreversible, and there is evidence that some wastage occurs because of the poor preparation they have received in school. The work of MacArthur (20) and Summerskill (21) in the United States, Mann (22) in Britain, and Olsen (23) and Hughes (24) in Australia suggests that research links between schools and universities could lead to findings that could have a strong influence on teaching in schools. MacArthur found persistent differences between state-sponsored schools and private schools in the United States. Summerskill urged more rigorous research on the psychological content of the learning experience and the meaning of scholarship for secondary-school pupils. Intellectually well-endowed students who lack the inclination for scholarship are familiar to teachers, and the studies reviewed by Summerskill suggested that there may be identifiable attitudes to school and school work which limit their chances of graduation from college should they enter higher education.

The studies reviewed by Olsen pointed to inadequate preparation in school as a principal cause of failure at the university, and showed that the need to assimilate, synthesize, and evaluate knowledge is not met by many schools. Several researchers in England and Australia have found that certain schools help their students to achieve matriculation or other entrance qualifications by cramming, spoon-feeding, and excessive coaching, and in some of these schools authoritarian methods are used which are inimical to preparation for higher education. Mann studied the differences between successful and unsuccessful student teachers. There were few differences in intelligence, social class, or academic record.

* Joan Brothers and Stephen Hatch have now completed a study of halls of residence in Britain in the Department of Higher Education at the University of London Institute of Education, and Marie Clossick has completed a study of a residential and study tower at the University of Essex.

The most striking differences were in their experiences of responsibility and opportunities for independent work while at school. Poorer students had had their studies over-directed and been given little responsibility throughout their school careers.

Olsen calls for more co-operation between schools and universities in preparing students to work by university methods. Freedom, self-direction, initiative, and use of a library are four examples of ways in which students could be encouraged. Schonell summarized the attributes of a good secondary school. It should help would-be university students to think for themselves in discussion, give them freedom in planning their time allotments, allowing for more free study periods and less formal teaching, and training in study techniques and even note-making and note-taking should be given. Failing students often complain of being overloaded, because they have not learned to work efficiently.

The research most urgently needed in this field is that aimed at discovering ways of influencing teachers in schools to modify their methods where this is necessary, especially in relation to prospective candidates for places in higher education. During the strike of schoolteachers in Sweden in 1966 it was found that secondary-school children could direct their own work better than had formerly been realized. Although they were not completely adequate to the task, the degree of success of which they were capable has encouraged the National Board of Education to sponsor research to explore how independent work in the schools can be extended. (25) All categories of students would probably benefit just as well from the sort of training which best prepares students for college or university work. Research might also be directed to studying which groups of pupils benefit the most and at what age these methods can be applied and for what intelligence levels. Ian McMullen, director of the Nuffield Resources for Learning Project, formerly headmaster of a large comprehensive school, inclines to the view that free study time, assignments, and seminar groups are methods which can be effectively applied at probably all ages and most if not all ability levels. He claims that such methods, properly used, increase children's motivation by allowing them a choice of activity and control over time, an increase in self-direction and organization and a relaxation of authority tensions. McMullen's work has shown that the schools with the most independent study were the quietest during breaks. These methods would clearly need to be more judiciously introduced into some schools than others. This could be done experimentally and assessment begun using appropriate controls.

With the current expansion of comprehensive schools' sixth forms, the danger is that directive methods will persist and even spread as sixth forms become larger. If this happens it is conceivable that wastage in higher education will be further encouraged at source, in the schools—in the ways the Hale Committee deplored. Students who might have been successful in higher education may thus fail in greater numbers because they were not properly prepared for higher education while in secondary school. Whenever research into this problem is done it would be prudent to extend it downwards to the lower forms and not confine the studies to the sixth-form level. It may be that students' potential for higher education could be improved at all levels of secondary education.

A National Data Bank

The need for research at the national level as well as local institutional and departmental research calls for a national data bank, on the lines proposed by Astin and Panos. (26) Storage of data by computer is simple, economical in space, and the data should be more accessible than they can be if retained in research departments scattered around many institutions as they are at the present time. Students and institutions, though they have individual characteristics, can be grouped nationally on certain criteria. Which data are worthy of collection would be a matter for informed consultation between interested parties. Wastage is not the only kind of study which would be facilitated. A national data bank would make possible research which otherwise would be impossible. Data concerning students could be collected by institutions as part of the normal entrance procedures. Intake data might be similar to that requested on the Freshman Information Form of the American Council on Education. The questions include occupational and study plans, preferences and reality choices, postgraduate degree ambition, kind of school attended, grades obtained at school, parents' educational level, social class, family size and birth order, age and sex, prospects of financing education, extra-curricular activities while at school, as well as self ratings on a range of abilities and orientations. Later information would also include performance in university and college studies, class of degree and first employment, whether students had gone on to a graduate programme or what stage they had reached before interruption of studies, any reasons for dropping out and whether students had transferred to other courses. Questions could be included concerning the kinds of accommodation used while undergraduates. It would also be useful to have data on personality and values, so that there could be some measure of students' growth towards liberalism during the process of higher education. If data were collected longitudinally, other supposed outcomes of higher education and development of professional attitudes in different disciplines could be studied.

Empirical evidence concerning the diversity of characteristics found in departments and institutions and the extent to which they are associated with wastage, and on patterns of supply of graduates to the professions, Civil Service, industry, schools, and universities would be valuable in forming educational policies. As Astin and Panos have pointed out, in formulating policy in the absence of systematized information of this kind administrators in institutions, government agencies, and elsewhere had been forced to rely upon educational folklore, and advocate the use of a data bank to facilitate the study of administrative practices, curriculum, and staffing. For continuous and comparative studies of wastage in different institutions data could be included concerning selection policies and criteria, the presence or absence of departmental quotas, evidence of flexibility in allowing students to change courses, the presence of other conditions such as allowing credits for successful studies, staff-student ratios, qualifications of staff, existing teaching and examining practices, systems of degree classifications, flexibility or rigidity of departmental pass rates, existence of student progress reviewing boards and their practices, and also sizes and rates of growth of departments and institutions.

Most of these data would help to discover means of analysing the problem of wastage and carrying out the Robbins Committee's (Robbins Report, para. 581) injunction to departments that they study continuously how to ensure that as many students as possible will graduate. Departments themselves were urged by the Committee to assume this responsibility, but regional or national studies should yield further clues to the solution of the problem. The common elements in wastage between institutions could be more clearly seen through comparative studies.

The greatest advantages of a national data bank would be in the long term. National sampling of large numbers of students according to a wide range of criteria would be practicable, where now it can be only fragmentary. Studies of the outcome of different kinds of student accommodation and flexibility of academic administration, and large-sample follow-up studies of the career and further study patterns of drop-outs and graduates in different disciplines by class of degree, and postgraduate students' research success are examples of the kind of research which would be facilitated by the ease in sampling which a data bank should make possible. National follow-up studies of the post-university career performance of groups of students in particular disciplines and by class of degree would be made easier.

Selection policies might well be capable of refinement, but, in view of the research literature reviewed earlier, the greatest benefit might be in the increased awareness of institutional characteristics and the impact of these on student performance. Lauwerys wrote, "In view of the stringent admission standards and by comparison with what is achieved elsewhere wastage rates in some [British] departments and universities seem excessive. If statistics were collected and published as a matter of routine, awareness of the problem would be stimulated and the adoption of remedial measures encouraged."* A national data bank would make it possible for a great amount of hitherto inaccessible material to be summarized, correlated, and published, and would be a first step towards continuous analysis of the effects of past policies and towards the synthesis of new policies based on empirical data.

Pass Rates and Measures of Productivity

As soon as we begin to discuss wastage, loss of productivity is directly implied. Throughout this study a satisfactory final definition of wastage has not been found. There is no single criterion. It is relatively simple to produce a formula for computing productivity, taking into account quantity only, but since higher education is concerned with quality the problem is complicated.† We have made reference to the way in which

---

Access to Higher Education, vol. II, section II, U.N.E.S.C.O. and the International Association of Universities, p. 557.

† For a statement on this topic see Maureen Woodhall and Mark Blaug, "Productivity Trends in British University Education 1938–62", *Minerva*, 3, 4, 1965.

the quality of student intake has risen over the last two decades, slowly and apparently continuously. Courses tend to grow in the amount of material students are expected to learn, and demand for the 'products' of higher education becomes more acute. It is fairly safe to assume that the quality of candidates has not declined, and has possibly risen.* In such circumstances is wastage at pre-War rates any longer justified? If students are now required to learn more in the same amount of time it is doubly wasteful to fail some who would have passed in former years, and there is much to be said for Lauwerys' proposal that some students should be given intermediate qualifications as evidence of having reached a certain level of learning. If we assume, then, that quality is rising, or is at least not deteriorating, we may, for the purpose of this argument, be justified in considering wastage in purely quantitive terms. With regard to quantity we can probably do worse than follow the simple formula posited by Hughes.

Hughes (27) put the problem in the following way. Quantitively wastage can be seen as loss of productivity—delay and drop-out being the clearest forms. For each student in a given academic year the university provides a certain amount of building space, equipment, and staff time, costing society, let us say, £500. If this 'student year' does not contribute to the award of a degree the £500 may be regarded as expenditure which is unproductive. 'Productive time' could be defined as the essential time required to gain a degree; for example, in a three-year arts or science course where 100 students graduate, the productive time is 300 student years.

Thus we might have the following:

	Productive time	Unproductive time	Total
Science	500 student years	500 student years	1000
Arts	600 student years	400 student years	1000

The resources of the university would have been used unproductively 50 per cent for science and 40 per cent for arts, or, in plainer terms, 45 per cent of the expenditure of the university on

---

* Darley obtained ability scores from freshmen entering 167 U.S. institutions in 1952 and 1959, and found that in these seven years the mean ability scores of the students increased, even though enrolments went up by 50 per cent in the same period. As measured by A-level performance there has been a similar general increase in the ability of British student intakes in the past decade.

students would not have contributed to the gaining of degrees. If the degree is taken as the sole criterion of success and we disregard any benefits which might accrue from failing students' having been at the university, then we can reasonably regard that proportion of universities' or colleges' expenditure as 'waste'.

Though this is admittedly a crude overall measure which does not take individuals into account, it constitutes an approach which is capable of development and refinement. As Hughes points out, wastage can be reckoned not only as student failure but also as waste of academics' research and scholarship time expended for no measurable result. If wastage is the price to be paid for high academic standards and failures are incapable of reaching those standards, then institutions should resist change. But this question can be satisfied only by careful investigation, not by discussion devoid of empirical evidence. From the point of view of policy, failure to anticipate the consequences of insisting on excessively high academic standards can also be disastrous. The present situation in England suggests that potential teachers of science in the schools are lost each year for this reason. This may account in part for the serious teacher shortage, and, in turn, the dearth of satisfactory science candidates for university places. The same may be true of other subjects.

Cunningham (28) advocated that universities should have machinery, standing rules, or guiding principles to ensure that excessively high failure rates do not occur in particular departments—or, if they do, to find out why. He maintained that if there were any lessening of autonomy by such a step it was justified by the need to safeguard the interests of the community as well as those of the student. The Robbins Committee (Robbins Report, para. 580) did not express themselves quite so forcibly, but they clearly advocated a serious assessment of the same problem in English universities.*

The problem of wastage cannot be satisfactorily solved by arbitrary administrative devices. It is vital that the kind of action suggested by the Robbins Committee, whatever form it might take, should not be arbitrary. Empirical studies are needed to ensure fairness to faculties with high wastage rates. Comparative studies are useful in showing where the problem is most serious, but local studies are also necessary to assess individual situations

* See page 197.

S.F.W.H.E.—Q*

and ensure that any administrative decisions which might be applied to reduce wastage are soundly based.

The practice of plotting students' examination results throughout their studies as shown in the diagram by Penney (p. 120) can serve several purposes: as a diagnostic method to spot which students will need most help; as a check on the reliability of the examinations; as a check on accuracy of selection; and to demonstrate at what point throughout the course accuracy in prediction begins to become possible. These purposes are not mutually exclusive; for example, the plottings will not show whether it is selection, teaching, examination-marking, or whatever else that needs to be improved. The essential thing is that once the students are plotted in this way, more accurate focus on the problem becomes possible and more intelligent questions can then be asked.

Responsibilities of Institutions and assessing the Effectiveness of Student Services

Apart from the global question 'what are the responsibilities of institutions of higher education towards students?', the more specific question of defining their responsibilities towards students in promoting purely academic success is in itself formidable. It may be right for autonomous institutions to please themselves, and perhaps the definition of responsibility is a domestic one. Institutions appear to vary enormously in the responsibility they are prepared to accept. The question here is how to reduce wastage, and once a department accepts responsibility for that, the next step is through consultation and experiment to test what measures are necessary to achieve that end.

Some of the possible measures have already been discussed. The roles of moral tutor, counsellor, adviser, and student-health-service doctor are not identical, and no research appears to have been done to assess the functions and relative merits of each. Few universities or colleges would desire or could afford them all. Which, then, should they choose to have? Should this decision be based on senior members' experience or hunch, or should students generally be asked about the nature of their problems to help us discover their needs? Perhaps a sample of, say, 10 per cent of students should be consulted, or it may be preferable to confine the study to those known to be failing or those who actually fail.

Alternatively it may be better to study the results institutions have achieved by using one method or another. One problem here would be that universities and departments may have different entry and examination standards. A well-planned research would control for both. The differences between the wastage rates, on the one hand, of institutions and departments who have reviewing boards and allow supplementary examinations and whose faculty feel responsibility for students' graduation and, on the other hand, a study of those who do not, but rather place all responsibility on the student apart from providing lecture courses, might produce some interesting results. As Sir Geoffrey Crowther once said, "What is extracted from the pool [of ability] depends less on the pool than on the pump". (29) Students are under an obligation to do as well as they can, but the differences between institutions in the methods by which they graduate greater or lesser proportions of students is a field in which empirical research is long overdue.

Studies of Special Groups of Students

Most urgently in need of study among these special categories of students are the clear drop-outs. In Britain they have been studied very little. Kendal's study of unsuccessful students from University College, London, and the University of Liverpool was very illuminating, and to some extent reassuring because it showed that a large proportion of these students succeeded elsewhere in the end. It would be interesting to know why they had to be failed in the first instance. Astin (30) in America found that 94 per cent of men drop-outs and 84 per cent of women intended to re-enrol.

If, as the small amount of research suggests, so many drop-outs have such strong motivation, and clear intentions to try again, it should be possible to avoid wasting them. Two possibilities immediately suggest themselves. They could be helped more by the institution originally accepting them as entrants. To discover ways in which they could be helped drop-outs could be asked to attend exit interviews conducted by sensitive interviewers who are sympathetic towards student problems, preferably with a psychological and sociological background and experience in student-counselling. Indeed, this would be a function of the counselling office. These interviews would be a valuable source of research data. Perhaps the course has been unsuited to these students; they may have had serious financial, social, or psychological problems, or antagonized their tutors; and the aims of the failed student may have been dissonant with those of the institution. Students may prefer to withdraw in favour of some more suitable alternative they have discovered, or feel they would like to withdraw temporarily with the intention of returning after a period in commerce, travelling, or other maturing experience. Research into the relative frequency and importance of these factors would suggest what, if anything, could be done to retain the student, and might show how to avoid wastage of the investment in grants and college resources. Shuman suggests that, where this is not done already, universities and colleges should make their appointments offices available to students who find they have to withdraw.

The second possibility is that of transferring the student to another course, perhaps in another institution, where he would be allowed credits in those subjects he has successfully completed. This would lead to a further programme of research and development, concerning those institutions and departments which might be prepared to accept the student and allow him credit. In turn it would be hoped the research would lead to negotiations concerning policy and administrative changes which would make it possible for more universities and colleges to accept students on these terms. Such flexible arrangements are effective, as demonstrated by Kendall's study in which he showed that up to 70 per cent of failed students made a further attempt to gain a degree or other qualifications, and, of these, two-thirds were successful.

The reluctance of departments to accept some other department's or institution's 'rejects' is understandable, and the reasons for this and its prevalence should be investigated. Kendall showed that not only do failed students often succeed, but sometimes they are successful to the extent of obtaining M.A. or Ph.D. degrees. American research showed that drop-outs most frequently go on to better institutions than the ones they left. (31) Reluctance to accept the older student also seems to be unfounded. One early Australian study showed that, compared with the general run of students whose graduation rate in minimum time was only 40 per cent, students who failed before enlisting in the armed forces came back to university after years of service and graduated in minimum time.*

* A. H. Iliffe (1969) has found at the University of Keele that students aged up to 40 and 50 years did as well as school-leavers.

Special sub-groups of students who should be studied are the promising students who are failing and the less promising ones who succeed. The concern of senior administrators at the frequency with which the achievement of extremely able students is disappointing and the recognition that seemingly mediocre students often achieve good results suggests the need for research to discover how this happens. It is tempting to believe that both categories of students reflect the limitations of selection and examination procedures. It would be desirable, if possible, to control for these. It would then be possible to discover which student variables can explain the unpredictable performance of these two groups.

It is possible that intelligence is a threshold variable, and that above a certain level, performance and ability are not highly correlated. In Anne Roe's study of eminent scientists, for example, there were some whose measured intelligence was only moderately above average. Given a certain moderately high level of ability, it was possible for some individuals to become not only successful, but eminent in their fields. If this is true of eminent scientists it probably follows that mediocre abilities in undergraduates are no essential barrier to graduation. We need to know more concerning the personalities, motivations, and aspirations of the two groups. Studies of this kind will yield indications for selection, student-counselling, and guidance.

Philistines and the All-round Scholar

Higher education's role is seldom thought to be limited to the production of mere holders of degrees. It is widely held today that scientists should know and appreciate something of the arts, humanities, or the social sciences. The cultured engineer, doctor, manager, or director should be the rule, not the exception. Engineers and architects who produce large, merely functional monstrosities of bridges and buildings to appal succeeding generations seem to some extent to be on the way out, and the philosopher, historian, and artist cannot escape noting at any rate some of the more spectacular scientific and technological achievements.

It is agreed that there should be something of the all-round man in the modern graduate. This raises a further question. In any field, who are the graduates who achieve the better class degrees and postgraduate eminence? Are Nobel Prize winners, Fellows of the Royal Society, and other of the best and most imaginative graduates necessarily those who while undergraduates performed well by avoiding interest in arts, humanities, or social sciences? Or, on the contrary, are they the ones who deliberately allowed their interests to range widely? It would be useful to know whether distinguished or mediocre students have the more catholic interests and greater culture. Decisions of scientists and technologists can have far-reaching social consequences, and this makes essential the inclusion of liberal content in their courses— at least enough for them to become able and willing to work with, for example, designers, sociologists, or town planners. Schonell has discussed how the increasing tendency towards specialization and professionalization may lead to a decline in the formative functions of universities, including their task of developing men and women as cultured persons with a broad education and awareness of social responsibilities and social values. This is a theme often discussed, but one in which there has been little research. It may be peripheral to the wastage problem, but it is closely related to academic quality in the fullest sense, and should be studied. Suppose we found, for example, that Philistines were generally awarded the best degrees in science and technology and narrow academics the best in arts, humanities, and the social sciences, or the opposite. Either finding would have far-reaching implications for curricula, teaching, and examining in higher education. We would then have to consider to what extent the professional orientation of higher education could or should be re-moulded.

Summary

In this chapter some main directions for future research into academic success, failure, and wastage have been suggested which follow closely the headings under which the literature has fallen and appear to follow as logical next steps. Both national and local studies are needed; national studies would yield general findings necessary for policy-making bodies, and local studies would guide the policies of particular institutions. A national data bank is desirable, containing data derived from each year's student intakes of all universities and colleges, one purpose of which would be to facilitate study of national samples of students in each discipline and to compare institutions and departments at different periods in time. The ethos of different institutions and its relation to students' performance could be studied. The effects of innovations in different institutions could be compared, and follow-up studies of groups of students on a national scale would be made possible. National samples could be made available of students who have had experience of student residence and those who have not; students who have dropped out and gained degrees elsewhere; highly gifted, and mediocre students; and students from different kinds of school; these are a few of the possibilities.

Young (32) stressed the importance of overall strategy to avoid unnecessary duplication of research and to heighten awareness of essential new research areas, and advocated institutes to sponsor defined fields such as higher education, teacher-training, economics and planning of education, and topics connected with schools. As previously remarked, although national research is essential, local research in institutions and departments is equally important. As Trow (33) has said, "Eventually . . . we want to know more, not about student attrition . . . in general, but about its causes in our own institutions. . . . We cannot easily assume that the conditions and processes we find in any one or any group [of institutions] are also present in another." This implies the need for an education research office manned by properly trained researchers on every campus, not as a luxury but as an integral part of the institution.*

Schonell and associates (34) have referred to informed and scholarly books, many of which represent expressions of opinion coloured by the experiences and attitudes of the participants. Important as these undoubtedly are, it must seriously be asked whether they are on their own adequate for policy formulation. Can research make a further contribution? The paucity of studies of students as they pass through university, and consequently the small amount of evidence available of a continuous kind on such matters as matriculation levels in relation to examination results, failure rates, and causes of failure, and the value or otherwise of particular changes in methods and courses, were singled out by Schonell *et al.* as examples of gaps in the knowledge of academics concerning their own institutions and departments. The Robbins Report advocated full and continuous

* See Abercrombie in *Universities Quarterly*, 22, 2, 1968, for a description of an English university education research unit.

inquiry as part of the university's responsibility to students. For this purpose independent research in each institution would clearly be required. It should be possible also to develop methods of indicating which students are most likely to falter, and which will be likely to benefit from remedial action to mitigate the influence of those factors which militate against success.

Research departments cannot impose research on unwilling departments. By offering consultative services and feed-back in the form of reports, confidential if necessary, it is possible for the interests of researchers and researched to be brought closely together in a common cause. If wastage is to be studied subject by subject, mutual confidence and consultation is essential.

Wastage or attrition in higher education is a major problem. The studies reviewed in this volume are a fair representative sampling of the literature. The main streams of research have been covered, and the indications are clear. Research on wastage, to be effective, must take into account institutional and departmental variables as well as the very wide range of variables more closely related to the student.

Apart from the implications for further research, two things stand out in bold relief. Academic wastage cannot be considered realistically as a problem which is separate from the goals and practices of institutions of higher education, because it is tied inseparably to organizations and their aims, and the personalities, policies, goals, and criteria of those within them, and to suppose that wastage can be eliminated by selection of better students is naïve. It may be hoped that institutions and departments will find by scientific means further ways of taking into account more of the individual differences which exist among students. Maintaining inflexible institutional characteristics which do not take students' individual differences into account is certain to inflate wastage unnecessarily. There is no implied suggestion that standards need be lowered, yet the research literature suggests many feasible innovations, apart from better selection of students. Research and innovation in one or more of these areas carefully chosen to suit particular institutions could lead to greater proportions of undergraduates successfully completing their studies while maintaining academic standards inviolate.

REFERENCES

1. A. H. Halsey, "Education and Mobility", in *The Listener,* April 18th, 1963.
2. Sir Fred Clarke, *The Study of Education in England* (London, Oxford University Press, 1943).
3. C. Sanders, "Factors and Research Problems in the Success and Failure of University Students", *Educand, 3,* 2, 1958.
4. Nevitt Sanford, "Personality Development during the College Years", *Journal of Social Issues,* 12, 4, 1956.
5. John Summerskill, "Drop-outs from College", in N. Sanford (ed.) *The American College* (New York, Wiley, 1962).
6. David E. Lavin, *"The Prediction of Academic Performance* (Russell Sage Foundation, and New York, Wiley, 1967).
7. Tokako Mori, "Structure of Motivation for becoming a Teacher", *Journal of Educational Psychology,* 56, 4, 1965.
8. P. E. Vernon, "Educational Abilities of Training College Students", *British Journal of Educational Psychology,* 19, 1939.
9. F. W. Warburton, H. J. Butcher, and G. H. Forrest, "Predicting Student Performance in a University Department of Education", *British Journal of Educational Psychology,* 33, 1963.
10. F. S. Dainton, "Dramatic Trend Away from Science", reported in *The Times Educational Supplement,* January 6th, 1967.
11. R. A. C. Oliver, "University Entrance Requirements: Whence and Whither?" *Universities Quarterly,* 20, 3, 1966.
12. John Summerskill, *op. cit.*
13. E. Rudd and S. R. Hatch, *Graduate Study and After* (London, Weidenfeld and Nicolson, 1968).
14. J. W. R. Whitehand, "The Selection of Research Students", *Universities Quarterly,* 21, 1, 1966.
15. Charles R. Wright, "Success or Failure in Earning Graduate Degrees", *Sociology of Education,* 38, 1964.
16. Howard Glennerster, *Graduate School: A Study of Graduate Work at London School of Economics* (Edinburgh, Oliver and Boyd, 1967).
17. G. D. Yonge, "Students", *Review of Educational Research,* 25, 1965.

18. E. A. Locke, "The Development of Criteria of Student Achievement", *Educational and Psychological Measurement,* **23,** 1963.
19. Doreen Langley, "Student Performance and Student Residence", *The Australian University,* **3,** 2, 1965.
20. C. MacArthur, "Sub-Culture and Personality during the College Years", *Journal of Educational Sociology,* **33,** 1960.
21. John Summerskill, *op. cit.*
22. J. F. Mann, "An Investigation into the Various Factors Influencing Success in Completing a Course in Teacher Training", Ph.D. thesis, London, 1961.
23. F. J. Olsen, "Failure in First Year University Examinations", *Australian Journal of Education,* **1,** 3, 1957
24. P. W. Hughes, "Academic Achievement at the University: An Analysis of Factors Related to Success" (Mimeo), (University of Tasmania, 1960).
25. S. Henrysson and E. Lövgren, "Independent Work in the Secondary School", *School Research,* 1967: 6. National Board of Education, Stockholm.
26. Alexander W. Astin and Robert J. Panos, "A National Research Data Bank", *Educational Record* (Winter, 1966).
27. P. W. Hughes, *op. cit.*
28. K. S. Cunningham, "Success and Failure in Australian Universities", Australian Council of Educational Research.
29. Lord Crowther cited in Sir Fred J. Schonell, "Student Adaptation and its Bearing on Academic Achievement", *The Australian University,* **1,** 1, 1963.
30. A. W. Astin, "Personal and Environmental Factors associated with College Dropouts among High Aptitude Students", *Journal of Educational Psychology,* **55,** 4, 1964.
31. Dorothy M. Knoell, "Undergraduate Attrition: Mortality or Mobility", (Mimeo), (Princeton, 1964).
32. Michael Young, *Innovation and Research in Education* (London, Institute of Community Studies and Routledge and Kegan Paul, 1965).
33. Martin Trow, "Social Research and Educational Policy", *Universities Quarterly,* **19,** 1965.
34. Sir Fred J. Schonell, *Promise and Performance* (Universities of Queensland and London, 1962).

INDEX

Figures in brackets refer to pages containing notes

ABERCROMBIE, M. L. J., 153, 154, 171, (217), (220)

Aberdeen University, 117, 160, 171

Ability, 28, 29, 30, 35, 36, 38, 51, 53, 54, 65–69, 74, 76, 77, 78, 81, 83, 107, 108, 113, 130, 134, 140, 214–216

Academic disciplines, 99, 111, 181, 201

Academic failure—*see* Wastage

Access to Higher Education, 243

Accommodation, 30, 32, 72, 76, 79, 149, 166, 173–182; at home, 32, 45, 177; and academic performance, 34, 176, 177, 178, 179; in halls of residence, 177, 238–239; in lodgings, 177

Achievement, pressures for, 52; over and under, 69; academic, 97, 98; need for (n Ach) 111, 112

Age, 28, 34, 50 ff., 65, 76, 133, 181. *See also* Maturity

Albright, L. A., 135, (147)

Albrow, M. C., 174, (221)

A-level examinations, 11, 57, 83, 84, 96, 100 ff., 113, 118, 119, 126, 187, 190, 231; correlation with tertiary education, 101; as predictor, 105, 121, 122, 229, 230; boosting results, 114 ff.

Allahabad University, 45

Altbach, P., 33, 57, 72, (85), 159, (218)

American Council on Education, 109

Anderson, A. W., 102, (142)

Anderson, C. A., (86)

Anderson, D. S., 103, 117, (142), (146), 163, 174, (219), (221)

Andrews, F. M., 66, 81, (92)

Anthropologists, 43, 136

Anxiety, 30, 69 ff., 73, 74, 78, 79, 112, 162, 168; and examinations, 73, 75

Arts, 16, 17, 21, 38, 40, 60, 96, 98, 109, 117, 122, 123, 136, 157, 203, 213, 244, 249

Asian students, 46

Aspiration, educational, 38, 46, 47, 56, 81; vocational, 38, 60, 199; level of, 112, 113, 154

Astin, A. W., 24, 33, 34, 35, 43, 45, 46, 51, 58, 60, 65, 77, 79, 81, (85), 107, 108, 110, (144), 158, 172, (218), (221), 241, 242, 247, (254)

Attrition—*see* Wastage

Australia, 21, 40, 49, 50, 105, 106, 116, 125, 126, 130, 163, 174, 182, 184, 186, 189, 215, 239, 248

Australian Council for Educational Research, 105

Austwick, K., (142)

BACIG, T. D., 175, (221)

Barnard, G. A., 205, 211

Barnett, V. D., (89)

Barron, F., 138

Beard, R. M., 63, (91), 152

Bentley, J. C., 134, (147)

Berdie, R. F., (141)

Berkeley, 47, 57, 140, 156, 235

Bernstein, B. B., 48, (88)

Biologists, 67, 136, 137, 155

Biology, 101, 136, 155, 156, 157
Birth rank, 43 ff.
Blaug, M., 22, (27), 96, (141), 215, (225)
Bloom, B. S., 135, 137, (147), 198, (224)
Bosworth, G. S., 200, (224)
Boyd, G. W. D., 64, (91)
Boyer, E. L., 132, (147)
Boyer, R. K., 52, (89), 181, (222)
Brannan, P., 126, (146)
Broe, J. J., 29, (84)
Brookover, W. B., 154, (217)
Brown, W. F., 56, (90)
Brunel University, 22
Butcher, H. J., 228, (253)
Butler, Lord, 115, (145)

CALIFORNIA PSYCHOLOGICAL INVEN-
    TORY, 67, 109–110
Cambridge University, 115, 134,
    164, 167, 188, 206. See also
    Oxford and Cambridge
Campbell, D. P., 159, 171, (218)
Canada, 12, 170
Career goals, 59, 170
Carr-Saunders, Sir Alexander, 28,
    29, (84), 187, (223)
Cassirer, H. R., 151, (216)
Certificate of Merit, 63
Chambers, Sir Paul, 200, (224)
Chaney, F. B., 66, 81, (92), 135,
    (147)
Chemistry, 62, 120, 151, 152, 155,
    156, 165, 198, 199, 205
Clark, B. R., 60, (91)
Clarke, Sir Fred, 226, 253
Classics, 151
Clements, R. V., 137, (148)
Cochrane, D., 130, 131, (147)
College Characteristics Index
    (research into student resi-
    dence), 182

College Entrance Examinations
    Board, 16
Connor, D. V., 152, (216)
Continental universities, 49
Corbett, J. P., (90)
Council for National Academic
    Awards, 205
Counselling and other services,
    30, 62, 73, 83, 149, 159–173;
    who should counsel? 166; and
    wastage, 170–173
Cox, R., 192, (223)
Craven, C. J., (145)
Creager, J. A., 24
Creativity, 56, 63, 68, 135; and
    research performance, 66, 82
Crowther, Sir Geoffrey, 247
Crowther Report, 116, 118
Cullen, A., (89)
Cunningham, K. S., 152, 162, 196,
    197, 199, (216), 245, (254)
Curiosity, 56, 64, 81, 113

DAINTON, F. S., 128, (146), 229,
    (253)
Dale, R. R., 57, (90), 113, 117, 125,
    (145), (146), 187, 189, 195, 197,
    (223), (224)
Dancy, J. C., 123, (146)
Darley, J. G., 19, (26), 100, (141),
    150, (216)
Data bank, 172, 241–243, 250
Dentistry, 17, 40
Department of Education and
    Science, 106
Derbyshire Education Com-
    mittee Report, 51, 53, 58, 110,
    186
Disciplines—see Academic disci-
    plines
Di Vesta, F., (144)
Douglas, J. W. B., 43, 44, 48, 79,
    (86)
Douglas, L. F., 57, (90), 208, (225)

256

Drop-outs, 20, 23, 33, 53, 57, 58, 64, 107, 108, 125, 168, 175, 181, 206, 209, 210, 216, 233, 247, 248; permanent and temporary, 20, 207, 208; and persisters, 60, 65, 81, 108, 173; satisfied, 112; and transfers, 207
Dropping out—see Wastage

ECKLAND, B. K., 20, (26), 59, (91)
Economic and Statistical Studies in Higher Education, Unit for, 22
Economics, 50, 101, 151, 199, 205
Education, and student teachers, 53, 59, 156; as regards universities, 191
Elder, G. H., 47, 69, (88)
Elvin, H. L., 128, (147)
Engineering, 17, 21, 31, 36, 38, 40, 42, 53, 59, 62, 63, 96, 97, 109, 121, 152, 156, 191, 199, 205, 210, 235
Engineering Science and Economics degrees, 205
English, 50, 101, 151
Entrance to university requirements, see A-level examinations; Sub-committee Report on, 119; and liberal admissions policy in first year, 121, 126
Essex University, 204
Evans, W., 183, (222)
Examinations, 19, 57, 96, 107, 121, 134, 149, 191–202, 236–237; and wastage, 10, 170, 191, 197, 215; procedures and pass rates, 18, 103, 109, 154, 170, 230, 243–246; and extroverts, 75; phobia and panic, 75; supposed purposes of, 191; and pass mark, 194–195; and the normal curve, 196; and research ability, 198; as faulty criteria and entrance to

professions, 198, 201–202; supplementary, 211; with course assignments, 211; open-book, 212
'Express streams', 114
Extroverts, 52, 71, 75, 97; neurotic, 70, 71, 74
Eysenck, H. J., 36, 70, 71, (85), (93)

FAILURE, 21, 23, 29, 31, 77, 104, 126, 129, 171, 237; rationalization of, 37, 34, 75; baffling, 45. See also Wastage
Family, conflict in, 30, 32, 73, 80, 181; size of, 34, 37, 43–45, 79; aspirations of, 38; support of, 38, 39, 57; characteristics of, 47–50, 82; democratic, 48, 68, 82, 227, 228; authoritarian, 68, 228
Farnsworth, D. L., 167, (220)
Feder, D. D., 166, (220), (221)
Fensham, P. J., 198, (224)
Finance, 33, 48–50, 57, 80–81, 175; self-support, 50. See also Grants
First-year results, as predictor, 121, 124; for selection, 124, 126, 128, 131; and correlation, 124; and intermediate qualifications, 126, 149
Fishman, J. A., 107, 108, (144)
Flecker, R., 31, 32, 50, 54, 66, 81, (84)
Fleming, W. G., (89)
Floud, J., (86)
Ford Scholars, 19
Forrest, G. H., 228, (253)
Forster, M., 45, 46, (84), 186, 195, (223)
Franks Report, 97, 98, 114, 183, 184
Frederick, W. H., 21, (26), 125, 126, (145)

Freedman, N. B., 64, 81, (91)
French, 151
French, E. L., (145)
Freshman Information Form of the American Council on Education, 241
Freud, S., 70, (93)
Funkenstein, D. H., 19, (26)
Furneaux, W. D., 28, 29, 41, 52, 70, 71, 74, (84), (87), 96, 99, 100, 109, (141), (144)

GALTON, F., 44, 45, (87)
Gardner, J., 201
Gazda, G. N., 167, 179, (220)
General Certificate of Education, see A-level examinations
Getzells, J. W., 69, (92), 106, (143)
Gibson, A. F., 202, 203, 204, 205, 211
Gibson, J., 35, (85), 134, (147)
Glass, D. V., (86)
Glennerster, H., 137, (148), 233, (253)
Glennon, J. R., 135, (147)
Goodrich, H. B., 155, 156, 157, 158, (217), 235
Goodstein, L. D., (144)
Gough, H. G., 133, (147)
Grace, H. A., 68, 70, (92)
Grants, 37, 49, 59, 136, 163, 232, 248; improved allocation of, 118, 125, 165, 209
Gray, G. A., 21, (27), 40, 53, 73, (87), 117, (143), (145), 162, 164, (219)
Great Britain, 10, 12, 16, 22, 29, 36, 41, 47, 50, 59, 79, 100, 105, 116, 117, 130, 135, 152, 153, 170, 182, 183, 231, 239
Greenbaum, J. J., 157, (218)
Gruber, H. E., (144)
Guilford, J. P., 69, (92), 106, (143)

HALE REPORT ON UNIVERSITY TEACHING METHODS, 152, 159, 186, 189, 190, 241
Hall, W. B., 133, (147)
Halmos, P., (25), (87)
Halsey, A. H., (86), 226, (253)
Hammond, S. B., 40, 55, (87), 153, (217)
Harris, D., 28, 43, 44, 50, 52, 54, 69, 70, 71, 79, (84), 101, 111, (142,) 164, 173, (219)
Hartog, Sir P., 191, (223)
Harvard Educational Review, 165
Harvard University Center for International Affairs, 57
Hatch, S. R., 232, (253)
Havighurst, R. J., (86)
Heilbrunn, A. B., (144)
Heist, P. A., 65, 67, 81, (91)
Henrysson, S., (254)
Hertel, J. P., (144)
Himmelweit, H. T., 34, 35, 53, 54, 62, 65, (85), (86), (90), 101, 103, 106, 107, 110, (142), (143), (144), 184, (222)
History, 50, 101
Hogben, D., 108, 109, 116, (144), 184, (222)
Hohne, H. H., 21, (26), (142), 195, (224)
Holbraad, C., 176, 177, (221)
Holland, 126
Holland, J. L., 67, 68, (92), 98, (141), 193, (224)
Holtzman, W. H., 56, (90)
Hood, A. B., (141)
Hopkins, J., 34, 35, 64, 65, (85), 173, (218), (221)
Hopson, B., 153, (217)
Horle, R. F., 167, 179, (220)
Howell, D. A., 32, 33, 49, 50, 57, (85), 160, 176, 177, 178, 183, (218), (221)

Hudson, L., 133, 134, (144), (147), 193, (223), 231
Hughes, P. W., 39, (86), 111, (143), 195, (224), 239, 244, 245, (254)
Humanities, 60, 62, 63, 96, 122, 123, 156, 157, 203, 206, 213, 235, 249
Hunt, S., (220)
Hunter, R. C. A., 62, (85), (91), 165, 167, (220)
Husén, T., 127, (146)

IFFERT, R. E., 50, 64, 81, (88)
Iliffe, A. H., 110, 127, (146), 249
Imperial College of Science and Technology, 119, 121, 232, 237
Incentive—see Motivation
India, 43, 46, 67
Introverts, 52, 67, 71, 76; neurotic, 69, 70, 75, 96, 109
I.Q., 21, 34–36, 46, 57, 60, 69, 70, 78, 101, 102, 113, 125, 162, 215; of science dons, 135

JACKSON, B., 105, (143), 163, (219)
Jackson, P. W., 69, (92), 106, (143)
James of Rusholme, Lord, 191
Jencks, C., 201, 213, (224)
Jenkinson, A. J., 18, (26), 152, (216)
Jex, F. B., 19, 20, (26)

KATZ, C., 101, (142)
Katz, F. M., 101, (142)
Katz, J., 204
Keele University, 12, 127, 128, 129, 206, 249
Kelsall, R. K., 12, (25), (87), 163, (219)
Kelvin, R. P., 52, 74, (86), 160, (218)
Kendall, M., 59, (91), 206, (225), 247, 248

Keniston, K., 57, (90)
Knapp, R. H., 155, 156, 157, 158, (217), (218), 235
Knoell, D. M., 19, (26), 59, (91), 165, 206, 207, 208, 209, (220), (254)

LAMKE, T. A., 154, (217)
Langley, D., 178, (221), (254)
Languages, 165, 195
Laslett, P., 188, (223)
Lauwerys, J. A., 115, 116, 119, 126, 128, (145), (146), 210, 211, 243, 244
Lavin, D. E., 70, 71, (93), 112, (145), 192, 193, 223, 228, 235, (253)
Law, 17, 38, 40, 50, 59, 63, 191, 193, 199, 202
Lawrence, R. M., 165, 170, (220)
Lea, R. C. G., 64, (91)
Learmonth, Sir James, 35, (85)
Leeds University, 164
Leverhulme Trust, 152
Levy, P. M., 63, (91)
Lewis, T., (89)
Light, P., (85), 134, (147)
Lipset, S. M., 33, 57, 72, (85), 159, (217), (218)
Liverpool University, 12, 247
Llewellyn, F. J., 99, (141)
Locke, C. D., 129, (147)
Locke, E. A., 97, (141), 236, (253)
London School of Economics, 12, 22, 28, 39, 57, 65, 101, 110, 208, 214, 233
London University, 176, 177; Institute of Education, 22, 152
Lovell, K., (86)
Lövgren, E., (254)
Lucas, C. J., 52, 74, 75, (86), 160, (218)
Lynn, R., 109, (144)

MacArthur, C., 184, (222), 239, (254)
McClelland, D. C., 111, 112, (145)
McConnell, T. R., 67, (92), 157, 213, (218), (225)
McCrum, N. G., (225)
McGill University, 62
MacIntosh, A., 19, (26)
McKeachie, W. J., 36, (85), 153, (217)
MacKinnon, D. W., 193, (223)
Macklin, A. D., 152, 160, (216), (219)
Maclaine, A. G., 40, (84), (87), 151, (216)
McLeish, J., (217)
McMullen, I., 189, (223), 240
McNeely, J. H., 11, (25)
Macomber, F. C., 151, (216)
Maddox, H., 63, (91)
Malleson, N. B., 17, 18, (26), 32, 34, 35, 38, 53, 54, 64, 65, 73, 75, 77, (85), (86), (93), (143), 153, 154, 160, 162, 165, 168, 169, 173, 183, 184, 203, (217), (218), (220), (221), (222), (225)
Mann, J. F., 239, (254)
Mansell Jones, P., (224)
Mansfield Cooper, Professor, 127
Marris, P., 38, 40, 53, (86), 164, 173, 184, (221)
Mathematics, 31, 66, 74, 82, 119, 120, 121, 151, 152, 165, 195, 205
Matriculation, 100, 103, 109, 116, 119, 130, 131. See also A-level examinations
Matsler, F., 67, (92)
Matson, R. E., 175, (221)
Matthews, T. H., (25), 29, (84)
Maturity, 30, 37, 50–52, 111, 133
Maxwell, M., 109, 110, (141)
May, R., 70
Medicine, 17, 21, 35, 40, 59, 62, 63, 96, 108, 109, 191, 193, 199, 202, 210, 235; medical students, 35, 60, 101, 116, 149, 153, 165
Melbourne University, 30, 45, 73, 160
Mercer, M., (89), (94), 112, (145), 185, (222)
Merrill, K. E., 47, 49, 80, (88)
Merrill, R. M., 19, 20, (26)
Mexico, 47, 156
Michael, W. B., 132, (147)
Middleton, I. G., (27), (84), (142)
Miller, G. W., 37, 48, 56, 64, 69, 71, 81, (86)
Minimum time, 21, 113
Minnesota Multiphasic Personality Inventory (M.M.P.I.), 68, 74
Minnesota University, 19, 100, 159, 171
Missouri Biographical Data Inventory, 108
Missouri University, 108
Mori, T., 228, 253
Morrison, R. F., 135, 137, 139, (147)
Mortality, of students; see Wastage
Morten, A. J., (145)
Moser, C., 22
Motivation, 22, 28, 30, 34, 50, 51, 54, 56 ff., 62, 66, 77, 80, 83, 107–113, 125, 213, 228, 233; and intrinsic interest, 28, 56, 64–69, 130; and vocational orientation, 30, 59, 60, 62, 63, 109, 231; and methods, 56; survival, 59; non-instrumental, 63; and higher degrees, 65; and selection, 124; and first year, 128
Mountford, Sir James, 17, 23, (25), (26), 99, (141) 150, 211, (216), (225)
Mumford, D. E., 129, (147)
Murray Committee, 21, 124
Murray, S., 111, (145)

NATIONAL CERTIFICATE, Higher, 19; Ordinary, 19
National Merit Scholars, 51, 58, 107, 157, 162
National Union of Students, 159, 190
New York City University, 33
Newcastle upon Tyne, University of, 134
New Zealand, 22
Nisbet, J., 104, 105, 117, (143), 171, (220)
Northern Ireland, 46
Nuffield Resources for Learning Project, 189, 241

OHIO UNIVERSITY, 19
Ojha, A. B., 52, 74, (86), 160, (218)
Oliver, R. A. C., 229, (253)
Olphert, W. B., 101, (142)
Olsen, F. J., 31, 32, (84), (143), 187, 188, 190, (223), 239, 240, (254)
Omnibus Personality Inventory, 139
Owens, W. A., 135, (147)
Oxford and Cambridge, 41, 114, 133, 153, 154, 163, 171, 176, 177; scholarships, 115
Oxford University, 73, 74, 184, 205, 206

PACE, C. R., 182, (222), 227
Pakistan, 46, 156
Panos, R. J., 24, 172, (221), 241, 242, (254)
Parents, influence of, 30, 37, 39, 48, 62, 64, 68, 159; educational background of, 39, 40, 41, 43, 65, 108
Parkyn, G. W., 21, (27), 81, 100, 123, (142), (170)
Parnell, R. W., 73, 93, 160, (218)

Peer relationships (need for affiliation), 28, 34, 47, 52 ff., 72, 76, 77, 108, 181
Pelz, D. C., 66, 81, (92), 137
Penney, Lord, 119, 124, 246
Persistence, 28, 30, 56, 60, 83, 113
Personality, 28, 52, 56, 65, 67, 68, 70, 83, 97, 99, 107–113, 136, 213, 229, 233
Personality Factor Inventory, 66, 154
Philosophy, 50
Philp, H., (89)
Physicists, 43, 67, 136, 137
Physics, 101, 120, 151, 165, 205
Piaget, J., 55, (90), 193
Plowden Report on Primary Education, 37
Pond, L., 54, 55, (90), 164, 187, (219), (223)
Prediction, 95, 97, 101, 107, 113, 122, 128; and school performance, 122, 123
Prediger, D. J., 108, 109, (144)
Presser, H. A., 64, (91)
Priestley, R. R., 30, 32, 45, 46, 73, (84), 160, 161, 162, 168, 169, 174, (219), (221)
Prince, R. H., (85)
Prusock, R. E., (222)
Psychology, 50, 60, 152, 199
Pye, Sir David, 199, (224)

QUEENSLAND UNIVERSITY, 41, 103
Queen's University, Belfast, 12, 45
Quotas, 29

REED, H. B., 70
Research, 138–140; and needs in higher education, 122, 226 ff.; students, 131–138, 140; and class of first degree, 134; and

Research—*continued*
grants, 134; into teaching, 235; into examinations, 236; and consultative services, 252
Rhodes, E. G., 191, (223)
Richards, J. M., 98, (141)
Riesman, D., 201, 214, (224)
Riker, H. C., 180, (222)
Robbins, Lord, 202, 213
Robbins Committee and Report, 11, 16, 23, 32, 39, 60, 96, 105, 122, 126, 149, 150, 160, 180, 196, 197, 209, 215, 233, 234, 236, 237, 242, 245, 251
Roe, A., 42, 43, 44, 45, 54, 67, 79, (87), 136, 137, (147), 228, 231, 249
Roe, E., (27), (84), (142)
Rosen, B. C., 46, (88)
Rowlands, R. G., 39, (86)
Royal Society, 133
Rudd, E., 232, (253)

SALLEY, R., 107, (142), (220)
Sanders, C., 22, 23, (25), 41, 50, 57, (87), (88), (89), 102, 103, 104, 106, 110, 111, 113, 117, 123, 125, (142), (144), (146), 164, (219), 228, (253)
Sanford, N., 10, 23, (25), 150, 158, 216, (222), (225), 227, (253)
Sarnoff, I., 34, 35, 65, (85), 173, (221)
Schonell, Sir Fred, 21, 22, (27), 32, 35, 40, 64, 83, (84), 103, 117, 124, (142), 163, 164, 165, 174, 181, 187, 190, (219), (223), 240, 250, 251, (254)
Scholarship-winners, 102
Scholastic aptitude tests, 105, 106, 229
Schools Council, 106
Schools, 239–241; Grammar, 28, 42, 70, 78, 184, 185; Secondary

Modern, 39, 42, 70, 185, 189; Primary, 48, 56, 64, 69, 71, 82, 190; and higher education, 51, 58, 65, 82, 182–191, 213; Independent, 78, 114, 184, 185; and I.Q., 185
Schwartzman, A. E., 35, 62, (85), (91), 165, 167, (220)
Science, 16, 17, 21, 38, 40, 60, 65, 101, 102, 109, 117, 119, 121, 151, 191, 195, 202, 203, 205, 213, 244, 249, 250; applied, 16, 60
Scientists, 35, 42, 43, 66, 82, 133, 205, 231, 249
Scotland, 40, 43, 67, 104–105
Scottish Union of Students, 159, 190
Segal, B. E., 74, (93)
Selection, 23, 57, 95–140, 162, 187, 210; improvement of, 22, 84, 95, 107, 131; of research students, 131–140; validity of, 215
Sgan, M. R., 175, (221)
Sheffield University, 12
Short, L. N., 21, (27), 40, 53, 73, (87), 117, (143), (145), 162, 164, (219)
Shuman, R. B., 19, (26), 248
Siegel, L., 151, (216)
Sinha, D., 43, 45, 46, 54, 60, 67, 70, (87)
Sixth-form colleges, 128–131, 188, 189, 230
Sixth forms, 11, 58, 83, 113–118, 124, 130, 165; third- and fourth-year sixth, 114 ff., 123; and teacher shortage, 115, 128
Social class, 28, 34, 37–43, 65, 74, 76, 77, 83, 97, 175, 177, 178, 184, 185
Social studies, 16, 60, 62, 63, 67, 101, 122, 123, 136, 156, 157, 203, 206, 235, 249

Social work, 59
Sociology, 60, 101
Sokol, R., 74, (93)
South Africa, 36
Specialization, 114, 116, 119, 123;
  and 'backwash effect', 114, 119
Spencer, M., 156, (217)
Spencer, S. J. G., 74, 75, (93)
Spielberger, C. D., 74, (93)
Srole, L., 159, (218)
Standard deviation, 21, 29, 121
Standing Conference on Univer-
  sity Entrance, 106
Stanford University, 16, 204
Stern, G. C., 182, (222), 227
Still, R. J., 75, 76, (93), 167, 168,
  (217), (220)
Stirling University, 213
Stringer, P., (221)
Strong Vocational Interest Blank,
  65
Study habits, 28, 54–56, 61, 82
Subject choices, 67, 128, 129, 163;
  unsuitable, 83, 163; enforced
  commitment to, 123
Suddarth, B. M., 175, (221)
Suicide, 72, 73
Summerfield, A., 34, 35, 62, 65,
  (85), 107, (144)
Summerskill, J., 12, 23, (25), 45,
  46, 49, 50, 53, 57, 66, (88), 112,
  113, (145), 164, 168, 185, 216,
  (219), 227, 231, 239, 253
Surrey University, 203
Survey of Study Habits and
  Attitudes (S.S.H.A.), 56
Sussex University, 172
Sweden, 126, 127, 240

Taylor, C. W., 106, 138, (143)
Teachers, 97, 118, 189, 190;
  remoteness of, 32; shortage of,
  202, 203, 245

Teaching, 63, 81, 149, 150–153,
  155, 186, 187, 215, 234–235
Technical colleges, 18, 42, 124,
  162, 194
Technological university, 53
Texas University, 19
Thematic Apperception Test,
  111, 112
Theobald, M. J., 117, (145)
Thistlethwaite, D. L., 63, (91),
  154, 157, 162, (217)
Thompson, M., (89)
Thorndike, R. L., (92)
Tibble, J. W., 191, (223)
Toronto Vice-Principals, Com-
  mittee of, 30
Trow, M., 60, (91), 251, (254)

United States, 10, 11, 12, 16, 20,
  23, 36, 37, 40, 43, 47, 49, 50, 51,
  52, 58, 59, 64, 66, 72, 80, 105,
  126, 132, 135, 153, 156, 162, 167,
  170, 182, 184, 204, 206, 231
Universities, British, 10, 20, 36,
  49, 57, 96, 106, 113, 117, 126,
  162, 173, 176, 215; Australian,
  20, 21, 36, 46, 57, 117, 124, 131,
  162, 174, 194, 211; American,
  36, 100, 151, 154, 167, 170, 171,
  179, 211; South African, 36;
  Canadian, 170; Dutch, 211
Universities of Great Britain and
  Northern Ireland, Conference
  of, 22
University College, London, 12,
  34, 59, 74, 171, 184, 248
University Grants Committee, 11,
  12, 13, 14, 16, 17, 149, 150

Vaizey, J., 22
Van Noorden, R. J., (225)
Venables, E., 18, (26), 30, 36, 42,
  43, (84), (87), 124, (142), (143),
  (144), 162, 195, (219), (224)

263

Veterinary science, 17
Vernon, P. E., 12, (25), 36, 38, 67, 83, (85), (92), 128, (142), 194, 195, 229, (253)
Vice-Chancellors and Principals, Committee of, 106, 230

WALSH, W. B., (222)
Warburton, F. W., 228, (253)
Warwick University, 205
Wastage, 76, 78, 107, 149, 186, 233, 234, 236, 252; rates in Britain, 10–18, 40, 150, 162; cost, 17, 194; dropping out, 32, 33, 43, 46, 49, 60, 62, 81, 108; lessening of, 95, 96, 149, 162, 165, 171; how much is tolerable? 215. See also Examinations
Watson, G., 33, 36, (85) 159, (218)
Wechsler Adult Intelligence Scale, 134
Weigand, G., (89)
Weintraub, R., 107, (142), (220)
Weiss, R. J., 74, (93)
Welford, A. T., (223)

Welsh, J., 104, 117, (143), 171, (220)
West Germany, 48
Western Australia, University of, 21, 102
White, G. E., (86)
Whitehand, J. W. R., 134, 135, (147), 232, (253)
Wilkinson, J., (145)
Williams, E. M., 101, (142)
Williams, F. E., 106, (143)
Williams, P. A., 65, 67, 81, (91)
Wilson, K. M., (218)
Winfrey, J. K., 166, (220), (222)
Wisconsin University, 19
Woodhall, M., 22, (27), 96, (141), 215, (225)
Woodruff, A. D., (144)
Worswick, G. D. N., 183, (222)
Wright, C. R., 132, 133, 138, (147), 232, 233, (253)
Wurzburg University, 20

YONGE, G. D., 182, (222), 235, (253)
York University, 191, 212
Young, M., 52, 251, (254)
Young, R. M., 167, (221)